NIETZSCHE'S FINAL TEACHING

Nietzsche's Final Teaching

MICHAEL ALLEN GILLESPIE

The University of Chicago Press   *Chicago and London*

The University of Chicago Press, Chicago 60637
The University of Chicago Press, Ltd., London
© 2017 by The University of Chicago
Published 2017
Printed in the United States of America

26 25 24 23 22 21 20 19 18   2 3 4 5

ISBN-13: 978-0-226-47688-9 (cloth)
ISBN-13: 978-0-226-47691-9 (e-book)
DOI: 10.7208/chicago/9780226476919.001.0001

Library of Congress Cataloging-in-Publication Data

Names: Gillespie, Michael Allen, author.
Title: Nietzsche's final teaching / Michael Allen Gillespie.
Description: Chicago ; London : The University of Chicago
     Press, 2017. | Includes bibliographical references and index.
Identifiers: LCCN 2016049886 | ISBN 9780226476889 (cloth :
     alk. paper) | ISBN 9780226476919 (e-book)
Subjects: LCSH: Nietzsche, Friedrich Wilhelm, 1844–1900. |
     Nihilism.
Classification: LCC B3317 .G5155 2017 | DDC 193—dc23
     LC record available at https://lccn.loc.gov/2016049886

♾ This paper meets the requirements of ANSI/NISO
Z39.48–1992 (Permanence of Paper).

CONTENTS

I first encountered the work of Friedrich Nietzsche as a first-year college student. The excitement and enthusiasm that that experience engendered is hard to describe or recapture, but it was real and compelling. Nietzsche speaks to the reader with an intimacy that is unusual among authors and unique among philosophers. When first reading Nietzsche, one feels as if one is being invited into a secret society, offered knowledge and insight available only to a select few, and allowed to experience feelings unknown to the rest of humanity. To read Nietzsche is to be suffused with a sense of soaring above the world and looking down on everything and everyone. To read Nietzsche especially when young is often simply to be carried away.

When so gloriously flying over humanity, however, it is difficult if not impossible to maintain any critical distance on oneself or on the author. I certainly had none in those faraway days. Such enthusiasm is not accidental. Nietzsche's goal is not to persuade but to enthuse, entrance, and overpower the reader, to initiate him into sacred mysteries and impel him to action. For many he is hard to resist. Over time, however, the attentive reader experiences a nagging suspicion that he has missed something, that exhilaration cannot be all of the story, that Nietzsche demands something more. The suspicion arises, to paraphrase the subtitle of *Zarathustra*, that Nietzsche does indeed write for all and for none, and that if one is not suspicious and critical, if one does not read Nietzsche "as good old classicists read their Horace," as he puts it in *Ecce Homo*, one will simply be taken in (KGW VI 3:303).[1] As I have gotten older and turned a more critical eye not only on Nietzsche but also on my own reaction to Nietzsche, I have had to confront questions that in my initial enthusiasm I did not even realize existed. I have asked myself again and again, what is so compelling about his books? Where do his haunting exhortations lead? Is this all just a virtuoso performance that signifies nothing, or at least nothing real, or is there some fundamental teaching that he means to impart? And if so, what is it, and where does he want to take humanity? I wish that I could say that after forty-five years of effort I had final answers to these questions, but that would be an exaggeration.

Nietzsche tells us repeatedly that he thinks the forbidden and traverses entire lands of thinking that others do not dare to enter, and raises questions that others are unable to endure. I think that this is correct and explains in part his phenomenal impact. On the surface Nietzsche's texts are filled with images and ideas that whirl about and are borne aloft by the flames of his passion, but underneath this spectacular bonfire, questions pile upon questions, relentlessly, burning red hot. Indeed, for one who has gained some distance on Nietzsche, Nietzsche himself becomes questionable, questionable in ways that admit of no unequivocal answers. He himself seems to be on fire.

The question of questions and of questioning is itself close to Nietzsche's heart. At the beginning of *Beyond Good and Evil*, he asks, "Who among us here is Oedipus? Who is the Sphinx?" (KGW VI 2:10) The depth and importance of this question is hard to exaggerate. It is a question that in a sense goes to the heart of thinking and reveals its dangers. Oedipus, as he first appears on Sophocles' stage, describes himself as the one whom all men call great, great not because of his physical prowess but because of his ability to solve riddles and answer questions. And yet what he himself does not realize is that he is the greatest of all riddles, the deepest of all questions. And when he stumbles on the question of his own identity, he is driven by his own hubris to seek an answer to it, fatefully and disastrously, destroyed in horrifying fashion by his own virtue. Nietzsche like Oedipus lived in questions, and he too happened upon the question of himself. Who was he? What was his role in life? What was his task or calling?

Many of us at one time or another face these questions. Nietzsche asked himself these questions over and over, as his repeated autobiographical efforts demonstrate. His restless movement from one field to another at university, his dissatisfaction with theology and his turn to classical philology, and then despite his early success, his turn to philosophy and cultural criticism; his enthusiasm for the Wagnerian project, and his subsequent critique of everything Wagnerian, his hopes for the future of Germany followed by his rejection of everything German—all bespeak a restlessness in search of a goal, someone on a quest for he knows not what, constantly dissatisfied, constantly moving on, repeatedly leaving things undone. However, when all else had failed and his life had come to a crisis, physically near death, and intellectually isolated and forgotten, Nietzsche found what he came to believe was the answer to his questions, and from that point forward he was a man possessed, caught up in his fate as inescapably as Oedipus, and in many respects just as tragically and disastrously. In that moment he became convinced not only that he had a task that could give meaning to his life, but that this task was of world-historical importance, and that his role was equal to that of Socrates, Buddha, or Christ. In his view, and contrary to what many commentators today suggest, this task was not merely a task of thinking but also of doing, deeply practical and political. Nietzsche's goal was not a professor's goal or even a poet's or philosopher's goal. He did not intend merely to fence with ideas, even with the ideas of the greatest poets and philosophers. His task, he came to believe, was nothing less than the re-valuation of all values, the complete transformation of European civilization.

Not only did he recognize his goal but also the means to attain it, and they were not pretty. He quickly came to see that to give birth to a new Europe, the old Europe had to be destroyed. Such a destruction in his view was in any case inevitable and indeed was already under way. His hope was that out of the wars he saw coming a hardened elite would arise who would hear and respond to his message giving birth to a group of superhuman creators. Only in this way could the decadence and degeneracy of the current nihilistic world be overcome.

Nietzsche was also well aware that the only means he had at his disposal were pen and paper. Fortunately or unfortunately depending on one's point of view, he had a capacity for using them that has seldom been equaled. With these tools alone, he sought to set in motion the development of an elite who would construct a new world on the rubble nihilism would leave in its wake. The pursuit of this goal was his sole and unrelenting task from 1881 until he slipped into madness in early 1889. It would not be too great an exaggeration to say that in this effort he expended all of his life force trying to fully articulate his teaching and foster the apocalyptic transformation it entailed.

This volume is an attempt to lay out Nietzsche's final teaching. It is by no means a full or comprehensive account. That would require many, many more pages. Nietzsche claims with some justification to say more in ten sentences than others say in a book (*TI*, KGW VI 3:147). It thus seems unlikely that I can encapsulate and explicate everything that Nietzsche says in seven books in a single volume. This volume instead consists of a series of essays that try to come to terms with what I take to be the principal ideas that shaped Nietzsche's final project.

The volume is divided into five parts. In the introductory essay, "Nietzsche's Deepest Thought," I describe the moment of insight that gave rise to the idea of the eternal recurrence of the same. It was this idea, I argue, that gave his final teaching its coherence and direction, providing the basis for an (anti-)metaphysics that rejects traditional metaphysics but still operates within the larger horizon of metaphysics, constituting a new *metaphysica generalis* (ontology and logic) and a new *metaphysica specialis* (theology, cosmology, and anthropology). I thus suggest that Nietzsche's rejection of systems and systematizers does not mean that his own thought is simply a disordered collection of aphorisms, as has often been suggested, but (at least from *Zarathustra* onward) a comprehensive whole shaped and guided by a poetic/musical logic.

The second part of the book, "Nihilism and the Superhuman," looks at the new anthropology that Nietzsche deploys in his efforts to come to terms with the nihilistic consequences of the death of the Christian God in *Thus Spoke Zarathustra*. In the first essay in this part, "Nietzsche and the Anthropology of Nihilism," I argue that while Nietzsche did not use the term "nihilism" in print until 1886, his understanding of the forms of nihilism was rooted in the anthropology that he laid out at the beginning of *Zarathustra*. This anthropology not only clarifies the character and varieties of nihilism but also reveals the necessity of the great decision that confronts humanity in the aftermath of the death of God. Humans, in Nietzsche's view, must choose between the last man and the *Übermensch*.[2] I examine the reasons Nietzsche believes it is necessary to choose the latter, despite what he readily admits are the cataclysmic consequences of this choice.

In the following essay, "Slouching toward Bethlehem to Be Born: On the Nature and Meaning of Nietzsche's *Übermensch*," I lay out in greater detail how Nietzsche believes this *Übermensch* will come to be, and focus in particular on the extraordinary burden that the *Übermensch* must bear in order to escape from the dead hand of the past and create a new world, what he has to do in order to become active and not merely reactive, and thus become truly creative rather than driven by the spirit of revenge.

The next part of the book examines Nietzsche's acceptance of his own decisive role as the teacher of the eternal recurrence of the same. The first essay in this part, "What Was I Thinking? Nietzsche's New Prefaces of 1886," examines in a comprehensive way Nietzsche's attempt to reconfigure and re-present all of his earlier works as erroneous but necessary steps on the way to the realization of his great idea, the formation of his final teaching, and the advent of the Great Noon. It details his passage through perspectivism, relativism, and nihilism, before coming to the idea of the eternal recurrence that became the bedrock for his final teaching and for the transformation of European civilization.

"Nietzsche's Musical Politics" discusses Nietzsche's work *Twilight of the Idols*, which Nietzsche himself characterizes as the most complete introduction to his entire philosophy (KGB III 5:414). It examines his critique of Greek philosophy, Christian morality, and German politics as well as modern French, English, and German culture in an effort to construct out of them a new Greco-Christian-European cultural synthesis drawing on his understanding of tragic Greek culture and the idea of the Dionysian. The essay shows the way in which Nietzsche deploys his new musical logic to bring this about, appealing not just to his critical psychology but to the rhythm, melody, and harmony of his language to move the emotions in an effort to foster the good Europeans that he believes are essential to the success of his cultural-political project.

In the final essay of the part, "Life as Music: Nietzsche's *Ecce Homo*," I discuss the last work Nietzsche completed before collapsing into madness. This work was to be a prelude to Nietzsche's planned-but-never-completed magnum opus. He believed it was necessary in order to let his European audience know who he was. They needed to know that he was not a mere scholar or cultural critic or a Wagnerian or a nationalist or an anti-Semite but the teacher of the eternal recurrence and the harbinger of the Great Noon. As in *Twilight of the Idols*, Nietzsche deploys his musical logic here not to give an account of European civilization but of his own life. The work is thus not autobiographical in the traditional sense but an account of how he became what he is, that is, the herald of his god and the one destined to usher in the apocalyptic transformation of European civilization.

In the fourth part of the work, "Nietzsche's Final Teaching in Context," I juxtapose Nietzsche's final teaching to his two foremost antagonists, Dostoevsky and Plato. The first essay in this part, "Nietzsche and Dostoevsky on Nihilism and the Superhuman," considers the impact of Dostoevsky's thought on Nietzsche and the fundamental differences between them. Nietzsche and Dostoevsky follow similar paths in their concern with European nihilism. In contrast to Nietzsche, however, Dostoevsky concludes that there is no human solution to nihilism and that the attempt to achieve one leads to murder, suicide, or madness. For him there can be no man-god or *Übermensch*, and we must rely instead on the man-God, that is, on Christ for our salvation. Viewed in light of Dostoevsky's account of nihilism, the incredible demands and the titanic dangers of Nietzsche's proposed path become apparent.

The second essay in this part, "Nietzsche and Plato on the Formation of a Warrior Aristocracy," measures Nietzsche not against his most powerful contemporary (Christian) competitor but against the thinker who is his foremost Western antagonist, Plato. I focus here not on the ontological question that is so central to the differences between them but on the practical question both want to address, the necessity of an aristocratic regime and the role of the genius who both believe must lead it. For Plato the principal political problem is how one restrains both the demos and the warrior class to ensure the rule of philosophic reason. He sees this problem in Homer and treats it as endemic to the Greek world, arguing in his *Republic* that a solution to it involves not only a precisely constructed set of political institutions but also an extensive system of education. Nietzsche, who is more concerned about the danger of democracy and the demos in the form of the last man, seeks to revive a master class that will topple the liberal democratic civilization that he sees as the final outcome of Christianity. Out of these conquerors he believes will come the *Übermensch*. What he fails to do, however, is to provide any sense of how such a regime should be constructed or how this new warrior class should be educated to transform it from "blond beasts" into a Dionysian aristocracy.

The conclusion of the volume, "What Remains," is concerned with determining why Nietzsche was unable to complete the magnum opus that was to crown and complete his final teaching. I ask, however, not merely why *he* could not complete it but also whether it could have been completed, and then finally whether the assumptions that underlay it were reasonable or even plausible. In this sense the essay serves not merely as a summary but as a final evaluation of Nietzsche's teaching and the political cultural project he wants to set in motion.

After this short summary of my argument, it might be useful to detail what I do not intend to assert in these essays. I do not claim that Nietzsche's final teaching is his only or even his definitive teaching. Nietzsche himself identifies three different teachings (corresponding to the three different periods of his thought), and there are several others that are at least partly developed in material that was unpublished during his lifetime but that has since come to play an important role in our understanding of his thought. This is especially true of the short fragment, "On Truth and Lie in the Extra-Moral Sense," which has played such an important role in the post-structuralist reading of Nietzsche. The early Nietzsche in my view was more communitarian and Romantic and developed what he called an artist's metaphysics. During his middle period, Nietzsche was more an experimentalist on the model of Emerson, Montaigne, and La Rochefoucauld, and more open to democratic possibilities. It is no surprise that those who want to use Nietzsche to support democratic theory turn to these works. I am concerned here only with detailing and in part reconstructing what I take to be Nietzsche's final teaching that he developed in this later thought. And by final here, I do not mean definitive. Had Nietzsche been able to continue his work, it is conceivable that he might have developed other views or have returned back to his earlier positions. I also do not claim that his final teaching is preferable to or better than his earlier teachings. As we will see, I have many reasons to doubt his conclusions. What I am trying to show in these essays is how one single great idea impelled him to reorganize his thought into a new whole during the last seven years of his life. His final teaching was not unrelated to his earlier work. In fact, I believe it draws on and develops much of the material from his earlier thought but reshapes it in response to the idea of the eternal recurrence.

I also do not mean to suggest that Nietzsche's thought was responsible for Fascism, National Socialism, or totalitarianism. That a version of his thought was used by the Fascists and Nazis is clear enough, but it is equally clear to us now that this version was only made tractable for them because of his sister's distortions of his texts and her misrepresentation of him in her biographical accounts of his life. It was her duplicity that made it possible for his readers to imagine that he was pro-German and anti-Semitic, in diametric opposition to what he actually wrote and believed.

It is certainly true that Nietzsche's praise of warrior virtues and manliness was appealing to Fascists and Nazis, but Nietzsche was hardly alone in holding these opinions. In fact, a renewed emphasis on manliness was widespread during this period and was typified by the push to reinstitute the Olympic Games. Moreover, the emphasis on a nationalistic and militaristic education was almost universal in European countries during the period leading up to World War I. If anything, Nietzsche's antinationalist rhetoric stands out as exceptional. Nowhere in his late thought does one find anything like the claim "dulche et decorum est pro patria mori" decried by so many of the later war poets. Finally, it is the height of irony that the Fascists and National Socialists who were so decisively driven by ressentiment and a desire for revenge should have drawn on Nietzsche who spoke out so decisively against both.

All this said, Nietzsche was convinced that the old European order rooted in Christianity was coming to an end, and that its collapse was inevitable. He also believed that this collapse would end in centuries of wars of unprecedented magnitude. This catastrophe in his view could not be avoided. That he welcomed such a collapse despite its consequences seems equally clear, not because he was enamored of violence, but because he believed this collapse would make possible a new beginning. To use a medical analogy, his concern was not with stopping the disease, which he believed was impossible, but with how the patient would emerge from this crisis. He believed humanity could become either much weaker or much stronger and laid out a plan of recovery that he believed would promote the latter.

On this point, I think that Nietzsche was mistaken. First, European culture and civilization were not as decadent and diseased as he believed. Second, even if they were, his reduction of the future of Europe to two stark alternatives was stunningly simplistic, closer to caricature than reality. It may be true that many human beings living in conditions of relative prosperity in market societies are as decadent as he believes, but that does not mean that everyone is bereft of the capacities for awe, wonder, and love as he suggests. Even a critic of democracy as vehement as Plato recognized that multiple human possibilities could and generally do exist in democratic regimes.

While there are reasons to question Nietzsche's analysis, however, it is hard to completely dismiss his critique. In part we do often see in our fellow citizens the narcissistic hedonism and consumerism that Nietzsche derided, and it is hard for us not to wonder whether this problem may not be deeper and more widespread than we believe. Critics on both the Left and the Right have pointed to this issue time and time again. I am convinced that Nietzsche presents us with this argument in both its starkest and most profound form and that we would be remiss if we did not give it our utmost attention.

In concluding this preface, I would like to thank a long list of people who have helped me think about Nietzsche over the years, including my teachers, Sam Beer who first introduced me to Nietzsche and Patrick Riley who listened to a naive sophomore try to make sense out of *Zarathustra*, Mark Blitz and John Rawls who supervised my senior thesis on *Twilight of the Idols*, and Joseph Cropsey, my graduate mentor; my friends Dennis Sepper, who wandered with me through the many abysses of Nietzsche's thought and whose friendship sustained me for many years, and Lowell Lindgren, who helped me understand the music of Nietzsche's thinking; my coauthors Tracy Strong and Keegan Callanan; and the colleagues and students over the years whose conversation and questions have stimulated my thinking about Nietzsche, including Catherine Zuckert, Stanley Rosen, Robert Pippin, Laurence Lampert, Ruth Grant, Babette Babich, Giacomo Gambino, Thomas Heilke, Christopher Rickey, and Edward Walpin.

Nietzsche believed that everything he undertook and everything he hoped to bring to pass, all of the pain and misery his teaching would inevitably entail, was justified as a remedy to nihilism. His goal was the elimination of all negativity and the formation of a deep gratitude for all things. I do not believe that I either can or would want to affirm as absolutely as Nietzsche believes is necessary, but I do know that I want to affirm all of these teachers, students, and friends and to express my gratitude to them for all they have contributed to my thinking, my character, and whatever in this volume has any value. As a small recompense for their kindness and in remembrance of comments and conversations that have stimulated my thinking about Nietzsche over so many years, I dedicate this volume to them.

INTRODUCTION

Nietzsche's Deepest Thought

Lake Silvaplana is located in the Upper Engadine, not far from Saint Moritz. It is surrounded by the high mountains of southern Switzerland, which are overhung with glaciers, cut by rivers, and covered with Alpine forest. There is a path around the lake, open only in the summer season when the snows have melted, which winds pleasantly in and out of the forest that sweeps down the mountainside. It is a favorite walk for locals and visiting burghers who have come to the area for a *Luftkur*, a curative week or two of exercise in the open air. The path is genial but generally unremarkable with the exception of one massive, pyramidal stone deposited on the edge of the lake by the glacier that carved the valley twenty-thousand years ago. And by the fact that it was on this spot in August of 1881 that a solitary walker was struck by a thought that transformed him from a little-known former academic into a philosophic visionary whose thinking has shaped our world in fundamental ways ever since.

This thinker was, of course, Friedrich Nietzsche. At that time he was living in a rented room in a small house on the edge of the Sils-Maria, a village at the southern end of the lake. He was a sickly wanderer, who had moved from place to place since he had retired from teaching in 1876, in search of a climate and a situation that would make it possible for him to live on his limited means and endure the ravages of his searing eye pain, persistent migraines, and intestinal disorders. He came to Sils for the first time in 1881 and was to return often thereafter. He was a deeply thoughtful man, but also a man who had failed to live up to the extraordinary expectations of his teachers and colleagues. He had obtained a professorship in classical philology at the University of Basel at the unheard of young age of twenty-four, without even completing a dissertation, on the basis of a few articles and what everyone recognized were extraordinary abilities, but from then on, everything seemed to go awry. In some part his failure was due to his poor health, but more important was his unwillingness to produce the kind of scholarship that was expected of those in his field. Instead he seemed only to indulge his passion for Schopenhauer and Wagner. To be sure, his first work, *The Birth of Tragedy: Out of the Spirit of Music*, had begun with an analysis of Greek drama, a traditional scholarly subject in classical philology, but it had then devolved into what most readers perceived to be little more than a polemic in support of Wagnerian music. Almost all of his fellow classicists treated it with derision or disdain. The work did attract the attention of many Wagnerians, but their interest in him and his subsequent work waned as a result of his break with Wagner in 1877.[1] He continued to write and publish although without any real success. His work grew increasingly idiosyncratic, aphoristic, and disjointed, highly critical of contemporary European, and particularly German, life and culture. His thought during this period was rooted in radical critique. He employed an approach he called *Entlarvungspsychologie*, which attempted to show that everything most people considered high and noble in fact had a low or mercenary psychological origin.[2] He was indebted during this period to the cynical realism of the seventeenth-century French aphorist La Rochefoucauld as well as the work of Montaigne.[3] While his insights and remarks, like those of his predecessors, were often quite penetrating and revealing, they also seemed scattered and at times exaggerated, and it was difficult for even his friends to understand his overall intention. Indeed, it is not clear that Nietzsche himself had any idea what it all added up to. His work during this period was positivistic in that it accepted nothing on faith, and more perspectival and experimental than his earlier and later thought. He thus seemed less the genius he is now often taken to be and more a sick and dyspeptic ex-scholar destined for a life of obscurity.

And yet by 1884, he had completed a work, *Thus Spoke Zarathustra*, which was to become the best-selling and most widely read philosophical work of all time. And from 1884 to 1888, he completed six additional works that have become more or less required reading for Western intellectuals ever since. His thought had a profound impact on an astonishing array of writers, thinkers, artists, and composers including Alfred Adler, Theodor Adorno, Hannah Arendt, Alfred Baeumler, Georges Bataille, Samuel Beckett, Henri Bergson, Martin Buber, Albert Camus, E. M. Cioran, Joseph Conrad, Gilles Deleuze, Jacques Derrida, Isadora Duncan, Michel Foucault, Sigmund Freud, Stefan George, André Gide, Knut Hamsun, Martin Heidegger, Hermann Hesse, Karl Jaspers, Carl Jung, Ernst Jünger, Franz Kafka, Nikos Kazantzakis, Jack London, Gustav Mahler, André Malraux, Thomas Mann, H. L. Mencken, Eugene O'Neill, Rainer Maria Rilke, Richard Rorty, Franz

Rosenzweig, Jean-Paul Sartre, Max Scheler, Giovanni Segantini, Lev Shestov, Georg Simmel, Oswald Spengler, Leo Strauss, Richard Strauss, Paul Tillich, Ferdinand Tönnies, Max Weber, Mary Wigman, Ludwig Wittgenstein, William Butler Yeats, and Stefan Zweig.[4] In fact, his influence has been so pervasive that his aphorisms are often scrawled on restroom walls and repeated as maxims by those who have never read his books or even heard his name.

What then was the source of this remarkable transformation? What was this singular thought that struck him as he made his way around Lake Silvaplana, "6000 feet," as he put it, "beyond man and time" (*EH, KGW* VI 3:333)? And how did it shape his thinking, transforming his profound cultural pessimism into a project for "the revaluation of all values," a total transfiguration and redirection of European life and thought?[5] The essays in this volume are an attempt to come to terms with this question through an examination of the teaching that Nietzsche developed on the basis of this thought, hinted at in the first edition of *The Gay Science*, presented definitively in *Thus Spoke Zarathustra*, and then further illuminated in his succeeding works, and in the unpublished material of the 1880s. While a great deal of ink has been spilled in an attempt to come to terms with many aspects of Nietzsche's thinking, surprisingly little attention has been given to this astonishing moment and the idea that guided his thinking for the rest of his productive life.

NIETZSCHE'S DEEPEST THOUGHT

Nietzsche called this seminal idea "the eternal recurrence of the same."[6] He considered it his "deepest thought," and treated it with such extraordinary reverence that on the few occasions when he gave an account of it to close friends he spoke in hushed tones as if initiating them into a conspiracy or a secret society.[7] Even in *Zarathustra*, where the doctrine was first announced, it is presented only in dream images, songs, and from the mouths of animals. Openly, Nietzsche more characteristically spoke and wrote not about the idea itself but about what he understood to be its corollaries and consequences, that is, the death of God, the will to power, the *Übermensch*, the last man, and the superiority of poetry and music to reason—all of which have become integral parts of the conceptual universe we inhabit. To be sure, many of these notions were first broached in one form or another in his earlier thinking, but they were transformed and given philosophical coherence and purpose by this guiding idea. It was in his view the greatest of all ideas and the turning point of history.[8]

Nietzsche gives us some insight into the seminal nature of this thought in the passage from *Ecce Homo* cited above, where he describes the thought transporting him "beyond man and time." This is a strange formulation.[9] We might expect "beyond man and God," or beyond "space and time," or even "beyond being and time," but "beyond man and time" is as rare in German as it is in English. What does he mean by this? And what does this tell us about the nature of his deepest thought?

Aristotle famously claimed that it was only possible to be a human being within the polis, asserting that those who lived outside it were either beasts or gods. Nietzsche refers to this passage in *Twilight of the Idols*, noting that Aristotle failed to mention a third possibility, that one might be both, that is, a philosopher (KGW VI 3:53). What does he mean by this, and how does it relate to his claims about his deepest thought? Beasts live by instinct and are guided by momentary passions or desires and consequently do not understand that they have a life with a beginning and an end. Since they do not recognize their own mortality, they do not have plans, projects, concerns, and so on. For them there are no deadlines, and thus no fundamental choices that have to be made between various goods. In this sense they are not in time in the same way that human beings are. Gods like animals also exist beyond time, not because they are unaware of mortality but because they recognize their immortality, that is, that they are not subject to the laws of time. Like animals they too have no deadlines, no need to choose this or that, and thus no real projects or purposes that shape their lives.[10] While they may resemble human beings, they are thus more akin to the forces or flows of the cosmos that seem to eternally repeat their natural patterns, or they are utterly arbitrary beings whom we cannot understand. In different ways both animals and gods thus live in an eternal present. Time does not exist for them in the same way it does for us. They are one with what is everywhere and always the same, with the great cycle of becoming or with what Plato called *aei on*, ever-being. The philosopher who is beyond both man and time in Nietzsche's view is both beast and god. In the face of his mortality, he recognizes his immortality, that is, his connection to and participation in what is eternal and ultimately real.

Nietzsche's deepest thought, the thought that marks him out in his own view as a philosopher, is the thought of the eternal recurrence of the same. This thought catapults him beyond man and time and connects him to what eternally is.[11] What is new and revolutionary about the idea of the eternal recurrence and what thus distinguishes Nietzsche from other philosophers (at least since the pre-Socratics) is the manner in which it names and describes *how* what is is. The thought of the eternal recurrence as Nietzsche understands it leads to a radically new conception of the whole, which entails a new understanding of being and reason, and of God, nature, and man. Nietzsche's thought of the eternal recurrence of the same is thus his deepest thought because it transfigures everything that is by giving everything a new meaning, goal, and purpose.

Although Nietzsche described his realization of this thought as a mystical experience, using language akin to that of Paul, Augustine, or Luther, he did not imagine that the idea simply dropped out of the sky. In fact, he went to great lengths in the 1880s to show how this idea grew out of his earlier life and thought. In metaphorical form, this account is at the heart of *Zarathustra*. He considered the question of the development of this notion explicitly twice, first in the new prefaces he wrote for his earlier works in 1886 and then in *Ecce Homo* in 1888.[12] There are also remarks in his other works of the time and in his notes and the material he left unpublished when he collapsed in early 1889 that bear on this issue.

Truly profound thoughts, as Nietzsche understood them, arise in response to fundamental questions. In order to come to terms with Nietzsche's thought of the eternal recurrence, we thus need to understand not merely his earlier thinking but the questions that motivated him, questions that arose not only out of his personal history and the history of his time but out of the history of the European world since the tragic age of the Greeks. This, of course, is not a task that can be achieved in any more than a superficial way in this essay. I will thus only briefly lay out what I have argued in much greater detail elsewhere.[13]

What is a fundamental question? Martin Heidegger argued in his inaugural lecture at the University of Freiburg in 1929, "What Is Metaphysics?," that a fundamental question is a question about the whole and thus a question that also calls the questioner himself into question.[14] All fundamental questions are thus not abstract or merely theoretical but also and perhaps fundamentally existential questions, rooted in the totality of our existence.

The notion that thinking is rooted in questions rather than propositions has been defended by many different thinkers in recent times including Heidegger, Gadamer, R. G. Collingwood, Leo Strauss, and Quentin Skinner. Crucial to understanding the meaning of an assertion or an idea is understanding the question to which it is an answer, and that almost always involves coming to terms with the personal, social, political, and intellectual context within which the question arises. There are, however, profound disagreements among those who share this general view about what constitutes the true horizon of thought and thus the appropriate context for the interpretation of a particular thinker's work. Some see the personal biography of the thinker as decisive. Others look at the thinker's social condition and/or the socioeconomic conditions of the world within which the thinker lives. Some see the structure of political life in a thinker's times as decisive. Still others put much greater weight on the ideas and questions of his or her contemporaries, often confining the intellectual horizon very strictly to the specific time in which the text was written or the individual lived. Others who also recognize the importance of ideas imagine that all real thinkers address perennial questions that are present everywhere and always. Instead of deciding a priori which of these approaches to follow, I think it is important to examine the thinker in question in order to determine the context within which he or she understands himself or herself to operate. In this determination, it obviously matters a great deal what these thinkers themselves say about this as well as what they experienced or what they have read or have knowledge of. Of course, even this cannot suffice for a variety of reasons. First, we all operate with concepts whose origins and meaning elude our understanding. Moreover, no one is completely transparent to himself or herself. And finally, even when thinkers do have a reasonable idea of what they are doing, for a variety of reasons they seldom tell the whole truth about themselves to their public or even to their closest family and friends.[15] However, while hermeneutic suspicion is thus always justified and necessary, we must not be paralyzed by uncertainty but instead cultivate a practical sensibility in synthesizing the different elements that impact individual thinkers.[16]

Nietzsche presents us with a particular problem in this regard, because he asserts quite explicitly that his seminal idea was the result of everything that has occurred or ever will occur. This claim, in fact, is one of the principal corollaries of the idea of the eternal recurrence. While in some abstract sense this statement may be true, it is less than helpful since we want to know which specific people, ideas, feelings, things, or events were more or even most important for the formation of this idea. Nietzsche is not oblivious to this fact and thus, within his global claim, gives us more specific indications of what he believes (or wants us to believe) has mattered most in his personal life, what social and political factors have shaped his thinking, and most importantly what the most powerful intellectual and spiritual impacts on his thinking were. These indications help, of course, but they are not dispositive. That said, his claims in this matter do provide prima facie evidence that we should not merely be examining his personal biography or events in his contemporary milieu but also the larger history of the European tradition, as he understands it, if we want to understand his great thought.

WHO WAS FRIEDRICH NIETZSCHE?

Nietzsche's upbringing almost certainly disposed him to an intellectual and spiritual life. He was born in 1844 into the house of a Lutheran pastor, and both his maternal and paternal grandfathers were Lutheran pastors as well.[17] His father, whom Nietzsche dearly loved, died of a cataclysmic brain ailment (almost certainly a stroke) when his son was only five, leaving the boy in the care of his mother, his grandmother, his sister, and two maiden aunts. He attended the famous German boarding school Schulpforta from 1858 to 1864, where he excelled at Latin and Greek, and attended university first in Bonn in 1864 and then Leipzig in 1865, originally to study theology but soon switching to classical philology. In 1865 he also discovered Schopenhauer's *World as Will and Representation* and began what was to be a lifelong wrestling match with his thought.

In 1867, at the age of twenty-three, he entered military service but was released due to injury and returned to Leipzig where in 1868 he met Richard Wagner and became his close friend and a member of his inner circle. In 1869, he was offered and accepted a professorship at the University of Basel in classical philology. The following year he joined the Prussian army in the Franco-Prussian War, serving as an orderly outside of Metz where he contracted both diphtheria and dysentery and collapsed from exhaustion. He returned to Basel, took up his teaching position, and in 1872 published his first work, *The Birth of Tragedy*.[18] The work was the product of his admiration of Greek tragedy, his deep love of music, his friendship with Wagner, his grappling with Schopenhauer's cultural pessimism, his deep concern with the cultural aridity of German life, and his dissatisfaction with the pedantic scholarship of German philology. Wagner and his followers thought highly of the book, but it was panned by Nietzsche's fellow philologists.

Instead of trying to repair his scholarly reputation by returning to more traditional scholarship, he threw himself into the Wagnerian enterprise and adopted a stance in his succeeding works not of a scholar but of a cultural critic.[19] These works included the four works he called *Untimely Meditations* (1873–76). The works were read within Wagner's circle but at the time had little impact on the larger intellectual world. He began other pieces that were more professionally oriented, such as "Homer's Contest" (1872) and "Philosophy in the Tragic Age of the Greeks" (1873), but left them unfinished.

The first Bayreuth Festival (1876) marked a turning point in Nietzsche's life. It was the centerpiece of the Wagnerian plan for the cultural renewal of Germany, a project to which Nietzsche had dedicated the previous eight years of his life and for which he had sacrificed his academic reputation. However, much to his dismay the festival as he saw it was a total failure that shattered his hopes that a tragic age and culture could be reconstituted in Germany on the Greek model. Nietzsche was also angry with Wagner because he paid so little attention to the intellectuals who attended the festival and instead spent most of his time patronizing those Nietzsche considered philistines, that is, the nobility and wealthy patrons whom Nietzsche believed had no appreciation for the spiritual significance of art.[20] As a result, Nietzsche distanced himself from Wagner, which contributed to their ultimate break.[21] The publication of *Human, All Too Human* (1878–80), which turned away from Wagner's cultural project toward a critique of the religion and morality that underlay it, sealed the break and thus served as Nietzsche's declaration of intellectual independence.

The emotional trauma of this separation coincided with a severe crisis in Nietzsche's health that left him near death for an extended period of time, and that led him to retire from his position at the university. He thereafter subsisted on the meager income from a small endowment that had been made available to him by the efforts of his friends in Basel. With his recovery he returned to writing, publishing *Dawn* in 1881, and the first edition of *The Gay Science* in 1882 (the second edition with a new preface and a fifth book was published in 1887). In 1882 Nietzsche also met the young Russian Lou Salome through Paul Rée, and they became fast friends. Indeed, it seems clear that Nietzsche first broached many of his ideas, including the doctrine of the eternal recurrence, to her during their walks in the mountains that summer. By the end of 1882, however, all of this had come to an end. Lou apparently rejected Nietzsche's proposals of marriage, and she and Rée departed, leaving Nietzsche distraught and alone.

Thereafter Nietzsche's physical ailments waxed and waned but never really disappeared. During periods of relatively good health, he completed what are typically considered his principal works: *Thus Spoke Zarathustra* (1883–85), *Beyond Good and Evil* (1886), *The Genealogy of Morals* (1887), *The Case of Wagner* (1888), *Twilight of the Idols* (1888), *The Antichrist* (1888), *Ecce Homo* (written in 1888 but not published until 1908), *Dionysian Dithyrambs* (written in 1888 but not published until 1891, and in one case 1908), and *Nietzsche contra Wagner* (written in 1888 but not published until 1895). In contrast to the works written between 1878 and 1882, these works all have a sense of purpose and reveal an author who has found his way and turned all of his energies toward a single goal. While his physical wandering was to continue until his collapse in early 1889, his spiritual wandering thus came to an end that day in August of 1881 on the shores of Lake Silvaplana, and from that time forward he marshaled all of his energies toward the completion of his final teaching.

When we think of Nietzsche's social milieu, we are prone to think of it as essentially German. Indeed, this seems almost self-evident. After all, Nietzsche was born in Prussia and wrote in German. Moreover, his early work was principally concerned with a rebirth of tragic culture in Germany through Wagner's music. If Nietzsche thought of himself as German at this time, however, it had little to do with being a citizen of the German *Reich* and much more to do with being culturally German. Moreover, when he took up his position in Basel, he gave up his Prussian citizenship (but did not become a Swiss citizen, becoming in effect a stateless person). Many of his friends were Swiss, some of his closest friends were Jewish, and he had a scattering of friends and acquaintances from Russia, France, and even America. In later years he was highly critical of German nationalism and the power politics of Bismarck, which he believed were ruining German culture. In opposition to the growing romantic nationalism of his time, he held up the ideal of the good European, an ideal he believed he shared with Goethe and others. He was particularly critical of German bourgeois culture and philistinism, romantic German music (and particularly Wagner), German Christianity, and the German diet (and especially German beer), which he felt contributed to what he considered characteristic German stupidity. The victory over France in the Franco-Prussian War, which led to unification of Germany, he believed to have been a disaster, in part surely because it further divided Europeans from one another but also because the new German state was rooted in a sheer power politics that paid no attention to the necessary cultural foundations of political life.[22] While the German state thus may have "worked," perhaps even supremely well, it had no goal or purpose that could give it meaning. Nietzsche subsequently came to distinguish such petty politics from what he later called great politics, which was rooted in the attempt to found a European political realm modeled on the Roman Empire, rooted in a new set of values derived from his idea of the eternal recurrence of the same.

THE INTELLECTUAL ROOTS OF NIETZSCHE'S FUNDAMENTAL QUESTION

While Nietzsche's upbringing, poor health, life experience, and the social and political events of his time obviously were important for him and had an impact on his development, they were not decisive for his thinking. A deeper concern from his youth onward was his sense of a looming cultural or spiritual crisis and decline. As a boy and young man he believed this was mainly a German problem but came to recognize as he matured that it was both broader and deeper, a problem that was essential to European culture as a whole. In his late thought, he referred to this crisis in a variety of ways, but most famously as "the death of God" and "nihilism."

Already in 1860, he and his friends Pinder and Krug founded a small literary society among themselves that they called "Germania," and that they hoped would help to renew German culture. They composed music, wrote essays, delivered lectures to one another, and talked incessantly about German culture and what could be done to revive its greatness. Nietzsche was concerned with these issues during his school years and his years at the university. During his time at the university, his attempts to make sense of this problem and find a solution to it were deeply shaped by Schopenhauerian pessimism and the Wagnerian program for cultural renewal. Whatever came out of his life experience, it was his encounter with these men and their thought that gave his thinking its initial direction. Schopenhauer defined the problem for him, and Wagner pointed the way to a solution. This was the reason that the failure of the first Wagner festival and his break with Wagner was so devastating for him.

The question he immediately had to confront in the aftermath of this event was why the project had failed. Part of the failure in his mind was due to what he saw as Wagner's betrayal of their common aspirations, but that was not all. The dominance of bourgeois society and philistinism had also played a role. He also concluded that he and Wagner had vastly overestimated the power that a dramatic festival might have in the modern world. Such festivals may have played a formative role in shaping Greek life, but what had been successful in a relatively small city-state could not have the same impact in a society of millions.[23]

All of these factors contributed to the perceived crisis, but as his thinking developed, Nietzsche came to believe that the source of the problem lay much deeper, not just in the mode or nature of the performance or in the personality of Wagner, but in the philosophical or metaphysical foundations of the European tradition, in the domination of what he had called Alexandrian culture in *The Birth of Tragedy* and what he later referred to variously as Platonism, Christianity, and rationalism, the notion of progress, and the related utilitarian belief that human happiness and thriving could be maximized through the proper technical organization of society. The concern with this rationalism was already implicit in his argument in *The Birth of Tragedy*. He argued there that the optimistic rationalism of the tradition that began with Socrates and Plato culminated in German idealism, where "reason bites its own tail" (KGW III 1:97). What he had in mind with this claim was Kant's antinomy doctrine, which asserts that reason inevitably becomes entangled in contradictions when it attempts to grasp the infinite and can only be saved if subjected to a thorough critique and confined within its proper limits. The antinomies, as Nietzsche well knew, had inspired and motivated the pessimism of Schopenhauer. In his work from *Human, All Too Human* to *The Gay Science*, Nietzsche shows in great detail that the essence of European rationalism is itself not rational, but is rooted in the irrationality of various conflicting passions, drives, and instincts. The philosophical heights of European thought thus rested in his view upon low psychological motives that are seldom if ever recognized. This critique, however, was not accompanied by an answer to the questions that it raised. The glimmerings of such an answer, however, were suggested to him on the shores of Lake Silvaplana in the idea of the eternal recurrence of the same.

NIETZSCHE'S (ANTI-)METAPHYSICS

The idea of the eternal recurrence of the same lies at the core of what I will call Nietzsche's (anti-)metaphysics. Let me explain what I mean by this term. Philosophy or metaphysics in its traditional sense can be divided into two main parts—*metaphysica generalis* (ontology and logic) and *metaphysical specialis* (theology, cosmology or the science of nature, and anthropology). The decisive concepts that characterize Nietzsche's mature thought—1) the danger of the last man and the possibilities of the *Übermensch*, 2) the death of the Christian God and the rise of the Dionysian, 3) the will to power, 4) the replacement of reason by poetic or musical thinking, and 5) the doctrine of the eternal recurrence—define his (anti-)metaphysical alternative to traditional European metaphysics.[24] The notion of the *Übermensch*/last man is the basis of his transformed "anthropology"; the death of God (and the rebirth of Dionysus), the foundation of his new "theology"; and the will to power, the ground of his "cosmology." With those three concepts, he essentially redefines *metaphysica specialis*. His turn to perspectivism, the notion that there are no absolutes, that nothing that is unqualifiedly true, lies at the foundation of his new poetic or musical "logic." And, finally, the eternal recurrence defines his new ontology or notion of being. Together they constitute his new *metaphysica generalis*. Nietzsche's (anti-)metaphysics thus depends in its fundamental structures upon traditional metaphysics in the very moment it rejects the substance of that metaphysics.

This (anti-)metaphysics developed gradually but was given unity by the doctrine of the eternal recurrence. The notion of "power," for example, was a central concern in *Dawn*, although the notion of the "will to power" did not appear in Nietzsche's printed work until *Zarathustra*. The death of God appears first in *The Gay Science*, the idea of the *Übermensch* first in his youthful description of Byron, and an early version of the idea of the Dionysian in *The Birth of Tragedy*. The notion of perspectivism is characteristic of the middle period of his works but only becomes a coherent doctrine in the context of the eternal recurrence.

When considering Nietzsche's late thought, scholars of different persuasions have made one or the other of these concepts the centerpiece of their interpretation. Under the influence of his sister's publication of a compilation of bits and pieces of his notes as a completed magnum opus under the title *The Will To Power*, many interpreters placed this concept at the center of his thought. Others, especially during the Nazi period, saw the core of his thought in the notion of the *Übermensch*.[25] Still others, often with a theological interest, have argued that the death of God is central, while contemporary post-structuralists have emphasized what they see as his nihilistic rejection of logic and truth and his turn to a more musical or poetic way of thinking as his basic teaching. There is a great deal to be said for and learned from all of these interpretations and, insofar as they draw principally on Nietzsche's earlier thought, they often construct plausible and in many instances attractive interpretations of Nietzsche's work. Surprisingly, however, only a small number of interpreters take Nietzsche's own claims about the importance of the eternal recurrence seriously.

Among the works that recognize the centrality of the eternal recurrence for Nietzsche's thought, the works of Heidegger, Löwith, Klossowski, and Lampert are the most illuminating.[26] Klossowski is perhaps the most insistent on the centrality of the thought of the eternal recurrence to Nietzsche. In his view, however, it is an impossible thought that that despite or perhaps because of its depth and profundity is a thought of delirium that ultimately leads Nietzsche into madness since it dissolves both identity and reality. While Heidegger too agrees that the idea of the eternal recurrence is central to Nietzsche's thought, in contrast to Klossowski he sees it not as a lucid if unsuccessful (and insane) effort to think beyond Western metaphysics and language as such but as the culmination of the history of the Western metaphysics of presence and the modern metaphysics of subjectivity. Both clearly bend Nietzsche to fit into the context of their own thought. Both also connect the doctrine of the eternal recurrence to a Nietzschean metaphysics, although, as will become clear, I do not believe that their portrayals of this metaphysics are finally correct. Lampert, by contrast, presents us with an interpretation of Nietzsche and the idea of the eternal recurrence that is scrupulously fair to his texts and notes. In contrast to Klossowski and Deleuze, who believe that Nietzsche is the first philosopher to resist recodifying the world, Lampert argues (correctly to my mind) that Nietzsche does precisely that with the doctrine of the eternal recurrence. He also rejects the now common (but unjustifiable) argument that Nietzsche never seriously intended to give his idea a grounding in modern science. And finally, he points to the possibility that Nietzsche was finally able to present this idea in a clear and consistent manner that adequately captured both its depth and breadth.

There are other more recent discussions of Nietzsche's idea of the eternal recurrence, but since many of those produced in English do not deal with the *Nachlass* and instead actually draw exclusively on the long-since-discredited *Will to Power*, it is hard to take them seriously since most of what Nietzsche has to say about the eternal recurrence is only available in the *Nachlass*.

I agree with Klossowski that Nietzsche's thought of the eternal recurrence is central and decisive for his work, but despite the enormous demands it placed upon him, I don't believe that it led him to madness, although as I will suggest in my essay "What Remains," at the end of this volume, in his descent into madness he leaped to conclusions based upon the idea of the eternal recurrence that in sanity he had thought unwarranted. I agree with Heidegger that the idea of the eternal recurrence is part of a Nietzschean metaphysics or what I call an (anti-)metaphysics that formally has a great deal in common with Western metaphysics but substantively moves in another direction. I am convinced, however, that Heidegger misconstrues the role of the eternal recurrence in Nietzsche's thought as a result of his effort to differentiate his understanding of the relation of Being (*Sein*) and time from that contained in the idea of the eternal recurrence. As I have argued elsewhere, Heidegger's notion of Being builds in ways that Heidegger never realized or at least never admitted on Nietzsche's notions of the eternal recurrence and the Dionysian.[27]

Although deeply influenced by Heidegger, Löwith charts a different course. In contrast to the prevailing interpretation of Nietzsche as the teacher of the will to power propagated by Nazi sympathizers such as Baeumler, Löwith put the eternal recurrence in the center of Nietzsche's thought. He argued that it is this notion that ties all of his diverse aphorisms together and thus makes possible something like a wholeness to his thinking. The purpose of this idea in his view is to provide a new notion of eternity in a nihilistic world in which the old god has died and consequently in which the old eternity has also become unbelievable. In Löwith's opinion, however, this attempt to combine an atheistic religion and a physicalist metaphysics or cosmology (that draws on pagan thinking going back to the Stoics and Heracleitus) is an impossible task and ends in disaster. Nietzsche is forced in the end to conclude that he is god and thus lapses into insanity. Löwith offers a very plausible reading and one that in many respects has become widely accepted. I don't believe, however, that he adequately understands the crucial turn that Nietzsche takes away from his previous thought with the realization of the idea of the eternal recurrence nor the (anti-)metaphysical structures of Nietzsche's thought that Nietzsche imagines can contain the very contradictions that Löwith finds so destructive. I also think all four thinkers underrate the importance of music in Nietzsche's thought in an effort to portray his thought as essentially philosophical and at least proto-existential.

Of the other well-known interpretations of Nietzsche, Deleuze is the least sensible or perhaps the most inventive in interpreting the idea of the eternal recurrence of the same, arguing that Nietzsche really did not mean that the same was the same.[28] Deleuze (like many post-structuralists) wants to enlist Nietzsche in an attack upon the philosophy of identity. He has good reasons to think that this is sensible, at least if one focuses on Nietzsche's early thought, and particularly his unpublished fragment "On Truth and Lie in the Extra-Moral Sense." Deleuze's attempt to extend this radical perspectivism to his later thought, however, is undercut by Nietzsche own claim that the idea of the eternal recurrence offers a way to overcome the nihilistic consequences of the radical perspectivism.

In trying to make sense of the eternal recurrence in contemporary thought, most scholars (often unknowingly) follow Löwith in discounting the cosmological element of the eternal recurrence, arguing that Nietzsche never made such an argument in print, or that he was merely speculating about such a scientific justification in the hope that it might provide support for his ideas and hoped to spend several years studying natural science only in order to see if it might be verified.[29] While I certainly don't want to deny that the idea has an existential or psychological element to it, and do not want to argue that Nietzsche saw it primarily as a cosmological doctrine, I want to suggest that such readings miss the crucial ontological character of the doctrine in that it posits and affirms a new notion of being within the context of the (anti-)metaphysics that forms the core of Nietzsche's final teaching. As a moment of his (anti-)*metaphysica generalis*, it does not constitute a cosmology or an anthropology (in Nietzsche's language "a psychology") but must be compatible with both and with the new Dionysian theology he develops. I do not think that Nietzsche succeeded in reconciling all of these elements in his published writings or for that matter even in his notes, but I am convinced that this was at least in part the goal of his planned magnum opus. Whether he could have succeeded in this titanic effort, however, remains a deep and unanswerable question. The difficulties are obvious and Nietzsche's struggles to complete the task equally apparent.[30]

As I read Nietzsche's later thought, the doctrine of the eternal recurrence is the concept that gives everything in his thinking its meaning and purpose, not the will to power, the death of God, the *Übermensch*, or nihilism. Thus, while many of his fundamental concepts may antedate his notion of the eternal recurrence, it forms the bedrock of them all and the basis of his final teaching.

This fact is not merely evident in all of his later works but also in the plans for his never-completed magnum opus. While the title for the work that Nietzsche's sister gave to her construction from his notes, "The Will To Power," was one he considered, there were many others, including "Attempt at a Revaluation of All Values," "An Attempt at an Explanation of All Events," "The Innocence of Becoming," "The Hammer," "Philosophy of Eternal Recurrence," and "The Great Noon." Her choice of a title for the distorted compilation she published in his name, however, led to a long misinterpretation of Nietzsche's thought that recurs repeatedly even in our own time as scholars, particularly in the Anglo-American world, seek to use this concept to assimilate Nietzsche's thought to a naturalistic materialism. This was certainly not Nietzsche's goal or intention. Her distortions also clearly played a role in making Nietzsche's thought, which was antinationalist and vehemently anti-anti-Semitic, into something attractive and useful for the Nazis.

The eternal recurrence not only is important in itself but also gives meaning and purpose to each of the other parts of his (anti-)metaphysics. From Nietzsche's point of view, European metaphysics had become unbelievable for a variety of reasons. Traditional ontological notions had melted away in the face of early modern skepticism that overturned belief in the existence of substantial forms. While this skepticism was itself overcome by the new science developed by Copernicus, Kepler, Galileo, Descartes, and Newton that demonstrated that change itself followed lawful and mathematically demonstrable patterns, the certitude on which it rested was called into question in the late eighteenth and early nineteenth centuries by historicism. In this way, by the middle of the nineteenth century, many thinkers had become convinced that the ontology and logic that had sustained the European tradition since Plato was built on sand. For these thinkers, traditional *metaphysica generalis* thus became unbelievable.

The same was the case for *metaphysica specialis*. Theologically, the belief in the Christian God had been fading for a long time, and as a result of Kant's critique, it had become clear that a rational proof of God's existence was impossible. Moreover, scientific advances in the explanation of the origins of the cosmos were undermining Christian faith and opening the way to atheism. Cosmologically, the world was neither a closed geocentric system nor matter that moved according to natural laws but a play of forces that were driven by pure chance. Moreover, there was no natural or supernatural reason that directed everything toward the good nor a beneficent creator who would reconcile and redeem everything at the end of time. Nor finally could man stand on his own. He was not the rational animal that Aristotle had imagined, not the *imago dei* of medieval thought, and not even the rational ego that Descartes had posited. Rather, as Darwin had shown, man was a passionate, willing being who came into existence as the result of an evolutionary process and would eventually be displaced by another form of life that was better adapted to the biological niche humans currently inhabited. God, man, and nature were thus devoid of sense and meaning. There were no ultimate purposes and no transcendent guidance or goals for human beings.

Nietzsche's fundamental thought accepted and indeed was rooted in this critique of traditional metaphysics, but in the face of this apparent meaninglessness, he sought to restore meaning and purpose to things. Indeed, the thought of the eternal recurrence established the foundation for a new (anti-)metaphysics within which a new ontology, logic, theology, cosmology, and anthropology were combined to constitute a new vision of the whole. His new (anti-)metaphysics understands humans not as a rational beings but as a willing beings, nature not as a rational order of matter in motion but as the will to power, God not as a transcendent rational being but as a Dionysian will or life force, logic not as reason but as poetry or music, and ontology not as unchanging forms (of things or motion) but as the totality of becoming eternally repeating its self-same cycle. The keystone of this entire edifice is the idea of the eternal recurrence. Without this ontological foundation, everything else remains essentially meaningless, a chaos of contingent motion, pure flux.

Nietzsche remarks in a note in the *Nachlass* that the eternal recurrence is the closest approximation of becoming to being (KGW VIII 1:320). Heidegger and others have pointed to this passage as an indication that Nietzsche did not finally escape from the traditional metaphysical notion of being as presence.[31] Rüdiger Safranski remarks that Nietzsche thus turned time into being.[32] This reading of the fragment, however, lays greater weight on the term "being" than Nietzsche intended. There is no being for him, there is only becoming, but it is an eternal becoming of a finite set of possibilities and thus a becoming that Nietzsche believed inevitably had and has to repeat itself. Each moment is thoroughly ephemeral and yet absolutely meaningful as a necessary moment of the eternal whole. Without this metaphysical element, the rest of Nietzsche's thinking remains a kind of untrammeled Heracleitean fire, but with it, it is transformed into a philosophical system, an (anti-)metaphysical system that retains many of the structures of metaphysics.

The peculiarity of this doctrine or of any doctrine that makes a claim about the whole is that it cannot in principle be known or demonstrated by experience or by any kind of rational proof. It or at least its premises can only be asserted hypothetically. In this context, one might legitimately ask whether such an assertion of the doctrine differs in any meaningful way from mere belief. It is Nietzsche's contention that it does. All belief in his view is passive and reactive. The assertion and affirmation of the doctrine of the eternal recurrence, by contrast, is active, not a desperate effort to find a palliative for suffering, but a creative act that endows existence with meaning. This, he believes, is what distinguishes his (anti-)metaphysics from all previous metaphysical systems since the time of Plato. In this sense the doctrine of the eternal recurrence is concomitant with the other aspects of Nietzsche's philosophy: it is a manifestation of the will to power; it is the assertion of an *Übermensch*; it is not a rational deduction but a poetic assertion; and it relies not upon a distant God but upon the development of a superhumanity capable of living in a tragic combination of darkness and light. It is also for Nietzsche the supreme moment of nihilism in which nihilism overcomes itself, the ultimate moment of willing in which the will wills itself as a whole, in which the will to power becomes a whole, and finally it is the harmonization of the cacophonous primal music that is the core of becoming.[33]

The eternal recurrence in this sense is central to all of Nietzsche's later thinking. To become the *Übermensch*, it is essential to will the eternal recurrence, to affirm the whole in its entirety. This affirmation liberates one from the spirit of revenge and allows one to be active and creative rather than merely reactive. It redeems every moment from contingency and irrelevancy by establishing its absolute importance as a necessary moment of the whole. The doctrine is similarly essential to Nietzsche's new logic since it opens up the possibility of a creative artistic willing, establishing new values rooted in new words, that build new bridges between things that remain eternally apart. To will the eternal recurrence is also in his mind to bring Dionysus into being, to become the last disciple of Dionysus, the site of the god's advent, to will both the unity of the whole and the self-destruction or self-overcoming of the whole, and thereby to live according to what Nietzsche calls *amor fati*. Obviously, all of these are interlocking concepts, but the recognition and affirmation of the doctrine of the eternal recurrence is the keystone that gives them all meaning and holds them all together. To proclaim and affirm this doctrine is for Nietzsche to become the *Übermensch*, to demonstrate that the world is the will to power and nothing besides, to provide the ground for the advent of Dionysus, to overcome nihilism, and thereby to provide the opening for a radical transformation of the rationalist European culture that has been dominant since the time of Plato into a tragic culture on the model of the Greeks. If he can complete this task, Nietzsche believes he can carry on the task that he and Wagner had begun years before, but which they had been unable to bring to a successful conclusion. In view of what he sees as the consequences of the doctrine, it is perhaps not surprising that he titled the last chapter of his last work "Why I Am Destiny."[34]

The consequences of the affirmation of the doctrine of the eternal recurrence in Nietzsche's view are not merely theoretical, but terrifyingly practical. In fact, he asserts that the proclamation of the doctrine will produce a world-historical event he refers to as the "Great Noon," an apocalyptic moment that will fundamentally transform the future humanity.[35] In this context he believes that the doctrine will serve not merely as an ontological teaching but as a psychological hammer that can sculpt a higher humanity, crushing many in a series of wars of hitherto unexampled horror, but at the same time creating a hardened type of human being and a new people out of whom a few superhuman poet-tyrants will arise to become masters of the earth.[36] Practically, the doctrine is a complete rejection of modern liberal/democratic/socialist life, a rejection of the notion of rights, of human dignity, of the value of work, of the nation-state, of peace, and of what he sees as the somnambulant consumerism of the "last man." The next two hundred years (1888–2088) in his view will be characterized by the collapse of European morality and the inception of a monstrous logic of terror and war, but all of this in his view will be a prelude to the establishment of a new tragic culture, a thousand-year Dionysian *Reich*[37] that will be much healthier and much more affirmative than anything seen since the tragic age of the Greeks.[38]

This great project grows out of and is connected to Nietzsche's earlier work in ways that I will describe in what follows, but at its core it is something new, in part a coalescence of earlier notions, but also a broad and startling plan for redeeming and overcoming humanity, a plan for the cultivation of beings who are not motivated by the spirit of revenge, and who are not reactive but active and creative. Nietzsche thus abandons the experimentalism and critical positivism of the middle period of his thought where like Montaigne he explored a variety of possible ways to live and think about life. *Why* he abandons this earlier path—which in light of succeeding events strikes almost all readers today as much more appealing—is spelled out in the drama of *Zarathustra*, which in many respects retraces his own spiritual development, and in the new prefaces he wrote for his earlier works in 1886.

Given the uses of his thought in the first half of the twentieth century, we might reasonably want to condemn his (anti-)metaphysics as antilife, but to be fair we have to remember that this project was not completed as Nietzsche intended. He was unable to finish even a draft of the great final work in which he intended to announce to the world in the clearest terms the doctrine of the eternal recurrence. Instead of this his sister presented a radically distorted version of his thought that was then adopted by a variety of intellectual, social, and political movements, many of which were anathema to him and deeply at odds with his goals and intentions. While this clearly lessens Nietzsche's culpability for what actually occurred, this does not necessarily mean that what Nietzsche actually foresaw and longed for would have been more palatable. There is no doubt that he wanted to have a truly explosive effect. He was quite sincere when he declared, "I am dynamite," and when he asserted that his name would be associated with wars of unprecedented destruction (*EH*, KGW VI 3:163). Thus, while he would almost certainly not have been happy with the catastrophic manner in which events unfolded, he clearly foresaw and even longed for a catastrophe.[39]

The effort to bring humanity to such a cataclysmic moment of decision is evident in his works of 1888 that are a crescendo preceding the announcement of his deepest thought. This is clear not only from his notes and letters, which are unequivocal on this question, but also from a number declarations in the works themselves.[40]

The preparations for the presentation of the magnum opus and the Great Noon that Nietzsche imagined would follow its publication are also evident in his correspondence in the last few months before his breakdown.[41] During this time he was deeply concerned with the publication of *Ecce Homo*, in which he intended to present himself to humanity as the teacher of the doctrine of the eternal recurrence and thus as destiny. Although the work was completed, he delayed publication, for several reasons. First, he wanted to show that the critique of Wagner in his recently published *The Case of Wagner* was not merely a recent change of course but a continuation of a long-standing effort that began in his earlier works. He thus hastily assembled a collection of earlier aphorisms into a work he entitled *Nietzsche contra Wagner*. He was concerned that the perception of him as merely an anti-Wagnerian would distort the message he intended to deliver. Second, the publication of *Ecce Homo* was further delayed by his belief that the work needed to appear simultaneously in multiple languages in order to avoid the appearance that he was merely a German thinker thinking about German problems. He hoped to secure translators for the simultaneous appearance of the work in at least German, French, and English, as well as, if possible, Danish, Swedish, and Russian. He was unwavering in his opinion that this work needed to be published before the *Revaluation of All Values*. Understanding who he was, he believed, was a prerequisite for understanding the magnum opus and its fundamental teaching. Under his sister's control of his work, however, this plan was not carried out. This key work, which Nietzsche himself believed was necessary to understand his project, thus was unknown during the crucial first twenty years in which his thought was received, and was only published in 1908. Moreover, in its place his sister's lengthy and repeated accounts of his life presented a vastly distorted view of her brother to the world.[42]

Nietzsche's collapse in Turin in early 1889 thus prevented the announcement of the idea that struck him on the shores of Lake Silvaplana in the manner he intended and made possible the many distortions of his work over the following decades by his sister and others. Of course, this does not mean that his magnum opus would have had the catalytic effect he imagined had he been able to complete it and see it through to publication. That said, there can be no doubt about his prescience on a number of matters. Twentieth-century Europe did experience the moral collapse and the advent of a monstrous logic of terror he had predicted. Moreover, he was correct in his prediction of the looming advent of wars of hitherto unimagined ferocity. These predictions notwithstanding, the *Übermensch* he imagined has not come into being, his notion of the will to power as a universal principle of natural motion has not been verified, and the Christian God in many ways still seems to be alive and well if considerably attenuated and more distant than in Nietzsche's own time. We do continue to struggle to make sense out of things, but the concern with nihilism, rightly or wrongly, seems now largely confined to an academic elite. It thus seems that the doctrine Nietzsche hoped to announce was not as necessary to the salvation of humanity as he imagined. But then this is perhaps the wrong way to look at the matter. After all, Nietzsche believed that humanity faced a choice between an upward path that led to his *Übermensch* and a downward path that led to the last man, the utilitarian consumer who was concerned only with maximizing his own happiness. Such a man in Nietzsche's view has no need of his doctrine and in fact must fear and reject it. He lives entirely on the surface and is incapable of love, wonder, or awe. Here again Nietzsche's prescience may not have been far from the mark. Indeed, the triumph of bourgeois life and its rabid consumerism may simply indicate that despite the wars and destruction, humanity simply chose the path that Nietzsche despised.

In light of all this, the question thus remains what meaning Nietzsche's doctrine can have for us. Or to put it another way, was Nietzsche in fact "destiny" as he claimed or just a historical cul-de-sac that we wandered into and have now escaped from and left behind? Or did he perhaps open up the way to a new path that leads in a direction quite different from both of those he imagined? In what follows, I will try to prepare for a more careful consideration of these questions by spelling out as clearly as possible Nietzsche's final teaching, rooted in his (anti-)metaphysics, and the practical consequences he imagined followed from his "revaluation of all values." Only when we have a better understanding of his later thought will we be able to begin to think about answers to the question of the significance of this thought for us today. The essays that follow are thus an attempt to come to grips with this teaching.

It is hard for anyone who has visited Sils-Maria and walked around Lake Silvaplana, a place of remarkable beauty and calm, surrounded by spectacular mountains, to miss the awe-inspiring character of the place. It is no accident that Nietzsche like Zarathustra retreated to this spot to recuperate and rethink the course of his life and his world. Nor in view of the majesty of the peaks is it hard to imagine that in that moment he was able to conceive of being elevated into a higher, eternal order of all things. What is hard to recapture in this locale is his sense of the throbbing heart of the world, filled with contradiction and violence, that he perceived as so intimately connected to this supernal vision. Like Heracleitus Nietzsche saw an eternal fire at the core of existence that would eventually consume and transform all things. In uniting this catastrophic fire with the cool and quiet eternity of the eternal recurrence, he poses a question for us that is extraordinarily challenging and terrifying, and unless we come to terms with its deeply problematic majesty, we will remain no more than casual wanderers meandering on a path whose end we cannot see and whose purpose seems little more than a curative recreation in the hustle and bustle of modern life.

NIHILISM AND THE SUPERHUMAN

Nietzsche and the Anthropology of Nihilism

It has become commonplace to portray Nietzsche as the preeminent philosopher of nihilism.[1] This reading, however, is highly questionable, since the term "nihilism" does not appear in his notes until 1880 or in his published work until 1886.[2] In fact, nihilism is only one in a series of concepts that Nietzsche employed in his attempt to come to terms with the spiritual crisis of European civilization. Moreover, he used it only briefly and then abandoned it in favor of the concept of decadence.

Nihilism for Nietzsche grew out of the death of God. God, as Nietzsche's Zarathustra argues, died out of pity for human beings, that is, because humans were no longer powerful enough to sustain him. The death of God is thus the reflection of a fundamental degeneration of humanity. Humans are no longer capable of creating or sustaining gods. As Nietzsche remarks in *The Antichrist*, "Almost two thousand years—and not a single new god" (KGW VI 3:183). The death of God, however, opens up new possibilities, freeing human beings in a way unknown since the tragic age of the Greeks.

According to Nietzsche, humanity can now become more than it has been or less, rising to glorious new heights or sliding into dark depths. In his final teaching, he associates the ascending path with Dionysus and the descending path with the Crucified. The future of humanity, in his view, rests upon our decision for one or the other of these two possibilities. The contrast could hardly be more stark—choosing the Dionysian path is saying Yes to life in all of its terrifying chaos and complexity; choosing the path of the Crucified is rejecting life in favor of an imaginary beyond. It is within this formulation of these two possibilities that Nietzsche deploys the concept of nihilism.

Nietzsche's use of the term "nihilism" almost certainly derives from his reading of Ivan Turgenev, but Dostoevsky, Nikolay Chernyshevsky, Mikhail Bakunin, Alexandr Herzen, and Pyotr Kropotkin were also important sources for his understanding of the phenomenon (*NL*, KGW III 4:26; *GS*, KGW V 2:264; *GM*, KGW VI 2:424; *NL*, KGW VIII 1:2).[3] Nihilism, for Nietzsche, thus initially meant Russian nihilism. However, Nietzsche was misled about the character of Russian nihilism by Prosper Mérimée and the French critic Paul Bourget, who wrongly believed that the nihilist movement in Russia was essentially Schopenhauerian.[4] Nietzsche thus came to believe that nihilism was a consequence of resignation and rejection.

Although Nietzsche's use of the term "nihilism" is relatively rare in his published works, he developed the concept more fully in a series of late notes in which he lays out a morphology or genealogy of nihilism. First, he distinguishes incomplete and complete nihilism. Incomplete nihilism he identifies with positivism, materialism, and utilitarianism, which attempt to escape from nihilism without facing the problem of values that arises from the death of God. Complete nihilism, by contrast, is deeply troubled by God's death and the collapse of all eternal values. It takes one of two forms. It is either passive nihilism, which in Buddhistic fashion rejects the world, or it is active nihilism, which seeks to destroy it. Nietzsche identified the former with Schopenhauerianism and the latter with Russian nihilism. Both of these are fundamentally negative and stand in sharp contrast to an affirmative ecstatic nihilism or Dionysianism that Nietzsche saw as the outgrowth of and solution to nihilism.[5]

In trying to come to terms with Nietzsche's conception of nihilism, however, we are on treacherous ground because of the problematic status of this unpublished material. Fortunately, we do not have to rely merely upon these notes. Since the death of God is fundamentally an anthropological event, Nietzsche's conception of nihilism is ultimately concerned with the degeneration not of God but of man. We should thus be able to gain some purchase on Nietzsche's concept of nihilism through an examination of his anthropology.

In what follows, I will examine this anthropology as it is presented in the prologue and part 1 of *Thus Spoke Zarathustra*, showing how the argument that Nietzsche develops in this text already maps out the fundamental figures of his later conception of nihilism. I will then try to show that Nietzsche's anthropology and the normative conclusions that he draws from it not only fail to come to grips with the problem of nihilism but exacerbate it.

ZARATHUSTRA'S ANTHROPOLOGY

Near the beginning of *Thus Spoke Zarathustra*, Zarathustra leaves his isolated mountaintop to return to the world of men. Zarathustra declares that he "wants to be a human being again" (KGW VI 1:6). What, however, does it mean to be a human being for Zarathustra? He gives us an answer to this question in his speech to the crowd gathered to watch a tightrope walker in the town of the Motley Cow: "Man is a rope, tied between beast and *Übermensch*—a rope over an abyss. A dangerous across, a dangerous on-the-way, a dangerous looking-back, a dangerous shuddering and stopping. What is great in man is that he is a bridge and not an end: what can be loved in man is that he is a going over and a going under" (KGW VI 1:10–11).

Human being is a rope stretched between beast and *Übermensch*, a being whose being consists in being pulled in opposing directions, indeed, a being that only remains in being as a result of the tension generated by these two conflicting attractions. Thus, humans do not simply leave behind what they have overcome. As Zarathustra argues, human beings were once apes and are now humans, but they are still apes, still drawn toward the beast. Or to put the matter in other terms, even the wisest is "also a mere conflict and cross between plant and ghost" (Z, KGW VI 1:8). Even now, Zarathustra tells the crowd, fragments of the *Übermensch* can be found scattered within a fallen humanity, afloat in "a polluted stream" (Z, KGW VI 1:9). The line that defines human being in this sense is not a mere temporal transition from lower to higher but a continual and unending struggle of conflicting alternatives. Human being is the site of the contestation of these alternatives, and the principal question for Zarathustra is how the higher can be brought to predominance.

Zarathustra claims he has returned to human beings to bring them a gift. This gift is the vision of the highest human possibility, the *Übermensch*. It is not clear, however, that the people want this gift. Indeed, when he presents it to them, they do not appear to understand him, taking his speech about the *Übermensch* to refer to the tightrope walker who is about to perform in the marketplace. In a further effort to make himself understood, Zarathustra describes not the highest human possibility but the lowest, the last man. Zarathustra explains to them that just as they already in some sense are the *Übermensch*, so they are also the last man, the human who seeks mere happiness and has lost sight of anything beyond the momentary satisfaction of his desires. Despite the fact that Zarathustra characterizes him as "the most contemptible," the people cry out that they want this man, that they want to be this last man.

In what sense, though, is the last man last? I want to suggest that the figure of the last man must be understood in the context of Nietzsche's image of the tightrope. The last man is thus not the historically last man, the post-historical man that Hegel imagined, but the last man who is still man, that is, the last human possibility before the beast.

We could display this diagrammatically as shown in figure 1. The last man is only one of our possibilities of being, as is the beast and the *Übermensch*. However, these are not the only possibilities. Zarathustra has yet to describe the other human possibilities that lie on this line.

FIGURE 1:

←HUMAN→

Beast   Last Man   *Übermensch*

The crisis of our age, which Nietzsche for a time called nihilism, is a crisis of human being, a crisis that arises because of the necessity of a momentous decision about what human being is to be. Humans do not inevitably progress from beast to *Übermensch*, as humanity's decline since the time of the Greeks made clear to Nietzsche. Rather they are constantly in tension, pulled both upward and downward, and thus constantly in danger of falling, of becoming the last man, or indeed a mere beast. The production of the *Übermensch* is thus not inevitable but something that must be willed. Man must overcome himself, or more exactly it is only by a series of self-overcomings that man can become the *Übermensch*.

The path of these overcomings is outlined in "The Three Metamorphoses" at the beginning of part 1 of *Zarathustra*.[6] The spirit, according to Zarathustra, first becomes a camel, then a lion, and finally a child. I want to suggest that these possibilities must also be understood in terms of the image of the tightrope, and could be diagrammed as in figure 2. The camel spirit, Zarathustra tells us, is the dutiful spirit, the reverent spirit that would bear much, the spirit who lives according to a divinely sanctioned code of values, under the hegemony of the dragon whose name is "thou shalt." The camel spirit in this sense is a step above the last man, for the last man lives according to his momentary passions, while the camel's passions are ordered by an external or positive moral law.[7]

FIGURE 2:

←HUMAN→

Beast   Last Man   Camel   Lion   Child   *Übermensch*

The camel spirit, however, is not content with its lot and goes into the desert and is there transformed into the lion. The lion spirit is the next higher human possibility. In the desert, the camel liberates itself from the dragon that the spirit will no longer call lord and God.[8] The lion is thus the denier of God and morality. In place of the "thou shalt," the lion sets the "I will," denying the givenness of the moral law. The dragon asserts that all value was long ago created, and while the lion cannot create new values with its "I will," it does win its own freedom with its sacred No. This skeptical, destructive spirit thus obliterates the externally imposed ordering of the passions that lifted the camel spirit above the last man, but this destruction does not simply produce chaos because the lion spirit itself is made possible by a higher form of discipline, not imposed from without but generated from within.

It is this discipline that is the foundation for the transformation of the spirit into the child. The child is not a reactive but an active spirit. It is not driven by resentment or hatred of that which has hitherto imposed order upon it. In contrast to the lion, it is capable of forgetting and thus of a new innocence. Therefore, it can be a new beginning, a game, a self-propelled wheel, a first movement, a sacred Yes. This spirit not only denies its former oppressor, the great dragon and its "thou shalt," but it also affirms itself and creates new values. This spirit in other words wills its own will. Out of this child comes the *Übermensch*.

The rest of part 1 of *Zarathustra* is a discussion of these three possibilities. Aphorisms 2–7 deal with the camel spirit; aphorism 8 is a transition; aphorisms 9–14 treat the lion spirit; aphorism 15 is a transition; aphorisms 16–21 consider the child; and aphorism 22 is a conclusion.[9] The final metamorphosis of the child into the *Übermensch* is not detailed in part 1, because Zarathustra himself labors there under the mistaken impression that the child and the *Übermensch* are the same. In parts 2 and 3, however, he increasingly comes to see that innocent creativity is only possible for a being who has overcome the desire for revenge against the "it was" by replacing it with a "thus I willed it." It is this seemingly impossible feat that the doctrine of the eternal recurrence makes possible.[10] This was the step that Dostoevsky's Ivan Karamazov was unwilling to take and which led him to give back his ticket, that is, to rebel against God and life.[11] Zarathustra also has great difficulty taking this step since it means rejecting all pity, but he is ultimately able to say Yes to this most horrible thought and thus to become truly free and creative. It is, however, a freedom beyond good and evil.[12] Thus, insofar as the *Übermensch* can only come to be on the basis of the doctrine of the eternal recurrence, he is weighed down by this thought. The creation of the *Übermensch* thus depends upon a recognition of the tragedy of existence that undermines the innocence of the child. The possibility of the *Übermensch* is no longer an unqualified gift, but also a hammer that may shatter humanity.[13]

The psychological ground for this anthropology is laid out by Zarathustra in part 1. The essence of human being, he argues, is not the soul or the self-conscious ego but the body, and the body is nothing but affect or passion.[14] Passion, however, is not a unity but a multiplicity, and each of the individual passions constantly struggles for expression. Human being is thus fundamentally conflictual, for the body is constantly at war with itself. Human life is thus suffering, and most morality and religion aims at ameliorating this suffering, either by establishing peace among the passions or by devaluing this world of the passions and escaping into an imaginatively constructed beyond (NL, KGW VII 2:27).

If human being is passion, however, human thriving cannot be produced by eliminating passion. The first positive step for Zarathustra is thus the liberation of man from his servitude to the good. This is the task of the lion spirit. Such a liberation, however, is also a liberation of our wicked instincts, as Zarathustra admits in the aphorism "On the Tree on the Mountainside." The internal and external war that such a liberation entails is the foundation for a new internal discipline, the discipline of the lion or warrior spirit.

If human being for Zarathustra is passion, then the measure of one's position on the line that Zarathustra uses to define human being is determined by the strength of one's passions. This strength, however, depends not merely on the force of the individual passions but also and preeminently upon their hierarchical organization (NL, KGW VII 2:27). We can imagine them as vectors. If very powerful passions are pulling in opposite or multiple directions, they will counterbalance one another. If, however, they all stand in the service of one drive or master passion, their force will be similarly increased. Therefore, the farther one moves along the line from beast to Übermensch, the greater the discipline or rank order of the passions must be. The line that represents human being is thus a measure of power, for power is nothing other than the breadth and effective coordination of the passions under a single head.

For Zarathustra, the psychology of the passions is thus grounded in the will to power. This term first appears in Nietzsche's published work in the aphorism "On the Thousand and One Goals" in part 1 of Zarathustra. Zarathustra argues there that a people is constituted by its values. These values separate a people from their neighbors and give them a positive character of their own. The tablet of these values is a tablet of their self-overcomings, that is, a record of their triumph over themselves, over what was most difficult and indispensable for them. It is the record of the subordination of their often contradictory passions to one master passion aiming at a single goal.[15] In this sense, these values are the voice of a people's will to power, of what Zarathustra characterizes as a love that will rule and a love that will obey.

The psychological foundation of the passions in the will to power is spelled out more fully in "On Self-Overcoming" in part 2 of *Zarathustra*. Building upon his previous account in part 1, Zarathustra characterizes the will to power as the unexhausted procreative will of life: "Where I found the living, there I found will to power; and even in the will of those who serve I found the will to be master" (Z, KGW VI 1:143–44). The passions are moments of the will of life itself that constantly strives for power. Their energy and multiplicity are conceived in terms of a fundamental self-opposing, self-overcoming will intrinsic to life itself. In and through this discussion of the will to power, Zarathustra's account of human nature is put in the context of an interpretation of life as a whole. In this sense, the line that Zarathustra uses to define the human possibilities must be understood as a mere section of a longer line of life itself.[16]

Where then did Nietzsche imagine European humanity was on Zarathustra's line? As the tightrope image indicates, they were close to or nearing a crucial turning point, in the very middle of the line. This is the point that Zarathustra calls the Great Noon. This can be diagrammed as in figure 3. The death of God fatally undermines the "thou shalt" of Christianity's camel spirit. This is a disaster but also opens up a great possibility. Christianity in Nietzsche's view helped to constrain and order human passions in an age when other forms of restraint were breaking down. It did so, however, only by subordinating human beings to an external positive law, by inculcating an absurdly simplistic vision of a rational God and a rational cosmos. It succeeded in preserving human beings, in other words, only by transforming them into camels, into believers.

FIGURE 3:

←HUMAN→

Great Noon

| Beast | Last Man | Camel | ↓ | Lion | Child | Übermensch |

The death of God, and the consequent delegitimation of all divinely sanctioned commandments and moral imperatives, has brought to an end all external constraints on our passions. In the ensuing vacuum, European humanity is confronted with two possibilities, descending toward the last man or ascending toward the lion, the child, and ultimately the *Übermensch*.[17]

The former is a rejection of the existing rank order of the passions; the latter the establishment of a new discipline.[18]

Zarathustra preaches the necessity of the Great Noon, that is, the necessity of the decision at that moment in which man stands exactly in the middle of the tightrope between beast and *Übermensch*.[19] As we can see from our previous diagram, however, this is precisely the point at which the camel is transformed into the lion.[20]

Zarathustra's teaching in part 1 is thus a call to arms, a call for the appearance of the lion-spirited, not as an end in itself but as a necessary step on the way to the *Übermensch*.[21] We are given a metaphorical indication of this in the prologue, for the man who walks the tightrope but is unable to cross over the midpoint plunges to his death when his rival, the sardonic jester, leaps over him. This leonine jester, however, only foreshadows the true herald of the Great Noon, the laughing lion, who appears at the end of part 4 of *Zarathustra*.[22] The appearance of this lion indicates to Zarathustra that this metamorphosis is at hand and that his children (and thus the *Übermenschen*) are now near.[23]

THE ANTHROPOLOGICAL FOUNDATION OF NIHILISM

I want to suggest that this anthropology provides the framework for Nietzsche's understanding of nihilism. Nietzsche's work from 1886 on is clearly a further development of the final teaching that he first articulated in *Zarathustra*. Nietzsche had originally planned to end *Zarathustra* with part 3. What currently passes for part 4 was to be the first part of a second *Zarathustra* project in which Zarathustra presented his explicit teaching to the world.[24] In large part because the work was met with incomprehension and indifference, Nietzsche became convinced that Zarathustra could not serve as his spokesman, at least not without much greater preparation of his audience. As a result, he did not continue this poetic/metaphorical project and turned instead to a more literal and direct discussion of the crisis of his age and its solution.[25] His later work is thus not a repudiation of *Zarathustra* but its completion, a fuller articulation of his final teaching.

The concept of nihilism that Nietzsche developed during this period was one of his attempts to persuade humanity to choose the Dionysian path to the *Übermensch instead of* the Christian/bourgeois path to the last man. The decisiveness of this moment is reflected in Nietzsche's increasingly hostile attitude toward Christianity, most prominent in *The Antichrist*, but also evident in the other works of the later 1880s.

Christianity must be destroyed because nihilism, according to the late Nietzsche, is a peculiarly Christian phenomenon. The Christian falls into despair because he believes that the death of God and the concomitant collapse of all absolute values mean that life has no value at all. If God is dead, nothing is true and everything is permitted. This conclusion has different meanings for different human beings. For some, it means that they can simply follow their momentary passions. These are incomplete nihilists, the banal hedonists whom Zarathustra characterized as last men. They do not seek discipline and order of rank but a democracy of the passions in which each is satisfied in turn without repression or sublimation. These people do not see or understand the problem of values since this problem of values is always a problem of the appropriate order or discipline of the soul.

The passive nihilist is a second kind of human being, the Christian who can no longer believe in God but who needs such an absolute. He is driven to despair and resignation in the face of this nothingness. The third kind of man, the active nihilist, is also distraught by the death of God, but he does not fall into despair nor does he resign himself to the world as he finds it. Rather, he falls into a destructive rage and seeks to push over all the remaining idols, to have done with all "thou shalts." This active nihilist thus bears a striking resemblance to Zarathustra's lion spirit. Like this spirit, the active nihilist is free but without a home, filled like Turgenev's nihilist hero Bazarov with resentment, seeking to overthrow the existing order.[26]

If we could return to our diagram, nihilism might be represented as shown in figure 4. In his last productive years, Nietzsche came to believe that the Great Noon was at hand. In the notes of this period, he even laid out a timetable for the future development of human being. Year one of his new time reckoning was 1888, the date of the publication of the first book of the revaluation, *The Antichrist*. This is the date of the Great Noon that initiates the onset of active nihilism. It will last, according to Nietzsche, two hundred years. These centuries of war and destruction will produce a new group of harder, stronger, more disciplined human beings who will be able to bear Nietzsche's teaching of the eternal recurrence (*EH*, KGW VI 3:364).[27] Nietzsche often calls these new human beings artist-tyrants.[28] Out of these hardened men, as Zarathustra suggests in "On the Gift-Giving Virtue," will grow the *Übermensch* who will in turn produce as a reflection of his own superabundance the supergod, Dionysus. This two-hundred-year period of war and destruction will end in 2088 with the establishment of a thousand-year Dionysian *Reich*.[29]

FIGURE 4:

←HUMAN→

Great Noon

Beast	Incomplete Nihilism	Passive Nihilism	↓	Active Nihilism	Dionysian Nihilism	Übermensch

NIETZSCHE AND NIHILISM

Nietzsche's conception of nihilism is thus deeply rooted in his anthropology. Two questions remain for us. First, does Nietzsche correctly "map" nihilism as a historical phenomenon against this anthropology? And second, even if Nietzsche does not give us an adequate explanation of nihilism as it was previously understood, how should we evaluate his conception of nihilism in its own right?

The term and concept of nihilism originated in the late eighteenth century. The preeminent intellectual figure in the development of the concept was Friedrich Jacobi, who used the term to criticize Johann Gottlieb Fichte's absolute egoism. Fichte's assertion that the I is everything, according to Jacobi, makes God nothing, a mere product of the human imagination. Jacobi sees this conclusion as the "most horrible of horrors" because if everything is merely the representation of the I, then the good, the beautiful, and the holy are merely hollow names.[30]

The concept of nihilism as it was originally deployed thus located the source of nihilism not in the weakness of the human will but in the assertion of its omnipotence. God does not die out of pity for human beings but because humans attribute the entire act of creation to themselves. It follows from this titanic claim that there can be no goals or rules for human action that are extrinsic to the human will. Human beings, or at least the best of them, are imagined to be not merely free but creative, not merely actors but makers in the fullest sense, making themselves, their world, and the laws governing their own actions. It is this absolute egoism that the earlier nineteenth century called nihilism.

Few nineteenth-century thinkers imagined that every human being was such a titan of creative power. In fact, even the most egalitarian revolutionaries attributed such force only to a chosen few. In his early thought, Fichte discovered these world-creators in the race of scholars whom he believed to be free from the constraints of the world in a way that ordinary people were not. In his later work, he imagined this elite to be made up of divinely inspired tyrants (*Zwingherrn*) forging the German people into an instrument of human liberation. This Fichtean vision of superhuman beings employing their radical freedom to remake the world exercised a decisive influence on the entire sweep of nihilist thought in the nineteenth century, from the early German Romantics to the Left Hegelians and the Russian nihilists. The Jena Romantics such as Ludwig Tieck, the Schlegels, and Novalis (all of whom were Fichte students) imagined these monsters of will to be demonic human beings who establish themselves in opposition to God and morality. Indeed, these figures transgress all existing custom and law in search of a new kind of freedom. They are heroes of the will, but heroes who in a world governed by the moral law can only be antiheroes, criminals, seducers, conquerors, and in many cases actual monsters.[31] The Left Hegelians and the Russian nihilists, by contrast, saw this will embodied in a revolutionary class. In the case of Marx, for example, this is the proletariat under the leadership of turncoat bourgeois intellectuals. For Chernyshevsky and Dmitry Pisarev, it is the intelligentsia in general and among them hardened professional revolutionaries. The millenarian core of this nihilist movement is captured at its conclusion in Trotsky's claim that permanent revolution will make it possible for man to "raise himself to a new plane, to create a higher social biological type, or, if you please, a superman. . . . Man will become immeasurably stronger, wiser, subtler; his body will become more harmonized, his movements more rhythmic, his voice more musical. The forms of life will become dynamically dramatic. The average human type will rise to the heights of an Aristotle, a Goethe, or a Marx. And above this ridge new peaks will rise."[32]

Even this brief discussion of the history of the concept of nihilism should make clear that Nietzsche's attempt to "map" nihilism against his anthropology is a radical break with what theretofore had been called nihilism. The demonic Prometheanism of the earlier concept of nihilism is not a reflection of either Christian despair or a pure hatred of the present that has no care for the future. In fact, this Prometheanism has obvious affinities with Nietzsche's equally Promethean vision of the Dionysian *Übermensch*. Nietzsche here was misled by Schopenhauer and the critics of nihilism.

Schopenhauer like many of the other leading German thinkers of his generation had been a Fichte student. However, he was repelled by Fichte's vision of a class of world-transforming supermen. The world-will in his view did not aim at human happiness. In fact, it had no end. Life, as Schopenhauer saw it, was a meaningless and fruitless striving that produced only human misery. Conquest and creation thus offer no satisfaction. The only way to inner peace is renunciation of the world. This rejection of the will for the path of self-abnegation was rare in the nineteenth century. Nietzsche, however, took it as typical and read the history of nihilism through Schopenhauer.

He thus did not see that in rejecting Schopenhauer's absolute negation of the world in favor of an absolute affirmation, he was implicitly reversing Schopenhauer's reversal of Fichte and thus planting himself on essentially Fichtean soil. As a result, he did not see the obvious affinities of the Prometheanism of the earlier nihilists to his own doctrines.

This fact, however, does not mean that Nietzsche was necessarily wrong, for while he may have been mistaken about nihilism as it previously appeared and was understood, he may still have seen more deeply than his predecessors into the essence of nihilism. I want to suggest, however, that this was not the case. In *Zarathustra*, Nietzsche suggests that the choice for our times is between the banality of the last man and the tragic culture of the *Übermensch*. The latter possibility, as we have seen, depends in his view on a cataclysmic transformation, led by leonine spirits. As disquieting as this vision might be, it is rendered in even darker tones in his later discussion of nihilism. Here, there is no real choice for present-day human beings. The bourgeois world is characterized as incomplete nihilism, which must necessarily slip into complete (passive and then active) nihilism. Nietzsche thus expects the advent of widespread despair and the renunciation of life on the Schopenhauerian model. He describes this future in dire terms in a note that is typical of the period: "Inevitable appearance of disgust and hatred of life. Buddhism. European strength driven to mass suicide" (KGW VII 1:2). To avoid this inevitable possibility, Nietzsche believed it was necessary to choose the path of active nihilism, that is, the path of war and destruction. He clearly recognized that this path was fraught with danger and that humanity itself might perish in the attempt to traverse it, as the tightrope walker does in the prologue to *Zarathustra*, but he saw no acceptable alternative. Moreover, after his discovery of Dostoevsky, he came to the conclusion that many of the leonine destroyers might also be driven not by a will to freedom, by a holy No, but rather by the same resentment and despair that characterized the passive nihilist.

In fact, Nietzsche's fears about the inevitability of nihilistic despair and suicide have proven extravagant and unfounded. If the intervening years have proven anything, it is that bourgeois society can weather the death of God without collapsing into either passive or active nihilism. There are many explanations for the strengths of the bourgeois world. It cannot be denied that technological organization has increasingly come to constrain and direct human passions in the ways that Heidegger and others have described. But it is also the case that the bourgeois world has long been undergirded and interpenetrated by practices and ways of thinking that Nietzsche too easily discounts or doesn't even recognize. Anglo-American liberalism and pragmatism in particular place much less emphasis on will than the tradition in which Nietzsche finds himself and certainly deserve credit for opening up a much more positive view of the world. Moreover, the continued belief in rights and particularly human rights and dignity, which Nietzsche imagined were merely idols of a deceased God that would soon come tumbling down, have proven much more enduring than he imagined.

The real choice was thus not between passive nihilism and a revolutionary transformation of European culture, but between a pragmatic liberal bourgeois democracy and revolutionary tyranny. Nietzsche like many other millenarian revolutionaries of the nineteenth and early twentieth centuries preferred the latter, which in his view was more life-enhancing and noble. While one may share Nietzsche's disgust with the banality of bourgeois life or see the iron bonds of technology as a real threat to human freedom, it is certainly not obvious that either of these can justify the destruction that he foresees, welcomes, and promotes. While there is much that attracts us to Nietzsche, it is a great mistake to overlook his darker side because this darkness is not an accidental appendage of his otherwise positive thought, but a clear consequence of his philosophical anthropology.

Slouching toward Bethlehem to Be Born: On the Nature and Meaning of Nietzsche's Übermensch

Nietzsche's name in our time has been indelibly linked with four ideas, the death of God, nihilism, the will to power, and the *Übermensch*.[1] Although all of these concepts play an important role in Nietzsche's final teaching, they appear much later in his thought than we often assume. The death of God, for example, is not announced in his published work until *The Gay Science*. The idea of the will to power first appears in print only in *Thus Spoke Zarathustra*, and while it occasionally recurs in his later published work, it gains its preeminent stature only after Nietzsche's death, and then largely as a result of his sister's misrepresentation of some of his notes as a magnum opus called *The Will to Power*. The concept of nihilism, as we have seen, appears even later in Nietzsche's thought. Here again the posthumous publication of his notes gave readers a distorted view of the importance of this concept for his thought. None of these concepts, however, played as important a role in the public perception of Nietzsche as the idea of the *Übermensch*, which is certainly the most famous of Nietzsche's many powerful images. This idea, however, also plays a smaller role in both his published work and in his unpublished notes than we often assume. It appears only fifty-three times in his published works and seventy-eight times in the *Nachlass*. Outside *Zarathustra*, the notes for *Zarathustra*, or the discussion of *Zarathustra* in *Ecce Homo*, he uses the term only eight times and then in a different or at least in a derivative sense, typically referring to, "a kind of *Übermensch*," or "a mixture of non-man and *Übermensch*." In Nietzsche's work, the concept properly understood is thus really used only by a single character in a single work and then apparently abandoned. What then accounts for the astonishing popularity of the concept? And more importantly, is this concept as important for Nietzsche as its popularity would seem to suggest?

The later importance of this concept has perhaps less to do with Nietzsche than with those who came before and after him. The idea of the superhuman had already appeared on the European intellectual horizon in the eighteen century, largely as a product of the counter-Enlightenment.[2] The Enlightenment itself was an essentially egalitarian movement that articulated a notion of reason that was universally accessible, and a doctrine of the division of labor that imagined that all great things were brought about by the common and collected efforts of large numbers of human beings. Drawing on Milton's Satan and a few earlier models such as Prometheus, the Romantics emphasized not man's common humanity or reason, or even the general similarity of rudimentary human desires, but the enormous differences in the hidden depths of the individual soul or self. This view was conjoined to a theory of historical change that saw titanic individuals and not the masses as the decisive force in world history. Goethe, for example, saw demonic individuals as forces of nature, unpredictable and uncontrollable by human beings, and yet playing a decisive role in shaping the course of human events. He had in mind people like Napoleon, and personified them most famously in Faust. Byron portrayed a similar titanic individual in *Manfred*, and later himself became a model for such an exalted "demonic" individual, joining Napoleon, Beethoven, and others in this Romantic pantheon of supreme human possibilities. Hegel in a similar vein argued for the decisive role of world-historical individuals in effecting historical change, even while suggesting that they would not exist or be needed in the future.

What was decisive in all of these accounts was greatness, and not goodness. Indeed, like Milton's Satan, these titanic individuals were morally ambiguous at best. In some cases evil seemed to be almost essential to their greatness as a demonstration that they were not subject to the petty constraints of bourgeois morality. Drawing on Fichte's notion of the absolute I, Ludwig Tieck presented a classic picture of such a "criminal" hero in *William Lovell*. This figure appeared repeatedly in Romantic literature. Stendhal's Julien Sorel and Balzac's Vautrin are only two of many famous examples.

By the mid-nineteenth century, interest in such figures had become widespread. Thomas Carlyle, for example, laid out this ideal in great detail in his work *On Heroes, Hero-Worship, and the Heroic in History*. Nor were such figures merely literary phenomena. After the failures of the revolutions of 1848, European radicals began to present images of superhuman revolutionaries. Building on Turgenev's ambivalent portrayal of such a revolutionary in the figure of Bazarov in *Fathers and Sons*, and Nikolay Chernyshevsky's Rakhmetov, revolutionaries such as Sergey Nechayev and Mikhail Bakunin sought to play such superhuman roles. The deification of Lenin and the Stalinist cult of personality were only the final consequences of this movement.

All of this was buttressed by social Darwinism that looked for the formation of a higher being as a result of the operation of the laws of nature and in particular the evolutionary notion of the survival of the fittest. It is in this context that Nietzsche formulates and deploys his concept of the *Übermensch*, and it is in large part because it resonated so perfectly with so many other similar ideas that it became so popular. Hermann Hesse in Germany, Joseph Conrad and Jack London in the United States, George Bernard Shaw and William Butler Yeats in Great Britain/Ireland, and many others in various parts of Europe and America saw Nietzsche's notion as the epitome of what they believed to be the highest human possibility.

After the shattering experience of World War I, such unadulterated hero worship gave way to a more sober appreciation of the dangerous nature of such ideas, but even then thinkers like Ernst Jünger and Ernest Hemingway continued to sing the praises of Promethean individualism. Such a vision of the heroic, superhuman individual played a central role in Italian futurism, in the Stakhanovite heroes of socialism, and of course in Fascism and Nazism. The hard and horrible lessons of World War II and the Holocaust further chastened such hero worshipers, but even then thinkers like Ayn Rand and more popular authors and filmmakers could still point to and exalt such heroic, superhuman possibilities, even if for the most part they banished them to an imaginary realm.

This fascination with the superhuman is well known, but does it help us to understand Nietzsche? Is Nietzsche at heart just another Romantic who is disdainful of democratic culture, or is there something more at work here? It is certainly clear that Nietzsche was deeply attracted to such Promethean possibilities, but it also clear that he did not merely take this notion from his predecessors. In fact, he is careful to distance and distinguish himself from many of those like Stendhal and Carlyle who articulated doctrines similar to his own. Indeed, Nietzsche sees himself as the heir not of Romanticism but of the ancient world. What then is the meaning of the *Übermensch* in this context?

Nietzsche was fascinated with exceptional human beings from an early age.[3] In his youth he looked to the mythical Prometheus, the semilegendary Ermanarich, and Byron's Manfred as models of such superhuman characters. As a student, he studied classical thought, and particularly the poetry and philosophy of the pre-Socratic, tragic age. During this time, he also met Wagner and came to share in his hopes for the renewal of German culture through the transcendent power of art. At that time, he came to see the exceptional human being not as a *Übermensch*, but as a creative genius, that is, as someone who is one with the genesis of the world and the superhuman power that underlies it. The exceptional human being is thus exceptional not through his own power or greatness, but because he is inspired or possessed by a superhuman power, because he is the oracle of this power. When the lyric poet says I, Nietzsche tells us in *The Birth of Tragedy*, it is in fact not the individual but the will of life itself, "the primordial artist of the world," that speaks through him (KGW III 1:41). During the period of *The Birth of Tragedy* and his "artists metaphysics," this figure is preeminently exemplified by the Greek dramatists (Aeschylus in particular), Wagner, and Schopenhauer. Beginning already with *Human, All Too Human*, however, Nietzsche calls this notion of genius into question, and in the works leading up to *Zarathustra*, he repeatedly employs his *Entlarvungspsychologie* to demonstrate that even these extraordinary individuals are often not higher beings but themselves human, all too human. Wagner in this respect is revealed as an actor who pretended to be inspired, but who in fact only wanted to have an effect. The chief alternative to such playacting, or what Sartre later called bad faith, is the free spirit who in the fashion of Montaigne and other skeptics follows the path of science rather than that of art. This science, however, does not aim at truth but is used as a tool with which to shatter our subjection to all transcendent ideals. This highly critical period of Nietzsche's thought in which he seems to delight in adopting multiple, and often self-undermining, perspectives, practicing what he calls experiments in living, comes to an end in *The Gay Science*, which itself points toward a different and, as it turned out, final teaching. This is the backdrop against which the *Übermensch* appears.

Nietzsche's vision of the *Übermensch* cannot be simply identified with either his early notion of genius or with the free spirit who appears during his middle period but certainly contains elements of each. The vision of the *Übermensch* is inextricably bound up with Nietzsche's final teaching that begins with the argument he lays out in *Zarathustra*.

The figure of Zarathustra is clearly related to earlier figures in Nietzsche's work. In *The Birth of Tragedy*, Nietzsche points to an enigmatic figure that he characterizes as "a Socrates who practices music," or "a musical Socrates" (KGW III 1:98). This figure is clearly meant to combine the philosophic elements of Socrates with the Dionysian sensibilities of the earlier Greek tragedians. When this work was originally written, the general public almost certainly thought this enigmatic figure pointed toward Wagner, but we now know that Nietzsche secretly cherished the thought that he himself would play this role. This figure is further elaborated in the sketches for an Empedocles drama that Nietzsche began about the same time but never completed. Nietzsche's Empedocles is not merely a philosopher but also practices music, seeking, for example, to end the plague in a town by staging a Dionysian festival, in sharp contrast to Oedipus who relied upon a purely dialectical examination. The connection of this figure to Zarathustra is still dimly evident in the published portions of *Zarathustra*, as Jürgen Söring has demonstrated, and is manifest in the notes for the continuation of the work in the *Nachlass*.[4] One ending, for example, has Zarathustra like Empedocles throwing himself into a volcano. Both Empedocles and Zarathustra are thus intimately connected to the Dionysian as Nietzsche himself points out in his discussion of *Zarathustra* in *Ecce Homo*, and as Laurence Lampert has substantiated in great detail in his *Nietzsche's Teaching*.[5]

The idea of the *Übermensch* is related to this effort to find a Dionysian or musical Socrates, and is a part of Nietzsche's lifelong effort to bring about the cultural renewal that he believed was essential to rescue Europe from the consequences of the death of God, or what he later called nihilism. Because God is dead, the *Übermensch* now can (and indeed in Nietzsche's view must) live. The *Übermensch* in this sense moves beyond the inspired genius of his early work and the free spirit who dominates the work of his middle period but contains elements of each. He is both poet and philosopher.

In *Zarathustra* itself the idea of the *Übermensch* is presented not as Nietzsche's idea, but as the idea that came to Zarathustra during the ten years of solitude he spent in his cave on the mountaintop. Zarathustra, we learn in the second aphorism of "Zarathustra's Preface," had retreated to this cave "bearing his ashes," that is, bearing the ashes of his dead god and of the faith that had guided and sustained him. He now returns, as the hermit in the forest notes, bringing fire to the valley, reborn as a child, as one awakened. He is returning to the world of men, because, as he puts it, he "loves man," or, as he quickly corrects himself, because he "brings human beings a gift." As we soon discover, this correction is decisive, because Zarathustra does not love man as he *is* but man as he might *become*. In fact, he despises man as he is, and his "gift" is not intended to gratify human beings, but to bring them to despise themselves by teaching them to love something higher than themselves. This gift and goal is, of course, the idea of the *Übermensch*. It is this idea that Zarathustra proclaims in his first speech to the crowd in the marketplace. His presentation, however, is both negative and nebulous, for it is little more than an assertion of his contempt for present-day humanity and the need for his contemporaries to despise themselves. When the people laugh at him and willfully misconstrue his speech as an introduction for the tightrope walker who is scheduled to appear before them, he tries again, laying out the abysmal alternative to the *Übermensch*, the last man, the petty hedonist devoid of wonder, longing, love, and creativity. He thus tells the crowd not only that they are contemptible, but that they will become even more contemptible if they do not follow the path he lays out for them. Is it any wonder that they hate him and want to kill him? Socrates' critique of his fellow Athenians was private and oblique; Zarathustra, like a Hebrew prophet, derides them publicly and directly.

At the very beginning of *Zarathustra*, Nietzsche thus lays out the fundamental problem confronting contemporary Europe. This problem grows out of the death of God and the concomitant collapse of European morality and Greco-Christian civilization. In Nietzsche's view and for reasons we will examine below, this event leaves Europeans with a choice between two possible paths, one leading to the *Übermensch* and the other to the last man. Nietzsche knows that the path of least resistance leads to the last man, but he is convinced that the path to the *Übermensch* is more compelling. The first argument that he presents for his position in *Zarathustra* is anthropological and psychological. This argument, however, is not his final word on the subject, and rests on another argument that is both cosmological and ontological. The anthropological argument, as we saw in the previous essay, is presented metaphorically in the preface and "The Three Metamorphoses" from camel, to lion, to child. The psychological foundations of this argument are developed in the rest of part 1, and the cosmological and ontological arguments are laid out in parts 2 and 3.

Viewed anthropologically, the human for Nietzsche is thus not an unchanging category, but a process or motion from beast to *Übermensch*. Indeed, human being is always a vector pointed either toward beast or *Übermensch*. The differences between human beings are determined by their "aliveness," that is, by their relative strength or power. All of life, Zarathustra tells us in "On Self-Overcoming," is a struggle for power or dominance. For Nietzsche, this is not some abstract, disembodied, or transcendent principle, but the moving force in all things, which he later calls the will to power. In defining this notion, he draws heavily on Gottfried Leibniz's monadology. The world is made up of points of force each moving in its own direction, and each seeking to dominate and subordinate its competitors in order to augment its strength with their own. In living things these force vectors are drives, passions, affects, or desires. Humans for Nietzsche are thus bodies dominated by passions, and not egos governed by reason. In contrast to beasts (who are also dominated by desires), humans are not determined by instincts (that is, by a single fixed order of rank within the self), but are the battleground of their passions, drives, and so on. We are at war with ourselves, or to put it another way, our various passions struggle for mastery, struggle to dominate and drive the self. No one passion is programmed to rule.[6] Each of us is the site of a subliminal struggle between the passions for dominance, and each of these passions seeks not to eliminate the others but to master them, to subordinate them to its goal, and thus augment its own force with their psychic energy. Nietzsche's anthropology is thus a radical rejection not merely of the traditional notion of the soul but also of the Cartesian notion of the self, and a turn toward a more materialistic psychology and ontology derived in part from contemporary materialists such as Friedrich Lange, but more fundamentally from Schopenhauer and the Greeks.

To understand the differences that Nietzsche sees between the various stages on life's way, it is necessary to understand the type of subordination that characterizes the self at each point along the line. As we have seen, the camel spirit is the allegorical representation of the believer, whose self is organized by his belief in an abstract "theological" notion of right or justice. The threat of a "wrathful" God, of what Zarathustra calls the dragon, exercises a kind of hegemony over him and within him. The death of God removes the restraints that give order, purpose, and direction to this world and this self. The idea of absolute truth and everything that was built upon it thus dissolve. The psychic consequence of the death of God is consequently the liberation of the passions from an alien, external constraint. This liberation offers marvelous opportunities, but it is also fraught with great danger.

This is what Zarathustra realized and what drove him to his mountain. The disintegration of the self and the world that had been built on this faith left him with only the ashes of his god and a self at war with itself. This conclusion is prefigured by the madman in *The Gay Science*, who comes to announce the death of God and realizes he has come too soon because the news of God's demise has not yet reached men, even though they themselves were his murderers. Zarathustra is this madman, the first to realize that God is dead, and to experience in this event his own psychic immolation. He spends his ten years of solitude reflecting on this "greatest event" and its consequences, reconstituting himself, and developing a new goal for humanity. He recognizes that the time when such a camel-like faith in God could give direction to human life is coming to an end. Rather than receiving our direction from some distant God, we are left to our own devices. Under these circumstances, Nietzsche believes that there are two possibilities that open themselves up to us. The easiest and in a sense most likely is a democratic possibility in which all internal discipline or hierarchy within the self dissolves, and we simply wander this way and that satisfying our momentary desires. This is the existence of the last man before the beasts, that is, the last man who is still human and not merely a herd animal (*NL*, KGW VII 1:503–4).

The path to the last man is immediate and direct—it requires only the liberation from all repression, and the death of God in Nietzsche's view entails the disappearance of what Freud would later call the superego. It is this unrepressed man who is served by the market economy that imagines human happiness to consist not in restraint and moderation but in the maximal satisfaction of all desires, and that strives not merely to satisfy them but to continually uncover or liberate new ones. This possibility in Nietzsche's view leads to an increasing weakness and decay, to what he later calls decadence or degeneration. The other, more difficult path leads to the *Übermensch*. This is a more aristocratic possibility that requires the establishment of a new order of rank or hierarchy within the self under a dominant and dominating passion. This internal reordering of the soul is the prerequisite for the reordering of culture and society that Nietzsche calls the revaluation of all values. He discusses this reorganization and redirection of humanity in "On the Thousand and One Goals." In this aphorism Zarathustra argues that all previous peoples have formed themselves by choosing values that were antagonistic to those of their neighbors, and that thus set them apart from and at odds with those nearest to them. This is an expression of their will to power. What has hitherto been missing, according to Zarathustra, is the one goal for all of humanity. This is the goal that Zarathustra aims to establish with his teaching of the *Übermensch*, a supergoal that will trump all other lesser goals, and thus attract the strongest and most courageous to his cause, those he later called good Europeans.

The path to the *Übermensch* is not only more difficult; it is also more dangerous, because the *Übermensch* can only come into existence in the aftermath of the destruction of European civilization. As we saw in the previous essay, the collapse of European civilization will, Nietzsche hopes, produce a cadre of hardened warriors out of whom the *Übermensch* will arise (Z, KGW VI 1:96–97).

In part 1, Zarathustra believes that such destruction will make possible a new innocence beyond good and evil, portrayed metaphorically as the child. This innocence is based upon a forgetfulness of the old values. Only such innocence will be truly capable of a new, spontaneous creativity, of saying not merely "No!" to the old values in the manner of the lion, but "Yes!" to new values and ways of being. In Zarathustra's thinking in part 1, the child thus seems to be identical with the *Übermensch*.[7] It would be a mistake, however, to believe this is Nietzsche's or even Zarathustra's final word on the subject. Indeed, the rest of *Zarathustra* is in a certain sense nothing other than an account of Zarathustra's recognition of the inadequacy of such an understanding of the *Übermensch*. Zarathustra learns in the course of his development that mere forgetfulness is not enough, that the *Übermensch* is not a child at play but a mature and diamond-hard individual who realizes that his spontaneity is only possible on the basis of an extraordinarily difficult and terrifying act of will that is bound up with the realization, acceptance, and active affirmation of the doctrine of the eternal recurrence of the same.

Humanity's future in Nietzsche's view crucially depends upon the direction we follow from this moment forward. In contrast to Hegel, he does not believe change is always progressive. There is no ineluctable historical necessity that impels us toward the *Übermensch*. Nietzsche, however, also does not accept Schopenhauer's pessimistic conclusion that willing has no meaning, and that we simply have to resign ourselves to our fate. Willing matters. That is why this moment of time is so crucial in Nietzsche's view to the future of humanity. It is the Great Noon, as Zarathustra calls it, the moment in which the great decision is made about who will be lord of the earth. As we discussed in the previous essay, we cannot remain camel-spirited beings. That requires a faith that is no longer tenable. The failure to try to become greater than we are will thus inevitably lead us to become less than we are. The attempt to pass over this point, however, will certainly lead to the destruction of many of even the most courageous human beings. Even the higher men represented by the tightrope walker will be leaped over and fall to their deaths. Even though they are higher, they are not high enough. Nietzsche thus makes it at least metaphorically clear that the price to be paid for the attempt to move in the direction of the *Übermensch* is very high. It takes a rare internal strength to pass from despair at the death of God to the active destruction of revolutionary nihilism.[8] Indeed, one must be willing not merely to die but to leap over others, knowing they will perish. Such hardness is necessary to make the passage to the *Übermensch*.

For Nietzsche's contemporaries and still for us today, the choice that he presents looks like a choice between war and peace, between a prosperous society that aims at the maximal satisfaction of human desires and a world of discipline, destruction, and deprivation. How can Nietzsche reasonably believe that anyone would choose the latter path? Within *Zarathustra*, the argument for this choice rests not merely on his hope that the revelation of the decadence of the last man will so disgust people or generate such shame that they will pursue a more elevated lifestyle, but more fundamentally on his conviction that he can convince some of his readers of the irresistible beauty of the *Übermensch*. Nietzsche has to show this group that what lies beyond man is so attractive they will not be able to live without it.

The *Übermensch* is thus a rhetorical tool that Nietzsche uses to seduce the most courageous human beings to abandon the path that leads to the last man in favor of the path of revolutionary destruction. However, it is not merely a rhetorical tool, and Nietzsche's goal is not merely war and destruction. He himself is not lion-spirited and does not particularly admire the lion-spirited. There is little praise in his work for the "blond beasts," although he clearly recognizes that it may only be out of such violent men that a new aristocracy can arise. Indeed, he seems to believe that it is only such higher possibilities that can finally justify the violence that is necessary in the present. In part 1, Zarathustra represents these possibilities with the image of the innocent child. He thus seems to suggest and perhaps even to believe that on the other side of the wars of tomorrow there is a pacific creative future. This optimistic image, however, fades in the face of the hard realities that Zarathustra has to confront in parts 2 and 3. To believe that these "higher" possibilities will be more pacific and less destructive than those on our immediate horizon is thus problematic. To understand why this is so, however, we need to examine more carefully why the child's innocence is an insufficient foundation for the *Übermensch*, and what is necessary to bring about the final metamorphosis of the innocent child into the hardened *Übermensch*.

The child as he appears in part 1 is the image of spontaneous innocence, of a new beginning, of play, the first moving of a wheel as Zarathustra puts it, or of natality to use a term Hannah Arendt later made popular. This figure draws in obvious ways on the Romantic idealization of childhood as a time of innocence, as well as on Kantian and neo-Kantian notions of spontaneity. What is missing in part 1 is any serious engagement with the genesis of this child. There is a great deal of talk about the production of the child, of this as the end of marriage, and of the freedom necessary to such innocent creativity, but it is not clear how one gets from here to there. Being one's own law means as Zarathustra points out being one's own judge and avenger, following the loneliest of paths. Zarathustra gives us an indication of how personal a path this is for him, for as he says, "You must wish to consume yourself in your own flame: how could you wish to become new unless you had first become ashes!" (KGW VI 1:78). It is only in this way that the lion-spirited can come to follow the path of the lover, which is the true path of the creator. Despite its obvious reference to Zarathustra's own path up the mountain, there is no concrete explanation of what makes this transition possible. In this sense it depends on "creating a god for yourself out of your seven devils" (KGW VI 1:78), but Zarathustra himself apparently does not know and certainly does not explain how to bring this about. Parts 2 and 3 of *Zarathustra* are an account of his coming to grasp and will this awful necessity. The rest of the book is thus the account of the metamorphosis of the child into the *Übermensch*.

This knowledge is not something that Zarathustra has to discover in the world. It is already present within him and must therefore only be uncovered and remembered. But while he knows it, he doesn't want to recognize or articulate it. We see evidence of this already in the first aphorism of part 2, suggestively titled "The Child and the Mirror." This aphorism recounts Zarathustra's dream of a child, but this is not an image of innocent spontaneity. This child holds up a mirror to Zarathustra to show him that he is in fact a devil, that he has not created a new god out of his devils, but remains satanic. He misunderstands his dream here, still hoping that his lioness, his wild wisdom, can be taught to roar tenderly, but this is only an indication of the immense need for forgetfulness or repression that the horrifying truth of his deepest thought requires. How then does Zarathustra bring this thought to the surface?

Already in the aphorism that follows the account of his dream, he returns to his earlier, one might almost say inauthentic, notion that the *Übermensch* is something he can create by violence.

> O men, in the stone there sleeps an image, the image of my images. Alas, that it must sleep in the hardest, the ugliest stone! Now my hammer rages cruelly against its prison. Pieces of rock rain from the stone: what is that to me? I want to perfect it; for a shadow came to me—the stillest and lightest of all things once came to me. The beauty of the *Übermensch* came to me as a shadow. O my brothers, what are the gods to me now? (*Z*, KGW VI 1:108)

Zarathustra imagines the problem here to be how he can shatter the rock of humanity and liberate the *Übermensch*. What he overlooks is the self-reflexive character of this act. He must himself first be freed, and the violence that he believes is necessary must first be exercised upon himself. In order to understand this fact, Zarathustra must first understand that he is not free.

This begins with his realization in "The Tomb Song" that he is incapable of the innocence of a child, that he has lost this innocence in his struggles with his enemies. What remains is only "*my will*. Silent and unchanged it strides through the years" (KGW VI 1:141). This will, however, as he makes clear in the next aphorism, "On Self-Overcoming," is nothing other than life itself that wants only to overcome itself, is nothing other than the will to power. Creation is thus never innocent—it always requires destruction and domination. Even this insight, however, conceals the truth that becomes more apparent in "On Redemption."

Willing never creates ex nihilo because it always acts within an existing world. It thus always must destroy in order to create. Evil is thus a necessary part of goodness. All of this is reasonably straightforward, but Zarathustra also recognizes that not all destruction is creative. Indeed, the destruction of the lion-spirited is not a sacred "Yes!" to something new but always only a perennial "No!" to what is. The lion-spirited are motivated not by a vision of what might be, but by the hatred of what is, precisely because what is always limits the will. Willing for them is thus not a final liberation, but a repeated gesture that is continually frustrated by the fact that they are always only reacting to what already is. The present, in other words, is always guided by the dead hand of the past. The destructive spirit of the lion thus is motivated not by spontaneous love, but by what Zarathustra calls the spirit of revenge, the hatred of the "it was." In order to complete the metamorphosis from the lion to the child, it is therefore necessary to overcome the spirit of revenge, or to use Zarathustra's language, to be redeemed from the spirit of revenge. Here, however, Zarathustra runs into a rock wall, for he realizes that willing cannot liberate because the will itself is a prisoner (KGW VI 1:173–78). To be free the will would have to will backward, and this it cannot do. Who, he asks rhetorically, could teach him to will backward? While this seems to be an impossibility, the mere articulation of the question catapults him toward the answer, an answer, however, that he cannot face. The Stillest Hour thus tells him that he "must go as a shadow of that which must come," that he "must yet become a child and without shame" (KGW VI 1:185), but Zarathustra cannot do this, and indeed spends most of part 3 haunted by this unthinkable and unspeakable thought. It is this thought, however, that is essential to his metamorphosis and to the advent of the *Übermensch*. It is also this thought that destroys the simple innocence of the child and puts in its place the tragic seriousness of the *Übermensch*.

This thought is the thought of the eternal recurrence. To will spontaneously, to be a self-moved mover, is the goal of the will, but this seems to be impossible for everyone who lives within time. In this respect, it is not so much death but birth that puts a limit on our will. To use Heidegger's terminology, we are always thrown into the world and shaped by it. Our motives thus arise out of or are in reaction to this world. In Nietzsche's view this throwness produces a subliminal anger against the "it was" that causes the greatest pain to the strongest human beings because it frustrates them again and again. What is necessary to a true liberation is not merely the passive acceptance of our throwness, but a means by which we can actually will it. Zarathustra recognizes this fact and knows what needs to be done, but is unable to articulate it even to himself until part 3, first indirectly in "On the Vision and the Riddle" and then finally, excruciatingly, and decisively in "The Convalescent."

In "On the Vision and the Riddle," Zarathustra begins to come to terms with this thought in recounting another dream vision. This is the vision of his conversation with the spirit of gravity about the nature of time and eternity. After much back and forth, Zarathustra asks the dwarf finally, "are not all things so firmly knotted together that this moment draws after it *all* that is to come? Therefore—itself too? For whatever can walk—in this long lane out *there* too, it *must walk* once more. . . . must we not eternally return?" (KGW VI 1:196). Zarathustra, however, does not understand the deep truth of this vision. The dream images are after all only what Nietzsche earlier characterized as Apollinian masks of a Dionysian reality, a view of the abyss through a scrim. Indeed, even in this relatively benign form, Zarathustra is terrified by "my own thoughts and the thoughts behind my thoughts" (KGW VI 1:196–97). At this point in his journey, he is still unable to face the truth directly. It is presented to him in his vision in the form of a sleeping shepherd choking on a snake that has crawled into his mouth and bitten into his throat. The solution is also contained in this vision—the shepherd bites off the head of the snake and spits it out, arising transfigured and laughing with "a laughter that is no human laughter" (KGW VI 1:198). It is no human laughter because it is superhuman laughter. The dream image here is the story of the metamorphosis of the child into the *Übermensch*. It is, however, only the metaphorical expression of the final step that entails not merely recognizing the eternal recurrence but willing it. This is the terrible truth, the terrible act that Zarathustra must complete to free himself from the spirit of revenge and establish the freedom and spontaneity necessary for real creation.

The eternal recurrence as it is presented in "On the Vision and the Riddle" is a cosmological doctrine that looks at the process from the outside. What Zarathustra is unable to articulate is not the way in which he is bound up in this process but the way this process is bound up in him. He thirsts and longs for the laughter that he heard, but he still cannot face the psychological abyss that is necessary to produce it. He wants to be in that world, but he is unwilling not merely to do but even to recognize what is necessary to bring it into existence. What then is the difficulty in recognizing and willing the eternal recurrence of the same? The answer to this question is essential to understanding the nature of Nietzsche's *Übermensch*.

On the surface, it is not clear why it is so difficult to accept this doctrine, and many readers have found Zarathustra's hesitations histrionic. This dismissal of the difficulty of accepting the eternal recurrence, however, is a consequence of a misunderstanding of the meaning of the doctrine itself. It is clear from Nietzsche's notes and from everything Nietzsche had to say about the doctrine that he believed its effect would be devastating. Indeed, he often characterizes it as a hammer that will strike humanity, crushing the weak and tempering the strong. At other times he refers to it as Dionysus or the abyss. There thus can be little doubt that he perceives the act of thinking it and willing it as a titanic deed, sufficient in fact to make possible the transition to the superhuman. What then are we missing here?

To overcome the spirit of revenge, it is necessary to will backward, but the will can only will forward. The arrow of time moves only in one direction. The past can then only be willed if it is not just the past but also the future. In willing the future, we thus must also will the past. If each act of willing is bound up with every other act of willing in a necessary and ineluctable way, then to will one thing thoroughly is to will all things always. Or to turn the matter about, in order to truly will any one thing, it is necessary to will all things. One cannot like Faust seek out one moment and affirm it with a "Linger moment, you are so beautiful!" without at the same time not merely saying but also willing that everything else be also beautiful, loveable, and infinitely choice-worthy. To will the eternal recurrence is thus to will the whole, and in this way to reverse the absolute resignation of Schopenhauer (and the Soothsayer who represents Schopenhauer in *Zarathustra*) into absolute affirmation. This is what Nietzsche calls *amor fati*. It is this absolute affirmation of the whole that is essential to the eternal recurrence. Such an affirmation, however, is not just a passive acceptance, a mere saying of the word "Yes" but a willing, and as such it is also a taking on of absolute responsibility for the whole, for everything that has been and will be.[9] It is thus not merely saying that everything is good or even that all undesirable or horrible things are tolerable in light of the other supremely good things but that everything, every moment is itself something that I will, that I do, that I am responsible for, that is my deed, and that I want with all my being.

A comparison here with Hegel may be illuminating. Hegel argued in a Christian fashion that at the end of history all things are reconciled in absolute knowledge or science. Concretely, this means that at the end of time all of the suffering of what Hegel graphically described as the "slaughtering bench of world-history" is redeemed by the attained reason and unity of the whole. All of the apparently meaningless pain and misery thus proves not to be meaningless but utterly meaningful as the way to this end. The end of history in absolute knowledge is thus completely satisfying because there are no outstanding debts left to be paid. Willing the eternal recurrence for Nietz-sche is so difficult because it means affirming not just a reconciled world, but a world that remains eternally unreconciled, eternally contradictory not just theoretically but practically as well. To will the eternal recurrence is to will, and that means to *do*, all things, to bring them all about, to adopt the position of a god who brings all things that have been and/or will be into existence. To will the eternal recurrence means not merely accepting the murder and torture of children as necessary, but also committing those murders and carrying out that torture, and even more importantly, *wanting to do so*. The *Übermensch* in this sense is infinitely distant from the inno-cence of the child. He is beyond good and evil in a very literal sense, a sheer monstrous will that wills all things, doing and wanting all things good and evil. The *Übermensch* is thus innocent not through a kind of forgetting but in the way an infinitely powerful god is innocent or indifferent, wanting the world to be as it is for the same reason Augustine's God does, simply because he wants it so.

In this light, Zarathustra's reluctance becomes more understandable. When he is actually able to summon up this thought, it almost kills him, but in successfully willing it, he is transformed and liberated. He thereby be-comes free and overcomes the spirit of revenge. In his freedom, however, he is absolutely responsible for everything that has occurred, and wants every-thing that is or has been, or will be. Yet in willing, in doing the most horrible things, he remains innocent. It is thus perhaps fitting that in describing this supreme possibility in his notes Nietzsche characterizes his *Übermensch* as "Caesar with the soul of Christ" (KGW VII 2:289).

If the decisive step in the coming into being of the *Übermensch* is will-ing the doctrine of the eternal recurrence, it would seem that Zarathustra himself must thereby become this *Übermensch*. This, however, is not the case. Zarathustra's recognition and acceptance of the doctrine of the eternal recurrence is necessary to but not sufficient for becoming superhuman. If one were to employ the Lutheran categories of Nietzsche's youth, Zarathus-tra may be justified by this act of will, but he is not yet sanctified; while he can understand and will the doctrine, he has not yet embodied it in himself because he is not hard enough to live it. Indeed, in Nietzsche's view, neither he nor anyone else can embody this doctrine without passing through the crucible of war that lies just over the horizon. This becomes clear when we examine his plans for the continuation of *Zarathustra*.

The second *Zarathustra* project, which began with what is now gener-ally treated as part 4, demonstrates that while Zarathustra recognizes what he has to do and wants to do, he is not able to do it because he still has to overcome his "final sin," his pity. To use his own language, he must "become hard." Only by overcoming pity will he be able to deliver his message as the teacher of the doctrine of the eternal recurrence to humanity. It was not enough to accept and will the lowest thing heretofore, that is, the last man, as he does in part 3, he must also will the destruction of the highest thing, the higher men, those who are his friends and companions.[10] He accomplishes this in the course of part 4 and declares at the end that his children are near. The sign of their approach is the appearance of a laughing lion surrounded by a flock of doves.[11] This is the sign because it is the metaphorical depiction of Caesar with the soul of Christ (*NL*, KGW VII 2:289). In the notes for the continuation of the work, Zarathustra descends the mountain, finds the world at war, delivers his teaching to a now more receptive humanity, and dies. He thus completes the promise he made in "On the Gift-Giving Virtue" at the end of part 1:

> Now I bid you lose me and find yourselves; and only when you have all denied me will I return to you. .... And once again you shall become my friends and the children of a single hope—and then shall I be with you the third time, that I may celebrate the great noon with you ... when man stands in the middle of his way between beast and *Übermensch* and celebrates his way to the evening as his highest hope: for it is the way to a new morning. (KGW VI 1:96–98)

His second return is at the beginning of part 2. He is about to embark on his final return at the end of part 4.[12] That is the time of the Great Noon, which we discussed in the previous essay, and which signals the end of European civilization and the advent of a harder humanity capable of grasping and accepting the eternal recurrence.[13] Zarathustra is thus not the *Übermensch*, but the one who proclaims the *Übermensch*, analogously not Christ but John the Baptist. However, in contrast to his predecessor, Nietzsche proclaims not the *Reich* of God, but what in his notes he calls the thousand-year *Reich* of Dionysus.

This *Reich* is ruled by the *Übermensch* (or *Übermenschen*) whose psyche has been hardened by years of war, whose will has been tempered by the doctrine of the eternal recurrence, and whose power is augmented by all of those he has overcome. Zarathustra points to this distant advent in "On the Great Longing" near the end of part 3. Nietzsche's original title for the aphorism was "Ariadne," which clearly points to Dionysus.[14] This is still reasonably clear in the version of the aphorism in *Zarathustra*. The object of Zarathustra's great longing is what it has always been, the *Übermensch*, but here he describes it as a longing for the arrival of the bark, the golden wonder around whom all good, bad, wondrous things leap . . . toward the golden wonder, the voluntary bark and its master, but that is the vintage who is waiting with his diamond knife—your great deliverer, O my soul, the nameless one for whom only future songs will find names. (KGW VI 1:276)

The object of Ariadne's, Zarathustra's, and Nietzsche's longing are one and the same, although it appears behind different masks and bears different names in Nietzsche's thought. In *Zarathustra* it is typically presented as the *Übermensch*. This name, however, is finally only a mask for the god of masks Dionysus. And even Dionysus, the last of the Olympians, is himself only a mask for what Nietzsche in *Birth* referred to as the contradictory primordial one (KGW III 3:207), the infinite and incomprehensible will at the heart of the world. It is thus no accident that Zarathustra here suggests that only future *songs* will find names for him. He is infinite and thus in Kant's sense sublime. Consequently, he transcends all names. To name him is to misrepresent him as something finite. However, Nietzsche realized from a very early period that such misrepresentation was essential, for it was only by transforming the sublime into something beautiful that it could be made bearable. It was just such a transformation that characterized the tragic age of the Greeks, which was the result of what Nietzsche calls the "dream birth" of the Olympian gods whose beauty alone made the experience of the sublimely tragic Dionysian abyss bearable.

Nietzsche's *Übermensch* is a similarly born in a dream, but this does not mean for Nietzsche that he is merely an aesthetic phenomenon. The dream of the *Übermensch* is the dream of the one who can look directly into the abyss and not be swallowed up by it. This is evident already in *Zarathustra*. The transformation that Zarathustra has undergone in the course of the work becomes evident if we compare "The Dancing Song" of the second part of the work, when he is at his most troubled, with "The Other Dancing Song," in the third part of the work after his recognition of the eternal recurrence and his convalescence. In both songs Zarathustra describes himself as peering into the eyes of life. But what a difference! In the first song, he declares that when he does so he seems to be sinking into the unfathomable. In the second song instead of losing himself in the abyss of life, he sees instead a golden boat, which is the boat bearing the golden wonder for whom only future songs will find names, that is, Dionysus. The sublime abyss in this way is transformed into the beautiful, and his fear into longing for the arrival of his god. It also then can serve as a rhetorical tool to convince his readers to face the Great Noon and everything it entails.

On one level it is thus the means by which the reader can come to see the eternal recurrence, not face-to-face, but through a glass darkly. For Nietzsche, however, his work is not merely a means of facilitating an aesthetic adventure for intellectuals who can otherwise continue to live comfortable lives. In fact, the *Übermensch* is the only hope for overcoming the banality of bourgeois life, for he alone can give humanity a goal that will enable them to will and endure the centuries of destruction necessary to bring it about. Only in this way can some portion of humanity become hard enough to will and survive the thought of the eternal recurrence. And perhaps then a few of those who survive this tempering process will be able to bite off and spit out the head of this Dionysian snake rather than being choked by it. And it is only these few who can will and redeem all that has been or is or will be. For Zarathustra as for Nietzsche, it is they alone who matter.[15] This transfiguration, however, lies in the distant future, and while it is the final goal of Nietzsche's project, it is also the means he uses to convince contemporary humanity to take the fateful step toward this end by choosing to become the lion. For contemporary humanity as for Zarathustra, there is thus only the longing for superhuman laughter and the superhuman joy that it betokens, the distant hope for the arrival of the golden boat and its wonder. Nietzsche believes that the present and near future by contrast are filled not with joy but only with pain and suffering, with war and destruction.

In his work after *Zarathustra*, Nietzsche almost entirely abandons the terminology of the *Übermensch* and returns to what at first appears to be his earlier Dionysian language, although in fact this too has been transformed by the recognition of the doctrine of the eternal recurrence. Part 3 of *Zarathustra* ended with the marriage of light and dark, of Apollo and Dionysus as the foundation for the coming into being of the *Übermensch*. In his later work, he accepts the consummation of this union and abandons his earlier dualist language in favor of a new concept of the Dionysian that includes in important ways the form-giving element previously attributed to Apollo. The idea of the superhuman, however, remains just beneath the surface of this later concept of the Dionysian (*GM*, KGW VI 2:352). In *Beyond Good and Evil*, for example, he refers to his guiding light as the genius of the heart whom he there calls Dionysus (KGW VI 2:247–48). In *Twilight of the Idols*, he describes himself as "the last disciple of the philosopher Dionysus" (KGW VI 3:154). Finally, he ends *Ecce Homo*, the last book he wrote, with the proclamation "Dionysus versus the Crucified." As he saw it, this book was the prelude to the long war that would end with the birth of the *Übermensch* and the establishment of the thousand-year *Reich* of Dionysus.

Nietzsche's image of the *Übermensch* and its later transmogrification into the Dionysian are supposed to be ravishing, to foster in the reader a longing comparable to that of Zarathustra, to make it impossible in other words to live without striving to bring such a being into existence. We cannot forget, however, that there is no certainty that this *Übermensch* will ever come into being. Zarathustra cannot live without the laughter of the *Übermensch*, but that does not mean that it is inevitable. Many die unfulfilled, and the price Nietzsche wants humanity to pay for the mere possibility of such fulfillment is high indeed. Thus, however much we may admire Nietzsche's genius or be moved by his works, we dare not overlook or minimize the monstrous character of this *Übermensch* and the doctrine of the eternal recurrence by which he lives. We dare not forget that this "genius of the heart" is in reality a vintager with a diamond knife (*Z, KGW* VI 1:276). And we must ask not what but whom he comes to harvest, and how many grapes will be left to rot when the best are chosen for his wine. Beneath the beautiful poetic imagery of the *Übermensch* lies a much darker reality.

The attempt to minimize the danger and horror of the *Übermensch* is, however, characteristic of our time. When Zarathustra gave the crowd in the marketplace a choice between the *Übermensch* and the last man, they chose the latter. We and the world in which we live are at least in part the products of their choice. Reading Nietzsche it is hard not to recognize this fact. We are thus moved by Nietzsche's critique and his appeal for something higher and more meaningful than the bourgeois world we find around us. In a strange way, we thus want the *Übermensch*, but we do not want him to disturb our comfortable lives. We want him as a kind of intellectual or cultural pleasure without having to pay Zarathustra's price. We want, in other words, a gentle *Übermensch* to save us from our gentle nihilism. And, of course, we want to imagine that we might be or become such superhuman beings, that we might become our own heroes.[16] There is nothing wrong with this if it is possible. If, however, the *Übermensch* must will the doctrine of the eternal recurrence in all its horror, as Zarathustra claims, and if this can only be brought about by the destruction of modern civilization, then we may need to conclude that it is a price too high to pay.

NIETZSCHE AS TEACHER OF THE ETERNAL RECURRENCE

What Was I Thinking? Nietzsche's New Prefaces of 1886

Interpretation
Leg ich mich aus, so leg ich mich hinein:
Ich kann nicht selbst mein Interprete sein.
Doch wer nur steigt auf seiner eignen Bahn,
Trägt auch mein Bild zu hellerem Licht hinan.[1]

The injunction of the Delphic oracle carved on the temple of Apollo, *gnōthi seauton*, "Know yourself," originally meant that you should know that you were a mortal human being and not an immortal god.[2] Heracleitus may have had this injunction in mind when he claimed that he had searched into himself, but whether he did or did not, in making the claim he established a new model for philosophic activity, moving away from the theological claim of the Delphic injunction and in the direction of something like human inwardness.[3] Perhaps more importantly, this notion of self-examination was also at the core of the Socratic claim that the unexamined life is not worth living. It is important to note, however, that neither Heracleitus nor Socrates claimed to know himself. Socrates in fact only claimed that he knew that he did not know. His self-examination thus seems to have led to skepticism. In fact, it was only with the development of Christian inwardness culminating in the notion of self-examination of the Protestant Reformation and the Cartesian *cogito* that the notion of true self-knowledge first appeared, and it was only with the Hegelian notion of subjectivity and absolute knowledge that the achievement of complete self-transparency came to be considered an actual possibility.

Friedrich Nietzsche like his Romantic predecessors rejected this notion. In fact, he doubted that humans could have more than a superficial knowledge of themselves. He repeatedly suggests that the conscious self is merely the tip of the human iceberg and that most of what we are is hidden beneath the surface of a psychic sea. In light of the discoveries of modern psychology and neuroscience, we no longer find this conclusion particularly surprising. What *is* surprising in Nietzsche's case, however, is not his skepticism about the possibility of self-knowledge but the fact that despite his doubts he repeatedly turned to autobiography in an effort to understand and interpret himself. How can we explain this apparent contradiction?

Nietzsche was undoubtedly an extraordinarily introspective and reflective individual.[4] He recognized this fact and in his late work described himself as a psychologist without equal. In part this was due to his belief that his own intense and long-standing physical pain had stripped away all ordinary human illusions and masks, allowing him understand himself in ways that others could not. But this interest in himself started much earlier. Already as a schoolboy, he began composing autobiographical sketches and between the ages of fourteen and twenty-four completed no fewer than ten.[5] While one might reasonably contend that these youthful endeavors preceded his later skepticism about the possibilities of self-knowledge, near the end of his life Nietzsche turned again to autobiography. *Ecce Homo* is the preeminent example of his late autobiographical reflections, but it is not the only instance of such concern.[6] The last section of *Twilight of the Idols*, "What I Owe to the Ancients," for example, is also explicitly autobiographical (and indeed was originally intended to be included in *Ecce Homo*). Nor were these autobiographical efforts confined merely to his published works. For example, in 1888 Nietzsche described his personal and philosophical development in letters to Georg Brandes.

In addition, Nietzsche composed another less well-recognized series of quasi-autobiographical reflections when he wrote new prefaces for his earlier works in 1886. They are particularly surprising because he wrote them only a few years after writing the passage in which he asserted that he could not be his own interpreter. We are thus forced to wonder about the nature of these prefaces. Are they interpretations of his earlier works and thus of his earlier self? And how does his decision to write these prefaces relate to his skepticism about the possibilities of self-knowledge? Or to put it more succinctly, what was he thinking both when he wrote what he wrote and when he wrote about what he had written? To answer these questions, we first need to consider more carefully what Nietzsche means by interpretation.

NIETZSCHE'S RECOGNITION OF THE PROBLEM OF SELF-INTERPRETATION

The poem at the beginning of this essay describes a hermeneutic paradox. "To interpret" in German is *auslegen*, which literally means "to lay out."

To interpret himself Nietzsche thus must lay himself out, that is, display himself as he is. In doing so, however, the self that is performing the laying out is necessarily left out of the account. In this way the self-interpreter in the act of interpreting inserts himself in a concealed manner back into the interpretation. Here Nietzsche uses the German verb derived from *einlegen*, "to insert," or literally "to put or lay in." Each act of self-interpretation thus requires another interpretation of the self doing the interpreting, leading to an infinite regress. All self-interpretation is thus always a self-re-presenting, a revealing of oneself that always also conceals the self that is doing the revealing. Nietzsche's re-presentation of himself in his new prefaces was thus not simply an explanation of what he had previously written but a re-presenting of himself and his earlier work in which the new self doing the interpreting remained masked and concealed. Self-interpretation is thus not a passive act of knowledge but a form of active willing that always constructs a new image of the self.

Although Nietzsche claimed that he could not interpret himself, he did not claim that interpretation as such was impossible. In fact he suggests that others who journey on their own path or track (*Bahn*) to a higher vantage point can reveal him in a brighter light. But what does he mean by this? To begin with, it is important to note that someone on his or her own path is not merely taking a random walk but has a goal and a direction if only that determined by the path itself. Nietzsche thus suggests that some light can be shed on his thought by those who are following their own paths. "Following a path" in Greek is *meta hodos*, from which we derive the word "method." As a classical philologist, Nietzsche was certainly aware of this fact. Hence, Nietzsche seems to suggest that he can be interpreted by those who are methodically pursuing their own goals. In doing so and carrying Nietzsche's image with them, they see him in brighter light and are thus able to interpret him, since they thereby gain a new perspective on *his* path and goal in terms of their own (and, of course, vice versa).[7]

Nietzsche does not thereby mean to assert that these others have a *true* interpretation of his thought. Indeed, during the period of his thought culminating in *The Gay Science*, Nietzsche was convinced that humans always only see and understand things from particular perspectives. This notion of interpretation assumes that all paths or methods offer us only partial views of things, and that no perspective offers an apodictic or even demonstrably *more* correct view of things. This insight led Nietzsche to examine matters from many divergent and often contradictory perspectives during this (middle) period of his thinking. These attempts or experiments (*essais* to use the French word that Montaigne, one of Nietzsche's heroes, made famous) produced an epistemological and moral skepticism about the possibility of an abstractly best path that allowed Nietzsche to explore which opinions, attitudes, and ways of life were most conducive to human thriving.

Such perspectivism is often thought to end in relativism and nihilism, and it is no accident that post-structuralist readings of Nietzsche draw heavily on the works written during this period of his thinking.[8] It is such a notion of the necessarily perspectival character of all knowledge that seems to underlie the claims he made about self-interpretation and self-knowledge in the poem at the beginning of this essay. This said, it would be a mistake to believe that this remained Nietzsche's view. Indeed, after the recognition of the doctrine of the eternal occurrence in 1881, Nietzsche came to a startlingly different conclusion. To be sure, in many respects he remained a perspectival thinker. He continued to be convinced that every perspective is based on a method that is set by following a particular path. Every perspective thus reflects the direction or vector of the path in question. That vector points toward a particular end or goal. The analogy to a path, however, gives us a somewhat misleading notion of what Nietzsche is arguing, since the image of a path predisposes us to think spatially. For Nietzsche, by contrast, the notion of a path is also and perhaps preeminently temporal.[9] We thus see the world in a particular way because we have an idea of a particular future or goal that determines the path (*hodos*) according to which (*meta*) we think. Our way of seeing is thus inevitably tied to a particular method. Interpreting something in the present is thus only possible because we project ourselves into an imagined future, and the method we employ is based on our intuition about the direction we need to go and the character of the path between here and there that we want to follow or establish.

The actual future, of course, is never merely one's own creation. We live in a world with others who have visions of what they as individuals and we as a community might be and become. Moreover, all of our and their hopes for the future are inevitably limited by facts of nature (*phusis*) and shaped to a greater or lesser extent by our peculiar cultural inheritance and tradition (*ēthos*). These factors place great limits on what we can imagine and thus upon the possibilities of interpretation. During the period of his thought from *Human, All Too Human* to *The Gay Science*, Nietzsche became convinced that he and his generation faced a unique opportunity. He came to believe that the death of God entailed the collapse of the authority of the European tradition that had constrained human thinking since the time of Plato. Thus, as he put it, despite the looming disaster the death of God entailed, it also opened up the world in a radically new way (*GS*, KGW V 3:253–56). Free spirits, that is, those freed from the constraints of tradition,

WHAT WAS I THINKING? 67

thus had the ability for the first time in over two thousand years to examine multiple competing perspectives, and to pursue what Nietzsche called *la gaya scienza* that could lead to a brighter, more vigorous future.

Nietzsche's understanding of his goal and task was fundamentally altered by his realization of the decisive importance of the idea of the eternal recurrence, which had a profound impact on his perspectivism. Many scholars have pointed out the performative contradiction implicit in Nietzsche's claim that all knowledge is merely perspectival, since that assertion itself seems to be absolute and not perspectival. To imagine that Nietzsche did not recognize this problem, however, is mistaken. Indeed, his idea of the eternal recurrence directly addresses this concern. To say that something is perspectival is not to say that it is false and therefore useless but to admit that it is only a more or less useful fiction, or to put it in the language of *Zarathustra*, one of many possible dream bridges of words connecting things that remain eternally apart (KGW VI 1:268). Moreover, insofar as knowledge is always only a tool with which we seek to attain our practical ends, the value of such knowledge does not depend upon its truth but upon the extent to which it helps us achieve those ends. But here lies the rub. All perspectives are determined by the way in which we stand toward the future, by the goals we see, or better foresee, at the end of our paths. The realization that our view of things is only one possible perspective, however, ultimately leads to despair since we recognize that our perspective, our way of life, and everything we value is merely partial and contingent and will eventually be surpassed and abandoned. Every perspective or worldview thus falls prey to the laws of time, or to what Nietzsche's Zarathustra calls the "it was." It ceases to be; it is overcome. Everything we do thus seems to be overhung with a great "In vain!" In other words, perspectivism seems to end in nihilistic despair.[10]

Nietzsche believed he had found an answer to such Romantic pessimism and despair with his realization of the idea of the eternal recurrence. The underlying assumption of the doctrine is that while time is infinite, matter is not and that there are consequently only a finite number of possible states of the universe.[11] Moreover, at every moment the current state of the universe depends upon all of the previous states. The universe understood from the perspective of the eternal recurrence is thus an interlocking whole through time, each moment of which is eternally the same as in every previous cycle. As a result no perspective is dispensable. Each is necessary to the whole. Moreover, all are preserved and recur eternally. Every individual being, every way of life, every event recurs over and over again endlessly. The great circle of becoming is thus eternally the same. The thought of the eternal recurrence thus does not demand a selection of one or even some set of perspectives, individuals, ways of life, and so on, and a rejection of others but the recognition that every one of them is necessary. We thus cannot select one or a few as preferable and condemn all of the others without condemning the ones we prefer. Thus, practically we can only either reject or affirm them all as a whole. Schopenhauer in Nietzsche's view had chosen universal rejection and that was the basis of his deep pessimism. For Nietzsche, however, such a rejection of the whole was itself only possible as a moment of the whole, which itself moves on, driven by a more fundamental force, which Nietzsche at times calls the will to power and at others life itself. Rejecting the whole is thus not a true rejection but only a sign of weakness, decadence, and declining life. Willing or affirming the whole, by contrast, is a sign of strength, health, and ascending life.[12]

Contrary to the claims of his later critics, Nietzsche does not present the eternal recurrence as an absolute truth, but as a perspective, a perspective that is affirmed not because it is true or false but because it is most life-enhancing. Indeed, from Nietzsche's point of view, we cannot possibly know whether it is true or false. To affirm the doctrine is rather an act of the will and means adopting a stance toward life that treats the doctrine as if it were true, and that consequently eschews all negation, affirming every possibility not merely as possible but as necessary. Affirming the eternal recurrence in this sense does not entail the rejection of any path or way of life, and indeed requires affirming them all. That said, the doctrine, as Nietzsche understands it, does entail a rank order of ways of life, and this presupposes a form of life that is superior to all others. But how is this possible? How can one affirm all possibilities and yet assert that one is preferable to all the others?

At its core Nietzsche's answer lies in his contention that truth is not the measure of life, but life the measure of truth. To affirm the eternal recurrence in Nietzsche's view is to affirm all forms of life. To be able to affirm the eternal recurrence is thus to be supremely alive, to be in fact the voice of life itself. Consequently, affirming or denying the eternal recurrence is the supreme test of the strength of one's will to life. In fact, it is a test that separates humanity into two camps, on one hand those who can affirm it and are elevated by it and on the other those who are crushed by it. The doctrine of the eternal recurrence is thus the one perspective on the whole that enables all other perspectives by asserting their necessity. It thus gives the broadest possible, most life-affirming view of the whole. For Nietzsche it thus also can serve as the basis for the evaluation of all other perspectives, and the development of an order of rank of these perspectives based on the vitality they produce.[13]

The affirmation of the eternal recurrence from Nietzsche's point of view is thus the highest moment of humanity, indeed the moment in which life affirms itself, the moment in which in a godlike fashion it pronounces itself good. There is thus no higher path than this, no perspective that looks down on this teaching. And the speaker of this teaching is thus destiny, the single moment at which everything aims and on which everything depends, the *kairos* or turning point of history.[14] It is only from this vantage point that one is able to definitively determine the rank order of all perspectives and ways of life. It is crucial to understand this point in order to make sense of all of Nietzsche's apparently hyperbolic claims about himself during the period of his thought from *Zarathustra* onward, for he sees himself as the teacher of the eternal recurrence, therefore as the supreme moment of life itself, or as he puts it, as the last disciple of the philosopher of life Dionysus, and consequently as destiny.[15]

RE-PRESENTING HIS EARLIER WORKS AS A PATHWAY TO THE ETERNAL RECURRENCE

In the aftermath of his recognition of the significance of the eternal recurrence, Nietzsche realized that his earlier works had all been missteps. He also realized, however, that they were necessary missteps. For him there could be no accidents. Nothing in his earlier life and thought could be dismissed because everything had been a preparation for his great insight and the task that it now imposed upon him. He also became convinced that the painful path he had followed was a path that his successors would also have to follow. While his earlier works had been errors, each had been a necessary error, and his readers had to understand how he had overcome these errors in order to facilitate their own passage through the abyss of relativism and nihilism to his great thought. The prefaces of 1886 were thus meant to speak to Nietzsche's future readers in their loneliness and despair as they sought a way out of decadence and relativism, to sustain them with the knowledge that he had walked this path before them, and to give them guideposts that would enable them to find their way as well.

These prefaces thus re-present Nietzsche's earlier works as a pathway to *Thus Spoke Zarathustra*, and the doctrine of the eternal recurrence. The occasion for the composition of these prefaces was the republication of his earlier works. Nietzsche's books from *Schopenhauer as Educator* onward had been published by Ernst Schmeitzner, whom Nietzsche had come to distrust and detest by the mid-1880s. He discovered that Schmeitzner had made no effort to publicize or distribute his earlier works and had not paid him his royalties. Schmeitzner also published many anti-Semitic tracts.

Nietzsche had detested anti-Semitism for a long time, but his sister's marriage to Germany's leading anti-Semite rankled him to the core and opened up the possibility that those who did not know him would misread his works as anti-Semitic.[16] The connection to Schmeitzner exacerbated this problem. Nietzsche's desire to find another publisher became more acute as he became increasingly convinced that he was on the verge of worldwide fame and that his works would soon sell in unprecedented numbers, earning him enough money not merely to live comfortably but to carry out his great project more rapidly. He even sought to borrow the relatively large amounts of money he needed to buy back the rights to his earlier works from his friends, but they all turned him down, believing that his expectations of success were the sheerest fantasy. In 1886 he was successful in regaining copyright as well as many unsold exemplars of his earlier works. After considering several alternatives, he convinced his first publisher, Fritzsche, to rebind and redistribute the existing copies of his works and publish further copies, all (except for his *Untimely Meditations*) with new prefaces and with some relatively minor changes and additions.[17]

Nietzsche, of course, was quite correct about his coming fame and the sales of his works, but what is of importance in this case is not his prescience, but the fact that when he wrote these prefaces, he was convinced that he was speaking not merely to a few dedicated friends but to a future pan-European audience. The new prefaces were an attempt to lead these readers, among whom he believed were some who would become free spirits and good Europeans, along his path to the realization of the idea of the eternal recurrence. In writing the prefaces, he thus lays out and inserts himself into his earlier works not merely in order to interpret himself, but in order to re-present himself to the public in a new light, not as a Wagnerian or Schopenhauerian, nor as a Romantic or German nationalist and especially not as an anti-Semite, but as the teacher of the eternal recurrence, and the herald of the Great Noon.

THE BIRTH OF TRAGEDY: "ATTEMPT AT A SELF-CRITICISM"

The autobiographical character of the prefaces is perhaps most evident in the new preface to *The Birth of Tragedy*, "Attempt at a Self-Criticism." Here Nietzsche roots himself in the events of the time in which the book was written, but reinterprets them from the perspective of 1886. In his discussion, he clearly wants to both dissociate himself from his earlier support of Wagner, Romanticism, and German nationalism and at the same time explain the decisive importance of this work as the first step on the path that leads to the realization of the eternal recurrence. This is reflected in the modification of the title from *The Birth of Tragedy out of the Spirit of Music* to *The Birth of Tragedy; or, Hellenism and Pessimism*, which de-emphasizes his connection to Wagner. Nietzsche's dissociation from the original text is already evident in the first section of the preface in which he refers to his earlier self exclusively in the third person, situating the original authorial self temporally in the "exciting" period of the Franco-Prussian War when the thunder of the Battle of Wörth was echoing over Europe, but spatially hidden away in an Alpine nook writing about the Greeks, asking whether the supposed optimism of Socrates and his followers was the height of Greek civilization or whether this optimism was not rather a sign of their descent from the pinnacle manifested in the pessimism of the earlier tragedians. Nietzsche thus puts himself both in his time and outside it, pointing toward what he later called his "untimeliness." However, he goes on to remark that the author of the text found himself several weeks later at the Battle of Metz and that he completed the book while recuperating from an illness contracted during the siege as the peace negotiations to end the war were under way at Versailles.

That he identifies the composition of the work with the Franco-Prussian War is no accident. Nietzsche suggests in this way the work's association with and dissociation from the concerns that dominated the period but also points to the failure of the Germans of that time to grasp the basic circumstances that characterized European civilization. His contemporaries understood victory in the war as grounds for optimism and pride, but from his point of view, this was a mistake. Indeed, the account he gave in *The Birth of Tragedy* suggested that optimism was not a consequence of success but of cultural decline.[18]

In this context his reference to the Battles of Wörth and Metz may very well be an allusion to the famous story of Hegel's completion of his *Phenomenology* with the guns of the Battle of Jena sounding in the distance.[19] The *Phenomenology* is one of the most famous philosophical examples of an optimistic theodicy and in this sense the final example of the optimistic metaphysics that Nietzsche argues began with Socrates and Plato. The *Birth of Tragedy*, as it was originally conceived, was rooted in this optimism although it replaced the Hegelian faith in the power of dialectical reason with a belief in the power of Wagnerian music to bring about a fundamental transformation and renewal of German culture. In Nietzsche's re-presentation of the work in the new preface (and in the new title), the optimistic element and particularly the expectation that Wagnerian music could transform German culture falls by the wayside and is replaced by a deeper appreciation of the wellsprings of Greek pessimism. He also admits that he now recognizes that he had then harbored hopes in the German spirit when there were no grounds for such hopes. By 1886 he had come to the conclusion that Germany could not be a vessel for the revival of antiquity because the Germans were the most un-Greek of all the European nations.

Looking back on this period, the later Nietzsche realized how vain the excitement and hopes of that time had been. Indeed, he now understood that the success of German arms and Wagnerian music had not portended the German cultural renewal he had hoped for, but a strengthening of Romanticism, rooted not in a pessimism of strength like that of the tragic Greeks but in a pessimism of weakness and decline.[20] He thus describes *The Birth of Tragedy* from this later point of view as an "impossible book," and laments that he could not find his own voice when it was written, since he was still too deeply under the sway of Wagner and Schopenhauer. All that said by way of self-critique, he focuses in the remainder of the new preface on what he sees in 1886 as the continuing contribution of the work, that it posed for the first time the question of the Dionysian.

Given the importance of the Dionysian for Nietzsche's final teaching, it is not surprising that he chose to emphasize this element in the new preface. Still, as many interpreters have pointed out, Nietzsche's notion of the Dionysian in his late works differs considerably from that of his earlier works where the Dionysian and the Apollinian are treated in Hegelian fashion as two contrary elements in need of reconciliation. In fact, by the 1880s, Nietzsche had almost entirely abandoned his notion of the Apollinian. With the exception of a few isolated passages in *Twilight of the Idols* and *Ecce Homo* in which Nietzsche discusses his earlier thought, the Apollinian is not mentioned in his later works, which focus almost entirely on the Dionysian that by then had come to play a more important role in his thinking in connection with the idea of the eternal recurrence. By his own admission, he abandoned his "artist's metaphysics" and beginning with *Human, All Too Human* had turned to an investigation of the world from many, often contradictory perspectives. The return to the concept of the Dionysian in the 1880s, then was not a return to this "artist's metaphysics" but, as we have seen, a turn to a new (anti-)metaphysics that interprets everything from the perspective of life and the eternal recurrence of the same. In keeping with his connection to Wagner and their mutual admiration for Schopenhauer, Nietzsche argued in *The Birth of Tragedy* that art alone could be the source of human salvation, famously asserting there that life was only justified as an aesthetic phenomenon. In the new preface, he reverses this claim, asserting that in the original work he posed his fundamental questions (including the question of the value of art) from the perspective of life. This turn away from art to life as the foundational moment in his thinking is also reflected in his turn away from Apollo, the god of beauty, to Dionysus, the god who like life itself repeatedly dies but is repeatedly reborn.

His attempt to understand things from the perspective of life is also a turn away from Christianity, which Nietzsche had come to see by the 1880s as antithetical to life, depreciating the actual world of living beings in favor of an imaginary afterworld. In the original text of *The Birth of Tragedy*, Christianity hardly ever appears and certainly is not the *bête noire* it becomes in Nietzsche's later thought. In writing the new preface, Nietzsche thus had to explain why he did not criticize Christianity in *The Birth of Tragedy* if he was already under the influence of a Dionysian view of life.

In attempting to answer this question, Nietzsche asserts that in the original text he remained *intentionally* silent about Christianity, suggesting that he had already recognized that Christianity was an essential part of the problem, but also that he was unwilling to bring it up in that context. Now this might be the case, but the claim is hard to justify on the basis of the original text. That Nietzsche already had doubts about Christianity is relatively clear but that he was then as critical of it as he suggests seem unlikely, in large part because at that time he was drawing on a tradition (which included Friedrich Hölderlin and Georg Creutzer) that saw Christianity as a moment in a continuing revelation that included Dionysus. All forms of religious life, according to this tradition, began with an initial revelation in India that spread westward taking on ever-new forms.[21] This account of the development of religion imagined that Dionysus was an earlier and incomplete version of Christ, a god who also dies and is reborn. Nietzsche's account of Dionysus in *The Birth of Tragedy* is indebted in many ways to this view. The archenemy of tragedy in the original text was not Christianity but Socratic rationalism. The Socratic turn toward an optimistic dialectic is portrayed as the source of the death of tragedy and the origin of what Nietzsche there calls Alexandrian culture. This rationalism, as he then saw it, was a symptom of the decline of the Greek world. In drawing his conclusions from this beginning, however, Nietzsche skips over the intervening two thousand years and suggests that the Enlightenment is the culmination of this Socratic tradition, which comes tumbling down when reason bites its own tail in the Kantian antinomies. Nietzsche thus can dispose of the entire philosophical tradition and clear the ground for what he imagines will be a new tragic age.

It was in fact only in his later work, beginning with *Human, All Too Human*, that Nietzsche began to consider more carefully the intervening period and particularly the role that Christianity played in this story, subsequently

eliding this rationalism with Christianity, which he increasingly characterized as "Platonism for the people." In the new preface to *The Birth of Tragedy*,
however, he asserts that the original text was at least implicitly an attack on
Christianity since it evoked Dionysus who is the model for the Antichrist.
Dionysus in this context represents the great Yes to life that Nietzsche juxtaposes in his later work to the No of Christianity. He seeks to read this
critique of Christianity back into *The Birth of Tragedy*, and claims that it
would have been more explicit except for his reliance on Schopenhauer and
Kant, but this seems to be something of an exaggeration, part of his effort
to reshape *The Birth of Tragedy* to better fit his final project. It is thus not
surprising that he concludes with the more tentative assertion, that while
he may not have openly criticized Christianity, he was at least subliminally
under the influence of a new god, Dionysus, and thus on the right track. Or
to put it in his later language, even if he was not yet the full-fledged disciple
of the god he had become by the 1880s, he was at least an initiate.[22]

HUMAN, ALL TOO HUMAN

Near the end of the new preface to *The Birth of Tragedy*, Nietzsche suggests
that the insistence upon truth and morality that characterize the Platonic/
Christian tradition is fundamentally at odds with the basic prerequisites of
life. Life is fundamentally competitive and contradictory. As a result, it crucially depends upon deception and thus upon art to make the pain of existence bearable. Greco-Christian rationalism and morality are consequently
not a great advance, as they have often been described, but a symptom of
decline, an attempt to ameliorate suffering by diminishing vitality. They thus
constitute what Nietzsche calls "the danger of dangers." However, the suggested solution that he leaves with reader at the end of that preface, learning
to laugh and dance, is obscure to say the least, almost certainly intentionally
so. The new preface to *Human, All Too Human* offers a more concrete explanation of such a "solution" in explaining how a person able to laugh and
dance in a tragic world could come into being. This is, of course, the figure
Nietzsche called the free spirit.

Nietzsche begins the new preface to the first volume of *Human, All Too
Human* remarking that people have imagined that all of his earlier works
aimed at undermining existing values, and that they thus promoted evil.
Nietzsche admits that his *Entlarvungspsychologie* did in fact aim at undermined existing morality and made him at times an advocate for the devil
and a critic of God, but he asserts that he is not therefore a proponent of evil.
Instead he claims that this hermeneutic attack upon existing moral beliefs

enabled him to stand beyond good and evil. As a result, he was free from the moral prejudices and constraints that limit most people's thinking. This freedom then made it possible for him to view and evaluate things from multiple, often contradictory perspectives.

He admits, however, that such a radical perspectivism is not necessarily a good thing. It often leads to relativism and to the recognition that there is nothing that is good in itself. He even admits that in his own case this relativism led to a deep disgust with reality, which he claims he was only able to endure by idolizing Schopenhauer and Wagner.[23] Since Nietzsche had come to believe in the intervening years that the images he had constructed of both men were inaccurate, one might imagine that he would simply admit that he had been wrong about them and move on. But he adopts a different tack. Instead of admitting that his admiration was a youthful mistake, he asserts that it was instead a necessary step in his development. Indeed, he claims that he *had* to imagine them to be much more than they actually were in order to keep from falling into despair. He needed to believe that he had allies and was not alone in his struggle. Although they did not live up to the heroic figures he had imagined, the image of the free spirit he constructed with them in mind was itself not merely imaginary, but a sketch of a human possibility that he realistically believed he could help bring into being.

The inadequacy of his heroes became clear to him after his break with Wagner when he could no longer sustain the illusion that Wagner and his music were the answer to European cultural decline. He was then filled with disgust and nausea in the face of reality. In his loneliness and despair, he needed friends, but none were at hand. To fill this void, he invented the free spirit. He claims that he knew at the time that no such spirits existed, but was able to convince himself that they were coming into being and hoped that he might nurture them and help them overcome their disgust and despair by describing his own experience.

The account of the origin and nature of the free spirit that follows in the new preface both mirrors and illuminates the account Nietzsche gives of the transformation of the spirit in "The Three Metamorphoses," in part 1 of *Zarathustra*. The problem with the modern spirit that Nietzsche described there was that it had been subjected for the last two thousand years to a moral "thou shalt" that established a standard for a virtuous life that directed human passions and desires in a particular way. In *Zarathustra*, he called this the camel spirit, because it bore the weight of its duties. In the new preface to *Human, All Too Human*, he describes the modern spirit similarly closed in and constrained not by some external force but by its own sense of duty, which reflects the power of existing conventions. Like the camel he describes in *Zarathustra*, those who live within this moral order have to bear the burdens that these duties impose. Their liberation, he argues in the new preface, comes about when they shudder before what they have hitherto loved. While the exact nature of the experience he is referring to remains unclear in the preface to the first volume of *Human, All Too Human*, in the preface to the second volume he clarifies this point, describing the collapse of his faith, and his subsequent inability to believe in anything. This spiritual crisis is identified in *Zarathustra* as the death of God.

This crisis of faith plunges the spirit into absolute relativism, allowing one at first to see everything from multiple and often contradictory perspectives, but ultimately leaving one believing that all values are false. If nothing is true, then as Nietzsche would later recognize, everything is permitted. Nihilism, as he would later name this experience, liberates all of the passions from the constraints of existing values and conventions. As a result, the spirit no longer has any ability to constrain its passions and falls into a lascivious lifestyle that transgresses all conventions.[24] This exploration of the forbidden, however, is merely the first assertion of the liberated will. As it continues, it explores multiple human possibilities. In many instances this leads to decadence and degeneration, but at least in some cases, and Nietzsche here is thinking of his own experience, the will to health proves ascendant. Thus, for the strongest and most vital, these experiments in ways of living lead to convalescence as one learns what is most advantageous to one's own vitality.[25] In this way, rather than retreating back into some faith or ideology that insists upon the illusory truth of only one perspective, the spirit learns to endure relativism. It thereby becomes free, no longer rejecting any way of looking at things as necessarily true and superior, no longer saying Yes or No to things, living beyond good and evil, concerned only with its own thriving. As it rises above all ideological and theological interpretations of the world, the free spirit is again able to encounter life without mediating concepts and illusions. After its long sickness, the spirit is consequently able once again to experience wonder. In this way it becomes continually healthier, having found a cure for the pessimism and despair that had paralyzed it.

The secret to Nietzsche's own liberation and to that of those who follow him, he asserts, is becoming master of oneself and one's virtues rather than remaining subject to them. This transformation assumes that while every value judgment is relative, the strongest humans have the capacity to establish an order of rank among values and perspectives that promotes their own thriving. For Nietzsche the crucial problem is how to rank order the various possible perspectives. This problem is central because determining which perspective is best only seems possible if one already has adopted a perspective. Which perspective we choose thus seems to be merely a reflection of who we are.

Nietzsche recognized this problem and took his stand on the side of life and vitality, which he believed was the bedrock underlying all rank ordering of perspectives and thus all values. Everything in Nietzsche's view is the result of the will to life, which in *Zarathustra* he characterized as the will to self-overcoming. Empirically there seem to be a number of objections to such a view. On many occasions, for example, individuals and peoples will choose to emphasize and elevate perspectives that seem to denigrate and deny life. Asceticism is one clear example. Nietzsche argues, however, that they do so only to enable themselves to survive under the harshest conditions when they are at their weakest. Such choices are still choices for life, but they are choices for the mere preservation of life that in the long run diminish the possibility of thriving. They are thus desperate measures that the sick and weak employ to save themselves. Nietzsche sees Socrates' turn to reason and the Christian turn to a loving and merciful God as examples of such extreme measures. Such efforts, however, are not cures for the disease but mere palliatives that ultimately limit vitality and undermine growth and the development of strength. Thus Nietzsche concludes at the end of the preface to the first volume that no psychologist will have any trouble recognizing where in this process the present book belongs, that is, that it is a trenchant critique of the psychic sickness of his contemporary Europeans. This he believes will be clear to the French where such psychologists exist and even to some in Russia, but almost certainly not in Germany, in large measure because the Germans continue to live within a Christian perspective that is antithetical to human thriving.[26] It is important to note here that Nietzsche's critique of the Germans is not merely a critique of Schopenhauer and Wagner and their followers but of his earlier self as well. He admits his own decadence in the preface to the second volume, and in this way believes he can help others like himself, potential free spirits, understand how they can overcome their own decadence and attain greater vitality.

In describing the way in which this sickness and despair appeared in his own life, he points specifically to the fact that he came to believe that no perspective was truer or better than any other, a fate he believes will soon beset all Europeans. Relativism is thus not an unadulterated good that merely liberates one from the constraints of morality, but also a great danger since it leads, or at least can lead, to a belief that nothing is true. It was this dark conclusion that he claims was reflected in his unpublished "On Truth and Lie in an Extra-Moral Sense."[27] He was able to recuperate from this debilitating condition not merely by rejecting it but by actively attacking the most dangerous instance of the prevailing moral outlook, Wagner. Nietzsche explains how Wagner, whom he had formerly seen as the great hope of German and European culture, had in fact thrown himself down before the cross and become a Christian. He had hoped Wagner was a Dionysian poet who could overcome Romanticism, but he turned out to be merely the most extreme Romantic.

Nietzsche claims at the end of the preface to the second volume that he found his way out of this abyss by taking sides against himself and, instead of doing what was easiest for him, chose to do what was most difficult. Like the spirit described in "The Three Metamorphoses" section of *Zarathustra* in the loneliness and desolation of his desert, Nietzsche claims he uttered a sacred No to what he had most loved. In this way and in the midst of his suffering, he claims, he found his own task, as he believes the future free spirits and his coming good Europeans can as well.

DAWN

In *Dawn* Nietzsche extends the examination of morality that he began in *Human, All Too Human*. In keeping with the subtitle of the book, *Thoughts on the Prejudices of Morality*, Nietzsche suggests in the new preface that "as long as the world has existed" morality has exercised such powerful authority that a real philosophic investigation of good and evil has been impossible. The task that Nietzsche believed he had discovered to be his own (and that he described in the preface to the second volume of *Human, All Too Human*) of moving beyond good and evil and establishing a new rank order of values begins with an investigation of the prejudices of morality. In the new preface to *Dawn*, he thus describes the author of the work as an underground man or mole who is digging away at the foundations of morality, undermining the blind faith that has sustained it.

His reference to an underground man may well be an allusion to Dostoevsky, whom Nietzsche admired as a psychologist who understood the decadence of modern morality that Nietzsche alluded to in the new preface to *Human, All Too Human*.[28] In this new preface, he describes the author of *Dawn* as engaged in a task very similar to that of Dostoevsky's underground man, patiently exploring the dark, nether regions of the self in search of a way to the surface and a new dawn. When Nietzsche originally wrote *Dawn*, however, he knew nothing of Dostoevsky. Indeed, he claims in the course of the work to have followed a path that was uniquely his own. His goal was to undermine the ancient faith that sustained morality. Morality in his opinion has never allowed itself to be questioned and criticized, and has used a variety of psychological, sociological, and political means to prevent an investigation into the nature of good and evil. Philosophers, as he sees it, have failed time and time again to pose this question. He thus concludes that morality is the "Circe of philosophers," the witch who has transformed all philosophers into domesticated animals.[29]

Even Kant, whose courageous goal was a fundamental critique of reason, failed to escape from this spell. He was at heart a pessimist, in Nietzsche's view, who realized in his consideration of the antinomies that reason itself was contradictory and thus could not serve as the foundation for morality, but he could not admit that morality was groundless. Instead he argued for another form of reason embodied in the moral law. This was not rooted in his critical thought but was due in large measure to the fact that he had been "bitten by the moral tarantula Rousseau" (*D*, KGW V 1:6), and had become as much of a moral fanatic as Rousseau's other disciple, Robespierre. Like Luther before him and Hegel after him, Kant recognized the inadequacy of reason but in typically German fashion turned to faith, in his case faith in the moral law and the categorical imperative.

Nietzsche admits in the new preface that he too like many of his predecessors is a pessimist, but he claims that in contrast to them he no longer has faith. The Christian God is dead, and everything that rested upon faith in that God, including all our distinctions of good and evil, can no longer be categorically affirmed. For Nietzsche the diabolically persuasive power of morality, which had infected and deflected all previous philosophers and which, he was convinced, continued to exercise its force in his own time, even on the supposedly atheistic anarchists, had come to an end. The abyss that this collapse of religion and morality opened up created room in his view for a genuine critique of morality and a new view of morality that could replace the Romanticism and idealism then ascendant in Europe.

The goal of *Dawn* was to move beyond good and evil toward moral realism. As a result it was at heart pessimistic about all previous forms of morality, hostile to all faiths, to Christianity, to Romanticism, to Fatherlandism, and also to hedonism and idealism (which he also refers to as European feminism). And yet Nietzsche admits that he was still driven by morality in the form of conscience, a conscience that was unwilling to accept anything as true that was not.[30] As an immoralist, he thus sees his earlier self as engaged in the self-overcoming or self-sublimation of morality. Being an immoralist, however, is merely something negative, and as Nietzsche knew you can't beat something with nothing. What is necessary then is not merely to critique existing values but to spell out the positive goals of his project. However, he does not do that here, but points instead toward his coming magnum opus in which these goals will be proclaimed at the Great Noon along with the doctrine of the eternal recurrence.

THE GAY SCIENCE

In the prefaces to *The Birth of Tragedy, Human, All Too Human,* and *Dawn,* Nietzsche presents us with an account of his intellectual development as the story of the decline of a Romantic into value relativism and despair, and his rebirth and ascent when he learns to free himself from the existing moral norms and establish his own way of living by reordering his life according to values that most enhance his vitality. The new preface to *The Gay Science* is a celebration of Nietzsche's return to health, a description of his joy at recovering from his long spiritual illness, but it is also a tribute to the power of the pain and suffering he has undergone and its capacity to sweep away all of the illusions by which we ordinarily live. Life for him is no longer something that can be taken for granted, and thus it becomes questionable again. Nietzsche consequently concludes that *The Gay Science* cannot really be understood by anyone who has not lived through the (painful) experiences behind it. Nietzsche in this way appeals to those who are suffering as he suffered, because he believes they are the ones who can be liberated from the constraints of the hegemonic moral outlook, and thus become free spirits, who can live experimentally, practicing what he here calls *la gaya scienza.*

The book consequently announces Nietzsche's liberation, a liberation brought about by having traversed the realm of nihilistic despair. In this way Nietzsche does not merely proclaim his own freedom, but also lays out a path for others to follow. This liberation produces a new cheerfulness despite the looming catastrophe that Nietzsche sees just over the horizon. He explains the reasons for his hopes perhaps most fully in the first aphorism of the new fifth book that he added to *The Gay Science* at the same time as the new preface. The title of that section is "The Meaning of Our Cheerfulness." He begins by describing the crisis that he alluded to in the earlier prefaces more explicitly as the collapse of the morality that has characterized Europe for the last two thousand years and the advent of a nihilistic despair of worldwide proportions. The greatest recent event, he claims, has been the death of God, which has begun to cast its shadow over Europe and that will bring in its wake the "collapse of the whole of European morality," and will usher in "a monstrous logic of terror," and "the gloom and eclipse of a sun whose like has probably never yet occurred on earth." In the new preface, he refers to this metaphorically as the coming onset of winter. This prediction is based on his own experience, which he sees as foreshadowing the experience of his fellow Europeans. For him the death of God and the collapse of moral authority led to a relativism that ended in disgust and despair with the realization that there is no absolute truth to guide our lives. He discussed this experience in his earlier prefaces. It is precisely his nihilistic despair in the face of relativism, however, that he believes he has overcome. He thus asserts at the end of this aphorism that "we philosophers and 'free spirits' feel, when we hear the news that 'the old god is dead,' as if a new dawn shone on us; our heart overflows with gratitude, amazement, premonitions, expectation. At long last the horizon appears free to us again, . . . the sea, our sea, lies open again; perhaps there has never yet been such an 'open sea'" (*GS*, KGW V 2:256).

This language is repeated in the new preface where he foresees the opening up of new seas where new goals are permitted again. He claims here that he has already lived through the crisis that will soon beset Europe, and that he offers a way out of it. This crisis takes on many different names in his thought. In *The Birth of Tragedy*, it was the advent of Schopenhauerian pessimism and the collapse of German culture; in *Human, All Too Human*, it was the decadence of Romanticism and idealism; in *Dawn*, it was the disgust and despair in the face of relativism; and in *The Gay Science*, it is the death of God and the looming collapse of the European moral order. What one must understand is that for Nietzsche there is no way to prevent any of this. It must be lived through. This is why he believes that those who have not yet gone through this experience cannot understand *The Gay Science*.

Nietzsche like Luther believes that it is only those who experience the depths of despair who can find their way to "redemption." Only those who have experienced the lasciviousness and immorality of Romanticism, the despair of pessimism, the disgust of relativism, and the abyss of nihilism can ultimately become free from the constraints of the existing moral order. The destruction of the old world makes it possible to imagine something new, opening up a realm without horizons, allowing one to set sail on uncharted seas.[31] Hence, the wars that he believes are coming are not a reason to despair but the source of his hopes for the future, and an explanation for the cheerfulness that pervades *The Gay Science*.

In this way the new preface and book 5 of *The Gay Science* complete the task of the new prefaces that began with "Attempt at a Self-Criticism." The prefaces as a whole describe the transformation of the spirit (already metaphorically described in *Zarathustra*) from the camel, to the lion, and finally into the child. In the new prefaces, Nietzsche tells us that he was a camel/believer not so much in Christianity but in the Romanticism of Schopenhauer and Wagner when he first wrote *The Birth of Tragedy*. In the new preface to *Human, All Too Human*, he explains how he became a leonine destroyer in the lonely desert he found himself in after breaking with Wagner. There he rejected and reversed everything he had hitherto accepted and believed, contradicting existing moral values as had never been contradicted before, seeking to bring down everything with his *Entlarvungspsycholgie*. Finally, in the new prefaces to *Dawn* and *The Gay Science*, he describes the manner in which he again became a child and was able to make a fresh beginning. He thus describes his own metamorphoses and transfiguration and simultaneously lays out the path for the future development of the free spirit and the advent of his good Europeans.

Nietzsche asserts in the new preface to *The Gay Science* that there are two kinds of philosophy, one that arises out of deprivation and another that arises out of riches and strength. In the first case, philosophy is needed as a palliative for sickness, while in the latter, it is a beautiful luxury that crowns a philosopher's health. The latter is much rarer than the former, but it does exist. In his discussion of his own experience, Nietzsche seems to suggest that he may be representative of both.

At the core of a philosophy for Nietzsche is the philosopher and his physiological experience.[32] This notion builds upon what he said in the earlier prefaces about examining the world from multiple perspectives. Morality insists that the world only be seen from a particular perspective. The liberation from the existing moral order that Nietzsche described in the new preface to *Human, All Too Human* leads to the morass of perspectivism and relativism. But as he made clear in the new preface to *Dawn*, this problem is solved by establishing a rank order of values or perspectives, and the basis of that order in his view is life itself, that is, the preference for a particular rank ordering is determined by what at that time and place and for that person is most conducive to vitality. Here he suggests that each of these rank orderings of perspectives represents a different philosophy. Philosophy here is thus not merely a set of ideas but, as he earlier argued in his unpublished fragment "Philosophy in the Tragic Age of the Greeks," a way of life (*NL*, KGW III 2:295–96). The sick and the weak need a certain philosophy to survive, while the strong need a different philosophy to prosper. The great advantage he believes he has in this regard is that he has passed through so many different states of health that he has developed multiple philosophies or outlooks on life and as a result is able to judge their value. He believes the predominate moral outlook or philosophy that arose from Socratism and Christianity is now coming to an end. It preserved life for centuries but now acts more as a constraint upon vitality than as a lifeboat for European humanity. His goal is to lay out a philosophy for a healthier and more vital superhumanity.

Crucial to great profundity in Nietzsche's view is great pain because it strips away illusions and undermines the simple trust we have in life. Nietzsche sees his own pain as the source of his liberation and as a result does not want to eliminate it or even (heroically) to endure it, but rather to express his gratitude for it. Dealing with his pain, he argues, made him a different person, a person for whom life itself became a problem. As a result, pain taught him to question more deeply. And this he tells us is the source of his cheerfulness.

For most human beings, this might seem to be an odd if not incomprehensible claim. How can intense pain, which shakes our faith in life, and calls everything we believe into question, be a source of happiness? One might very well imagine that long and continued pain and disillusionment leads not to cheerfulness but to the belief that life is a burden that we are better off without. In fact, this is the response that Nietzsche attributes to Socrates.[33] How can we explain Nietzsche's assertion in the new preface to *The Gay Science* (so strongly reminiscent of the last of the "The Three Metamorphoses" in *Zarathustra*) that from severe sickness one returns newborn, more childlike and innocent, subtler?

Nietzsche does not give us an explanation for this claim in the new prefaces, but he does give us at least a partial explanation for the absence of such an explanation. At the end of the preface to the first volume of *Human, All Too Human*, he remarks that "one remains a philosopher only by—keeping silent." But silent about what? The answer is what all of these new prefaces were meant to prepare his readers for, the announcement of the doctrine of the eternal recurrence. We see this prefigured in the last two aphorisms of book 4 of *The Gay Science*, "The Greatest Weight" and "Incipit tragoedia" (KGW V 2:250–51).

Pain makes life burdensome. It imposes a weight upon us that crushes us. The question is how we respond to this weight. The greatest question then is forced upon us by the greatest weight, our most burdensome and painful moment. In "The Greatest Weight," Nietzsche poses such a question. He asks the reader how he would respond to a demon who whispers into his ear that everything that has been must be again and again an infinite number of times, not better or worse but exactly as it has been into all eternity.[34] He asks whether the reader would throw himself down in agony or praise the demon as his greatest benefactor, the source of his greatest joy. The answer lies in something within the individual but what that something is remains obscure in this aphorism.

In the final aphorism of part 4, "Incipit tragoedia," however, Nietzsche points toward this answer, to which he gives the name Zarathustra, the teacher of the eternal recurrence and the herald of the Great Noon.[35] This answer was developed in metaphorical form in *Thus Spoke Zarathustra*, the work that immediately followed *The Gay Science*. It was further spelled out in the remaining works he completed in his productive lifetime and was the central topic of the planned magnum opus that he was working on when he wrote the new prefaces.

At the end of the new preface to *The Gay Science*, Nietzsche pulls together all of the themes of the previous prefaces. He returns back to the question that had motivated *The Birth of Tragedy*, the question of the role of art in human life. In *The Birth of Tragedy*, he had originally asserted that life could only be justified as an aesthetic phenomenon, that is, only by means of art. He now asserts that if we convalescents still need art, it is a different kind of art, a masking, fleeting art, for artists only. He also seems to suggest that the *Entlarvungspsychologie* of *Human, All Too Human*, which sought like Egyptian youths to search tombs by night, was a form of youthful madness, and a desire for a truth that was too demanding. Or as he puts it, truth no longer remains truth when its veils are withdrawn. Thus, he concludes echoing Heracleitus, philosophy must have respect for the bashfulness of nature, and if truth is a woman (the hypothetical with which he begins *Beyond Good and Evil*), her name is Baubo, the female correlate of Dionysus.[36] Here again we see a renewed emphasis on the Dionysian that Nietzsche put at the center of the new preface to *The Birth of Tragedy*. He concludes the preface to *The Gay Science* then by returning again to *The Birth of Tragedy*, declaring that the Greeks—and here he clearly means the Greeks of the tragic age—were superficial out of profundity, combining art and philosophy in the manner he attributes to a future Socrates who practices music in *The Birth of Tragedy* (KGW III 1:107). It is in this sense he claims that "we," that is, he and the other coming free spirits, are Greeks and artists.

WHO IS NIETZSCHE'S NIETZSCHE?

The realization of the doctrine of the eternal recurrence was the decisive turning point in Nietzsche's life, transforming a failed academic into a world-historical thinker. His first attempt to announce this great idea in *Zarathustra*, however, had no initial impact upon his contemporaries. Not unreasonably, Nietzsche blamed this lack of response on his publisher, but he was also acutely aware that, even absent his publisher's failures, his potential future audience would inevitably read (or not read) these works and those that he intended yet to write under the impressions drawn from his earlier works.

They thus would assume that he was a Schopenhauerian or a Wagnerian, or a relativist, or a dyspeptic malcontent who could see nothing positive in modern life, or even a nationalist or anti-Semite. He thus became convinced that he needed to explain to his future readers who he was. Nietzsche was convinced that the doctrine of the eternal recurrence superseded his previous positions and could be understood on its own. He also recognized, however, that these previous positions were steps that he had had to climb in order to become the person capable of thinking the eternal recurrence. The new prefaces as a whole were thus an attempt to integrate his earlier thought into the great task he saw arising from the realization of the eternal recurrence of the same. They are in this sense the account of the development through which he had to pass, and by analogy the development through which Europe must yet pass to come to terms with his apocalyptic idea.

The new prefaces that Nietzsche wrote thus also present a new Nietzsche. The Nietzsche who presents this new account of the development of the old Nietzsche, however, remains concealed within this account. His self-interpretation is always a self-re-presentation that is guided by the aims of the later Nietzsche who in many ways is distinct from the Nietzsche who wrote those books. The Nietzsche that Nietzsche presents as the author of those works does not recognize the fundamental thought that guides the author of the prefaces. The idea itself is never named. The author represents the earlier Nietzsche's path as a path to this great revelation, and in so doing lays out a path for his fellow free spirits, but he does not present the revelation itself.

In confronting the death of God and the advent of explicit and active nihilism, Nietzsche became convinced that the moral order of the European world was coming to an end and that as a result human life would be left without a goal, without purpose, and without meaning. In these circumstances, he concluded that human beings would have to choose one of two possibilities, the last man or the *Übermensch*. Nietzsche describes his path through relativism and nihilism to the establishment of a new rank order of values in the new prefaces to his works from *The Birth of Tragedy* to *The Gay Science*. What is only alluded to in these prefaces, however, is the final step that takes humans from the innocence of the new beginning to the maturity of the *Übermensch*, and that is the realization and affirmation of the eternal recurrence of the same. Thus, while the new prefaces help to reconfigure Nietzsche's earlier works as steps on the path to a superhumanity, they do not carry his readers to this goal. That was the task of *Thus Spoke Zarathustra* and of his unfinished magnum opus.

Nietzsche's Musical Politics

Nietzsche's late thought began with the proclamation of the death of God in the first edition of *The Gay Science* in 1882 and was to have ended with the proclamation of the eternal recurrence in the magnum opus that was left incomplete when he collapsed into madness in January of 1889.[1] This was a teaching for a Europe that Nietzsche believed had come to a crucial turning point. The death of God in his view was inevitable. Moreover, this death would undermine European morality, civil society, and the state, as well as art, religion, and philosophy. The traditional categories, methods, and values that had shaped European life since the time of Socrates in his view would consequently no longer suffice to make sense out of life and give it meaning and purpose.

In order to give life meaning, Nietzsche believed it would be necessary to think in a new way. The Greeks of the tragic age had combined what we think of as poetic, philosophic, musical, and mythological thinking, but beginning with Socrates, rationalism had broken them apart. Nietzsche was convinced that this was one of the principal sources of European decadence. He thus believed that it was necessary to rethink thinking. This notion, of course, was not new but had played an important role in European thought at least since the time of Kant. The effort to transcend the traditional categories of thinking, however, was particularly evident among the Romantics. Romantics such as Tieck, Novalis, E. T. A. Hoffmann, the Schlegels, Blake, Coleridge, and Emerson, to name only the most obvious, were deeply interested in new modalities of thinking. But perhaps the most famous Romantic effort to reunify modalities of thinking was Wagner's development of a new form of music drama modeled on Aeschylus that was characterized as a *Gesamtkunstwerk*. The early Nietzsche had been very taken with this Wagnerian idea and in *The Birth of Tragedy* had explored the idea and buttressed

Wagner's arguments with a reinterpretation not merely of ancient tragedy but also of the European philosophical tradition that had rejected this form of thinking. While Nietzsche soon concluded that Wagnerian music drama did not succeed in reconstituting a comprehensive form of art or thought, he remained deeply interested in this problem and after his break with Wagner, experimented with new forms of expression in an effort to constitute a more primordial form of thinking that brought together art, religion, and philosophy in new and more powerful ways, seeking to play the role of what he called in *The Birth of Tragedy*, "a musical Socrates" (KGW III 1:98). He realized that we do not think and communicate merely with clearly defined words connected in logically coherent sentences but with gestures, dance, music, words, song, and many other forms of expression.[2] The question for him was how to bring these all together in a way that would make possible a more profound and encompassing means of communication. *Twilight of the Idols* is one of Nietzsche's preeminent efforts to develop such a new form of expression. His models here are not merely the tragedians who informed his early *Birth of Tragedy* but also the pre-Socratic Greek thinkers as well as classical European poets such as Goethe and composers such as Mozart and Beethoven. In this essay I attempt to show that *Twilight of the Idols* is an attempt to develop and deploy such a new form of expression, and that in this way it plays a crucial role not merely in its criticism of existing modes of thinking and being, but as a demonstration of the new "logic" intrinsic to the (anti-)metaphysics that is at the heart of Nietzsche's final teaching.

The importance of this effort, however, has been obscured by a number of factors. Although written in August 1888, *Twilight of the Idols* was not published until late January 1889.[3] It thus appeared only after Nietzsche's breakdown and was almost immediately characterized as a work of madness.[4] This soon became the standard view of *Twilight* and of Nietzsche's late works in general, owing in part to his sister's distortions of his texts and manuscripts and to his extravagant self-praise, which many regarded as a sign of megalomania. There was some countervailing opinion. For example, Julius Kaften, who visited Nietzsche in August 1888, remarked that he saw no signs of insanity, but this view was exceptional, and it was not until scholars were able to examine Nietzsche's manuscripts in the 1930s that a new interpretation began to emerge.[5] Unfortunately, Nazism, the war, and the necessities of reconstruction delayed the reappraisal of Nietzsche's thought until the 1950s and 1960s.[6]

Even then, severe questions were raised about Nietzsche's philosophical legitimacy. Following Jaspers, many argued that his thought was fundamentally contradictory.[7] Others argued, in part because of Nietzsche's own denigration of all systems and systematizers, that his thought was intentionally unsystematic and therefore "fragmentary" or "aphoristic."[8] Such an assertion is questionable, however, for Nietzsche is equally scornful of such a fragmentary style (*CW*, KGW VI 3:21). Moreover, his letters and *Nachlass* indicate that he had a deep concern with the structural integrity of his thought and work.[9]

This view of Nietzsche as an unsuccessful philosopher arises out of a failure to grasp the true character of his thought. He is certainly not a systematic philosopher in the traditional sense: traditional systematization may produce a whole in his view but only by the "exclusion and negation of all artistically productive forms" (KGW III 1:162). His thinking during this period is an effort to move beyond the distinctions that have characterized thinking for the last two thousand years. He describes himself at times as a psychologist, a poet, a composer, a philosopher, an aphorist, a prophet, and as the disciple of the god (or at times philosopher) Dionysus. While he thus opens himself up to the likely critique that he is a bad poet, bad philosopher, and so on, the attempt to measure him by traditional disciplinary standards fails to take seriously his claim to go beyond them. In order to come to terms with his actual project, we thus need to pay more attention to the place of creative thinking and its expression within his (anti-)metaphysics. Within this framework he tries to develop a new logic, or to put it another way, to develop a form of thinking that is not subject to the limitations that have been put on thinking by traditional logic. This is reflected in his earlier exploration of multiple literary styles, but it is attained most fully only in the works of 1888 and in *Twilight* and *Ecce Homo* in particular. Nietzsche's new way of thinking thus may seem a form of madness to many traditional philosophers, but this is perhaps inevitable for a thinker who imagines himself to be a musical Socrates. To understand the character of Nietzsche's final teaching, it is thus necessary to carefully examine the mode in which it is deployed in *Twilight*, which I will refer to in what follows as his musical philosophizing.

Nietzsche understands music in a very broad sense.[10] There can be no doubt, however, that his concern with music in the narrower modern sense was also profound. Janz argues that "music and composition were not only incidental occupations for Nietzsche, they were a serious concern for him, rooted in his very essence."[11] Throughout his life, Nietzsche was devoted to music. At twelve, he was an accomplished pianist and shortly thereafter taught himself composition from the textbook of Johann Georg Albrechtsberger, the teacher of Beethoven. He soon began composing, but his music was little appreciated. Despite this, he continued to hope for success until the end of his productive life, as his letters and repeated efforts to secure the performance of his *Hymn of Life* (1887) indicate.[12] Moreover, many of his closest friends were composers, musicians, or gifted musical amateurs such as Wagner, Hans von Bülow, Carl Fuchs, and Heinrich Köselitz (Peter Gast).

That music should form a central topic of this thought is thus hardly surprising. Indeed, four of his works, *The Birth of Tragedy*, *Wagner in Bayreuth*, *The Case of Wagner*, and *Nietzsche contra Wagner*, explicitly consider principally musical subjects. Music for Nietzsche, however, was not merely a substantive concern but also played an important role in his style. As Janz has pointed out, Nietzsche's sketches for works often give only the number of pages, chapters, and so on, indicating "a musical-theoretical foundation, a musical architecture."[13] In his pursuit of a nonsystematic but coherent style that combined the various forms, Nietzsche drew very heavily upon existing musical practices. Perhaps already in *The Birth of Tragedy*, probably in *Zarathustra*, and certainly in his late works, Nietzsche employs musical forms to coordinate the various aphorisms within a larger whole.[14] In his new introduction to *The Birth of Tragedy* in 1886, Nietzsche characterizes the work "as 'music' for those who are baptized in music" (KGW III 1:3). In letters to Franz Overbeck (6 February 1884) and Paul Widemann (31 July 1885), he calls *Zarathustra* a symphony, a claim that Janz has shown must be taken seriously (KGB III 1:475; III 3:74).[15]

Twilight of the Idols was written in the shadow of Nietzsche's projected but never-completed magnum opus. During this period, he was deeply concerned with music. Not only did he avidly attend and write to his friends about all kinds of musical performances, he also worked on compositions of his own. Moreover, two works of the same year, *The Case of Wagner* and *Nietzsche contra Wagner*, explicitly consider musical subjects. At the time, he was studying the musicologist Hugo Riemann's theory of phrasing, as well as Fuchs' *The Future of the Musical Performance and Its Origin* (1884). He wrote to Köselitz on 15 January 1888 that "music now gives me sensations, as really never before. Life without music would simply be an error, a burden, an exile" (KGB III 5:231–32). Indeed, music cast such a powerful spell over him that he was continually distracted from his magnum opus. He wrote to Köselitz on 21 March 1888, "I recognize nothing more, I hear nothing more, I read nothing more; and in spite of all that there is nothing that really more *concerns* me than the fate of music" (KGB III 5:275).

His correspondence suggests that this concern with music conditioned his work. While completing *The Case of Wagner*, he wrote to Köselitz on 17 May 1888, "I lack a year of exact music studies, in order to get control of language for that" (KGB III 5:317). In a letter of 20 July 1888, he informs Overbeck that "just now a small musical pamphlet of mine is being printed" (KGB III 5:362). In a letter to Brandes of 13 September 1888, he calls himself a "musician from instinct" (KGB III 5:419) and in another letter to Köselitz of 18 November 1888 remarks that "*The Case of Wagner* is operetta music" (KGB III 5:419). In what follows I will argue that Nietzsche employed musical forms in structuring *Twilight* and will then try to demonstrate the central importance of these musical forms and music in general as the new "logic" at the heart of his (anti-)metaphysical final teaching.[16]

Twilight of the Idols by Nietzsche's own testimony is a summary of his entire philosophy (KGB III 5:414). It is written in classical sonata form, although the combination of form with image that Nietzsche employs is also strongly reminiscent of early Romanticism. From a musical point of view, this is hardly surprising. Nietzsche had had a preference for the classical in music since his youth, and while he was later attracted to the Romantics and especially Wagner, his own compositions often draw on classical models even as they adopt a number of early Romantic characteristics.[17] In a letter to Fuchs of 29 July 1888, Nietzsche asserts, "We are both very anti-decadence musicians, i.e., anti-modern musicians" (KGB III 5:374). Nietzsche was also well acquainted with sonata form from his previous musical studies and had read with interest Carl Spitteler's discussions of the form in his *Essays on Aesthetics*. He was also clearly concerned with the similarities between musical and poetic forms, as is clear from his letters to Fuchs of 29 July and the end of August 1888 in which he also lays great weight upon the way in which rhythm has an ethical purpose in shaping and controlling the passions (KGB III 5:401, 403–5).

Sonata form is often used for single movements of sonatas or symphonies, and usually consists of three parts—an exposition, a development, and a recapitulation—generally followed by a closing statement, or coda, and often preceded by an introduction. In the exposition, the main ideas are presented, usually in two or three different themes. Various aspects of these themes are developed in a wide variety of ways in the development, usually in a dramatic and dynamic manner, and the recapitulation then repeats the exposition with, however, certain harmonic changes that are usually "prepared" for by the development. The coda is then a short phrase used to bring the movement to a clear and dramatic close. *Twilight* follows this form.[18] The structure of the work might be schematized as shown below.[19]

Title	*Twilight of the Idols*			
Time Signature	"Forward"			
Rest	Place, date, comment, and signature			
Introduction	"Maxims and Arrows"			
Exposition	"Socrates"–"Germans"			
Theme I	"Socrates"–"Fable"			
a) "Socrates"	I(1–2)	II(3–10)	III(11–12)	
b) "Reason"				
c) "Fable"				
Theme II	"Morality"–"Improvers"			
a) "Morality"	I(1–3)	II(4–5)	III(6)	
b) "Errors"				
c) "Improvers"				
Theme III	"Germans"			
a) (1–3)	I(1)	II(2)	III(3)	
b) (4)				
c) (5–7)				
Development	"Skirmishes"			
Introduction	(1)			
Exposition	(2–31)			
Theme I ·	a(2–6)	b(7)	c(8–9)	d(10–11)
Theme II	a(12–14)	b(15–16)	c(17–18)	d(19–20)
Theme III	a(21–23)	b(24–25)	c(26–29)	d(30–31)
Development	(32–48)			
Theme A	a(32–33)	b(34–35)	c(36)	d(37)
Theme B	a(38)	b(39–40)	c(41–42)	d(43)
Theme C	a(44)	b(45)	c(46–47)	d(48)
Recapitulation	(49–50)			
Theme I*	(49)			
Theme II*	(49)			
Theme III*	(50)			
Coda	(51)			
Recapitulation	"Ancients"			
Introduction	(1)			
Theme I*	(2)			
Theme II*	(3)			
Theme III*	(4–5)			
Coda	"Hammer"			

TITLE

As originally conceived, the work was entitled *Idleness of a Psychologist* (KGW VIII 3:345).[20] In this form it ended with "Skirmishes of an Untimely Man." Köselitz wrote to Nietzsche on 20 September 1888 (KGB III 6:309–10) that the title was too unassuming, which prompted him to change it first to *Hammer of the Idols* and then *Twilight of the Idols; or, How One Philosophizes with a Hammer*, drawing the new title from the substance of the preface and making the minor changes necessary to harmonize the text with the new title, as Nietzsche notes in a letter to Köselitz of 27 September 1888 (KGB III 5:443).[21] Shortly thereafter and certainly before the middle of November, Nietzsche decided to expand the work and added the final two sections, "What I Owe to the Ancients" and "The Hammer Speaks." The title, according to the preface, betrays the work, as Nietzsche admits in a letter to Köselitz of 27 September 1888 (KGB III 5:443).

Twilight of the Idols (*Götzen-Dämmerung*) is an allusion to Wagner's music drama *Twilight of the Gods* (*Götterdämmerung*). In *The Birth of Tragedy*, Nietzsche had argued that a rebirth of tragedy and a new tragic age were possible because the philosophic tradition that had displaced tragedy had revealed itself as nihilistic in Kant's antinomies and because German, and in particular Wagnerian, music was animated by that same spirit out of which Greek tragedy had been born. By 1888, however, Nietzsche had not only long since lost hope in Wagner but had come to see him as the epitome of the forces that were leading European civilization into nihilism. His title is thus intended as both a critique and parody of Wagner. God, according to Zarathustra, is dead. In Nietzsche's view, however, the idols (including Wagner), the images of God, "what previously was called truth," continue to dominate human life (*TI*, KGW VI 3:352). Belief in God, which hitherto provided the light in which truth was possible, has degenerated into idolatry. Like the hermit whom Zarathustra encounters in the forest, mankind is not yet aware or at least does not yet admit that God is dead. In the absence of God, however, the idols that men worship are enveloped in the twilight of nihilism and like the old gods of Wagner's music drama are approaching their end. In the words of Brünnhilde, "The gods' end now dawns: so I throw the torch in Valhalla's resplendent citadel."[22] Nietzsche, too, in proclaiming the end of the idols casts his torch into the citadel of European civilization. There is no doubt in Nietzsche's mind that the twilight of the idols is an evening twilight for European civilization, but he hopes that the conflagration his torch will ignite will open up the space for the morning twilight of a new dawn, the dawn of the tragic age of the *Übermensch*. This conclusion, however, is left unstated in the work itself and thus remains only as a looming question for Nietzsche's readers, a question Nietzsche intended to answer in his magnum opus.

The subtitle, *How One Philosophizes with a Hammer*, further illuminates the work. The term "hammer" signifies in the first instance a tool used for building or destroying and is hence an image of power. Nietzsche uses the term in this sense in *Zarathustra* as the hammer that rages against the stone in which the image of the *Übermensch* is imprisoned (KGW VI 1:107–8; see also *BGE*, KGW VI 2:81). In commenting upon this passage in *Ecce Homo*, Nietzsche characterizes this use of the hammer as Dionysian, as the joy even in destroying (KGW VI 3:47). In the preface to *Twilight*, however, the hammer is described as a tool for determining sonority. The unity of this dual image becomes clear as an allusion to Wagner's *Ring* cycle. The image of the hammer appears twice in the *Ring*. In *Rheingold* the god Donner uses his hammer to bring a great thunderstorm to dissipate the twilight obscuring the way to Valhalla. The storm that the hammer evokes resolves into a rainbow bridge over which the gods cross into their new citadel. In *Siegfried* the hammer appears again as the tool Siegfried uses to form the irresistible sword, *Nothung* (Necessity), with which he defeats Wotan. Nietzsche's subtitle suggests that the world characterized by nihilism, by the death of God and the twilight that this event has spread over the old Christian God, and the idols shaped in his image, will be destroyed by the hammer in the hands of the philosopher who forges a new sword and a new necessity, who produces the lightning and the storm that disperse the twilight and prepare the way for the tragic age of the *Übermensch*.

The philosopher, reminiscent here of the Old Testament prophets, is portrayed as calling his people back from the worship of idols to the worship of the one true god. This god, however, is not Yahweh or the Christian God but the god of tragedy, Dionysus.[23] The hammer that reveals the hollowness of the idols is thus the god himself, whose music calls mankind to his festival and his tragic age. This is borne out by the *Nachlass*, which contains the proposed title "The Hammer (or Dionysus)" (KGW VII 3:205). Whether humanity will succeed in establishing a tragic culture or even survive the attempt, however, is uncertain. In the *Nachlass* the continuation of the *Zarathustra* project was to end with the "Last speech: Here is the hammer that overcomes men / Did man turn out badly? Well, let us test to the utmost whether he can endure this hammer!" (KGW VII 2:73). The meaning of this enigmatic passage becomes clearer in comparison with Wagner.

The rule of the gods in Wagner's *Ring* is based upon the justice of covenant, on the strength of Wotan's fidelity to written law. In pursuit of power and glory, however, Wotan breaks his word and thus dooms himself and his pantheon to destruction. The pursuit of power, symbolized by the ring, requires the renunciation of love, which is the basis for all communal life. Power in Wagner's view drives both men and gods into the self and thus assures the collapse of the old order. The world can be redeemed only through the renunciation of power out of love. Brünnhilde fulfills this task in igniting the final conflagration in *Götterdämmerung* and returning the ring to its rightful owners. It is this idea of redemption through love, the Romantic notion that order can be established without recourse to political power, through the evocation of the communal spirit of the *Volk*, which is the determinative theme of Wagner's *Ring*.

The destruction of the old idols by the hammer of Nietzsche's musical philosophy in *Twilight* is also a redemption that subordinates the old order within the new. The old idols are "redeemed" within the eternal order of things as necessary moments of the whole. This redemption, however, is not the result of a renunciation of power for love but rather of the will to power that loves only the *Übermensch* and its own completion in the recognition of the eternal recurrence and a new tragic age. *Twilight* is thus Nietzsche's *musical* alternative to Wagner's vision of death and renewal. He attempts to write the true music drama, to overcome the old idols or so-called truths of the European tradition, and to give birth to that which Zarathustra claims is beyond both God and the idols, to the tragic age of the *Übermensch*.

His work like that of Wagner is also a *Gesamtkunstwerk* although they differ on what this entails. Wagner had sought to unite the various arts that in his view had grown distant from one another since Euripides transformed Greek drama and to include elements of theology and philosophy as well. In *Twilight* and his late works in general, Nietzsche attempts to combine music, poetry, philosophy, epigrammatic and aphoristic prose, psychology, history, and theology, in a single expressive art, which is perhaps the best example of the new logic that is essential to his (anti-)metaphysics. In what follows I will try to make sense of what this means by focusing on the musical structures he uses to gather all of the other elements together.

PREFACE

The preface to the work is divided into two sections separated by a line of Latin. There are 135 words above and 180 words below the Latin line, which constitutes a proportion of 3/4.[24] This division suggests that the preface is the time signature, specifying 3/4 time (triple meter). Triple meter is more or less equivalent to ancient trochaic meter, which, according to Nietzsche, is the meter of the bacchic dance, used especially by Aeschylus in his choral odes; it does not imitate speech but instead remains fundamentally musical and thus ennobles tragic poetry.[25] It is hardly surprising then that Nietzsche should employ it in a work that seeks to revive the spirit of ancient tragedy.

The preface explains this use of musical forms.[26] Music is what Nietzsche needs to avoid the "all too heavy seriousness" of the revaluation. He remarks in *Nietzsche contra Wagner*, "My melancholy wants to relax in the hiding places and abysses of perfection: for this reason I need music. But Wagner makes one sick" (KGW VI 3:417). For Nietzsche, Wagner's music offers no relief since it is entangled in decadence. *Twilight* is Nietzsche's convalescence, his *idleness* (or leisure), as the original title characterized it, from the burden of the magnum opus. It is not, however, mere play but, as Nietzsche asserts, a "case," that is, a polemic or war, like *The Case of Wagner*, which he was working on at the same time as *Twilight*. This war, however, is a "relaxation because it releases tension, because it allows the drawn bow to release its 'arrow,'" because, as Nietzsche suggests in the Latin quotation, "spirit increases and vigor grows through a wound."

This is only one side of his convalescence, as he points out in the section of the preface below the Latin line. The other is striking idols with a hammer and hearing the famous hollow sound—the sound that they are empty and worn out.[27] This is not the destruction of the idols but the musical revelation of their emptiness, which, according to Nietzsche, can only be understood by those who have ears behind their ears. He apparently refers here to the third ear mentioned in *Beyond Good and Evil* for the musicality of language, for symmetry, crescendo, inflection, tone, and tempo (KGW VI 2:97–99; see also *EH*, KGW VI 3:302).

This musical revelation is Nietzsche's philosophizing with a hammer. The original title, *Idleness of a Psychologist*, gives a clue to the nature of this philosophizing. Nietzsche characterizes himself in this title not as philosopher but as psychologist. Nietzsche's philosophizing with a hammer, his sounding out the idols, is fundamentally an attempt to determine whether idols such as Socrates are psychologically healthy or unhealthy, whether they represent ascending or descending life.

The final paragraph of the preface indicates how these two projects are combined. This war is a recreation or convalescence because it is a musical war in which opposition is necessary to but not sufficient for harmony. Philosophizing with a hammer in the twilight of a world in which God is dead is the incorporation and subordination of both contemporary and eternal idols, that is, ideals or truths, within the musical form of a new necessity. In sounding out these idols, Nietzsche reveals their emptiness. However, it is precisely this emptiness that allows them to resound. The revelation of their emptiness is thus the source of Nietzsche's music and hence of the tragic age this music is meant to call into being.

This musical motif continues at the end of the preface: the place, occasion of composition, and signature are a rest inserted at the beginning of the piece—indicating that the work begins on an upbeat, which suggests, according to Nietzsche, that the piece will be lively rather than restful (*GR*, KGW II 3:112–14). The date is especially significant. Nietzsche remarks in *Ecce Homo*, "On the 30th of September a great victory; seventh day; idleness of a god along the Po" (KGW VI 3:354).[28] Here Nietzsche marks the idleness or rest of his seventh day, after the completion of his creation of the first book of the revaluation.

INTRODUCTION

A sonata introduction begins in the tonic key, modulates through various keys, and then usually ends with a closing cadence leading into the exposition. The deviation from the tonic in the introduction produces a tension that is resolved by the return of the tonic in the first theme of the exposition. The introduction also often introduces in compressed form the various themes of the work although not necessarily in the same order or key. Nietzsche's introduction follows this format and achieves all these objectives.

A central difficulty for our analysis is understanding what constitutes key for Nietzsche. In this regard, he apparently relies upon the Greeks, who distinguished various keys or modes and named them after the political cultures or ways of life they believed represented the passions or behaviors that these modes seemed to engender, for example, the effeminate Ionian and Lydian modes, the courageous Dorian mode, and so on. Nietzsche adopts and reverses this practice—the political cultures or ways of life represent different keys.

Each of these cultures or ways of life worships a particular idol that represents its dominant passions or drives, or its national character.[29] The idol thus reveals the true character of the political culture and an analysis of the idol reveals what is often hidden from view to those within the culture itself. Nietzsche's psychological examination and evaluation of the various idols is thus also an evaluation of the political cultures that worship these idols. His music is thus a form of political analysis.

The introduction, "Maxims and Arrows," begins with three aphorisms reminiscent of the Greeks. The first, "Idleness is the beginning of all psychology," recalls Aristotle's dictum that wonder is the beginning of all philosophy. This is even clearer in an earlier version of the aphorism extant in the *Nachlass*: "Idleness is the beginning of all philosophy" (KGW VIII 1:293; see also VI 3:225; and V 2:494).[30] The second aphorism, "Even the most courageous of us only seldom has the courage for what he really *knows* . . . ," recalls Socrates' assertion that the unexamined life is not worth living (cf. *TI*, KGW VI 3:67), and the third aphorism refers to Aristotle by name. Thus, classical Greek culture and the philosophic idol that it worships are apparently the tonic.

The introduction ends with eight aphorisms (37–44) that form a closing cadence in sharp contrast to the opening theme of the exposition ("Socrates"). Nietzsche's conclusion—"Formula of my happiness: a yes, a no, a straight line, a goal"—is opposed to the first sentence of "Socrates"—"About life the wisest of all times have judged alike: it amounts to nothing." This opposition between Greek philosophy, as symbolized by Socrates, and Nietzsche's musical philosophizing is the major problem that the work itself must resolve.

The solution is already implicit in the introduction. As Werner Dannhauser has pointed out, this section is implicitly an account of Nietzsche himself.[31] This is indicated perhaps by the number of aphorisms it contains (forty-four), which corresponds to the year of Nietzsche's birth (1844) and to the year of his life in which the work was written. This is more clearly indicated by the fact that much of the introduction is drawn from a collection in the *Nachlass* entitled "Maxims of a Hyperborean" (KGW VIII 3:271–74; see also VIII 3:345). In *The Antichrist*, Nietzsche characterizes himself as a Hyperborean, a man of the north who worships Apollo, the god of poets and the god whose oracle at Delphi proclaimed Socrates the wisest of men (KGW VI 3:167). The resolution to the problem of the introduction and the work as a whole—the contradiction between the Greek way, personified by Socrates, and the German way, personified by Nietzsche, is thus already implicit in the introduction: the epiphany of the Greek gods among the Germans, the return of Greek gods, and especially Dionysus wearing the mask of Apollo, to reconstitute out of the winter twilight of nihilism a new tragic age and culture.

EXPOSITION

The exposition ("Socrates"–"Germans"), which consists of forty-five aphorisms, is a sounding out of what Nietzsche calls *eternal* idols. The first theme is concerned with Greek philosophic ideals, the second with Christian moral ideals, and the last with German political ideals. The Greeks thus are the tonic of the work, while the Germans are the dominant, that is, the fifth above the Greeks. The musical problem of the work is to resolve the harmonic dissonance between these two themes, to reconcile the dominant with the tonic, the Germans with the Greeks, so that they can return in the same key in the recapitulation.

Structurally, the three themes are identical. Both the first and the second contain nineteen aphorisms (perhaps pointing, for reasons we shall examine below, to the nineteenth century), while the third contains seven. The themes are also historically sequential, beginning with the Greeks, passing through Christianity, and ending with the Germans. The form of the themes, however, remains the same, which seems to indicate that the inherent problem is not solved by the thematic development.

THEME I. The first theme is in three sections: "Socrates" (twelve aphorisms), "Reason" (six aphorisms), and "Fable" (one aphorism). It begins with an attack upon Socrates. It is not Socrates the man but Socrates the idol that Nietzsche attacks, and through his psychological examination or sounding out of Socrates he hopes to determine the health or sickness not merely of Socrates but of the philosophic tradition that idolizes Socrates.

In the first part of "Socrates" (1–2), Nietzsche opposes Socrates' view that life is no good to his own that the value of life cannot be estimated. He then attacks Socrates (3–10) employing his *Entlarvungspsychologie*, arguing that Socrates' "virtues" are merely symptoms of disease and a desire for revenge against life. Socrates, in his view, was only taken seriously because he seemed to offer a cure for the general Greek sickness, the chaos of the instincts, with his equation of reason, virtue, and happiness, but this was a misunderstanding, for his rationality was only a more complete manifestation of decadence and descending life (see *BT*, KGW III 1:81–90). Nietzsche then presents his alternative, ascending life, rooted in instinct and not in reason (11), and resurrects Socrates to admit his defeat (12).

This section presents the fundamental problem of the work as the opposition of Socrates' and Nietzsche's cultural/political prescriptions. Socrates is the antithesis to the tragic sense of life that Nietzsche seeks to foster with his music. In *The Birth of Tragedy*, Socrates was portrayed as the destroyer of tragedy whose optimistic dialectic drove music out of tragedy and gave birth to Hellenistic culture (*BT*, KGW III 1:91; see also *BT*, III 1:6, and *UM*, KGW IV 1:18–19). Nietzsche attacks Socrates to clear the way for the rebirth of tragedy, evaluating both in terms of the law of life, that is, according to whether they affirm or deny life, whether they are examples of ascending or descending life (*NL*, KGW VII 3:60).

In "Reason," Nietzsche categorizes the basic errors of the philosophic tradition, which idolizes Socrates, as manifestations of descending life and compares them with Heracleitus and science as examples of ascending life. The continuation of the theme in the tonic is signaled by Heracleitus, who, as an integral moment of the tragic age of the Greeks, here represents the real alternative to philosophic degeneracy, Nietzsche himself (see *EH*, KGW VI 3:311). Nietzsche concludes that the actual world has falsely been characterized as the apparent world in opposition to the "real" world by philosophy as a weapon against ascending or tragic life. The distinction between "real" and "apparent" is thus only a reflection of descending life. This philosophic rejection of life is juxtaposed to Nietzsche's alternative, that is, the Dionysian artist (6), who rather than renouncing life because it is terrible affirms it for precisely this reason. The antithesis of these two positions is resolved in the final section of the theme.

"How the 'true world' finally became a fable" is a cadence leading into the second theme. This section reasserts the tonic in the person of Plato, and in a manner characteristic of sonata form sums up the first theme. Nietzsche reinterprets the entire philosophic history of European civilization, from the destruction of tragedy by Socratism to the rebirth of tragedy in *Zarathustra*, as the process by which the Socratic premise is overcome.

THEME II. The second theme like the first is also in three sections: "Morality" (six aphorisms), "Errors" (eight aphorisms), and "Improvers" (five aphorisms). It also begins with the confrontation of Nietzsche and his adversaries (1–3)—here Christianity (in place of Socrates) as the champion or idol of morality (in place of philosophy). Christian morality, however, is really only the generalization of the Socratic equation, as Nietzsche indicated in "Socrates" (11). The second theme is thus an extension of the first, contrasting here two ways of dealing with the passions—the Christian practice of extirpation and Nietzsche's practice of spiritualization. As in the first theme, Nietzsche's psychological examination reveals that Christianity rests upon a denial of life, which he argues is impossible since it assumes a position outside life that is unattainable (4–5). Hence, it is merely a manifestation of descending life in contrast to Nietzsche's alternative, the immoralist (6), who recognizes and affirms the fatality of everything that is.[32]

The second section of the theme, "Errors," locates the source of this misunderstanding of life in the failure to understand that the apparent world is the actual world and the mistaken attribution of causality to the "real," noumenal world. This section ends with a further examination of Nietzsche's alternative, ascending life. Man, according to Nietzsche, is a piece of fate and cannot be disentangled from all that has been and will be—hence, he cannot judge life because it is the whole of which he is only a part. It is precisely this acceptance and love of fate, this *amor fati*, in Nietzsche's view, that characterizes the tragic artist, the Dionysian faith (of "Reason" 6) that grasps the necessity and beauty of Zarathustra and thus of tragedy. This is likewise the faith of the immoralist, the great affirmer mentioned in "Morality" (6). Indeed, an early draft of this section ("Errors") was entitled "The Immoralist" (*NL*, KGW VIII 3:348).

In the final section of the second theme, "Improvers," Nietzsche demonstrates (as in "Fable") that all previous morality was a rejection of life as it is and hence a manifestation of descending life. He then concludes that the improvers of morals know that he is right because they always claim the right to lie, that is, to be *immoral*. Like Socrates, they themselves are thus brought forth to admit their defeat.

THEME III. The final theme of the exposition is in the dominant, that is, German political culture, and is structurally identical to the other themes, although only about one-third as long. The dominant has a special significance in sonata form, since it is the fifth above the tonic and thus forms a perfect interval with the tonic. This interval, however, does not constitute a harmony of the melodies of the two themes; indeed, there is an express prohibition in sonata form against parallel fifths. Thus the harmonic dissonance within each theme between Socrates' way and Nietzsche's way is identical to the harmonic problem of the exposition and hence the work as a whole, the resolution of the differences between the Greeks and the Germans. It is only through the development and modulation of the dominant into the tonic in the recapitulation that this contradiction can be overcome, that the dissonance of the perfect interval between Greek and German life, between philosophy and politics, between Socrates and Nietzsche, can be resolved into harmony.[33]

In the first aphorism (as in "Socrates" 1–2 and "Morality" 1–3) Nietzsche contrasts the two opposing positions, the Germany he represents and the Germany of the *Reich*, the Germany of the mediocre. In the second aphorism (as in "Socrates" 3–10 and "Morality" 4–5), he sounds out this German spirit and argues that it is antithetical to life. In the third aphorism (as in "Socrates" 11 and "Morality" 6), he indicates that not merely the German spirit but German life itself that is in decline and then calls all Europe as a witness to support his case (as in "Socrates" 12).

In the second section of the theme (as in "Reason" and "Errors"), Nietzsche points to the source of this degeneration as the failure to recognize the antagonism of *Kultur* and *Staat* (4). In *The Birth of Tragedy*, Nietzsche had argued that German political revival and unification into a *Reich* were possible on the basis of the cultural unity fostered by Wagner's music drama. He soon became convinced of the futility of such aspirations and indeed came to recognize that such a politics was antagonistic to true "music" since it established political unity only by enervating spirituality. Nietzsche opposes nationalism and argues that one must be not a good German or Frenchman but a good European. A European in Nietzsche's sense, however, is not a characterless cosmopolitan but the embodiment of the 2,500-year-old European tradition (*GS*, KGW V 2:313). One can be such a European, however, only if one understands this tradition in terms of its unifying theme, that is, nihilism. The recognition that God is dead is thus the presupposition of a new tragic age. Zarathustra brings this truth down from the mountains, and it is with his going under that tragedy begins. The good European grasps Zarathustra's teaching of the doctrine of the eternal recurrence and understands it as the basis for the great politics of a new tragic age, something quite different than the petty politics of Bismarck and his contemporaries.[34]

In the third section of the theme (as in "Fable" and "Errors"), Nietzsche locates the source of contemporary decadence in the failure of educational institutions (5) and indicates his alternative, the educator who teaches men style.[35] Nietzsche here characterizes his own musical style in contrast to both Wagner and German *Bildung* as affirmative, dealing with contradiction and criticism only as a means (6).

In the *Republic*, Socrates argues that education begins with gymnastic and music and ascends through mathematics to dialectic. This relegation of music to a lower level is in Nietzsche's view the result of Socrates' optimistic dialectic, which drives music out of tragedy and thus out of the education that informed the tragic age (*BT*, KGW III 1:91). As he sees it, it is this dialectical optimism that characterizes European thought. The rebirth of tragedy thus presupposes the subordination of dialectic and hence of the entire post-Socratic tradition to music understood in the broadest sense. This is apparently the meaning of the conjunction of positive and negative elements in Nietzsche's thought. Nietzsche does not seek to remove or even to disprove his opponents but to incorporate and subordinate them within the harmonic structure of his music. He strives to sound out his opponents and demonstrate that they are necessary as harmonic moments of a musical cosmos, as necessary, even if abysmal, moments of life itself. The recognition of their necessity is bound up with his doctrine of the eternal recurrence of the same. The necessity of the contradictory elements within the whole constitutes the essence of the tragic, and their incorporation and harmonization is thus the affirmative musical teaching that underlies the negative or critical philosophic character of the work.

DEVELOPMENT

The development section of a sonata fragments and recombines the exposition themes in order to resolve their harmonic dissonance so that they can return in the recapitulation in their original order in the tonic. This means that for Nietzsche the problem of eternal idols must be resolved so they can return not as idols of a dialectical tradition but as elements of a tragic European culture that combines philosophy, morality, and politics in a neo-Greek synthesis. The third section of each exposition theme indicates the way to such a reconciliation: the problems of traditional philosophy, morality, and politics culminate in the nineteenth century. The solution to the problem of eternal idols thus presupposes the solution to the problem of the "idols of the age."

The development section itself is written in a sonata form more or less equivalent to that of the work as a whole. This seems to indicate that the problem of contemporary idols in the development is formally identical to the problem of eternal idols. The title of the development, "Skirmishes of an Untimely Man," supports this thesis—it is not Nietzsche's war with eternal idols but rather his skirmishes with the lesser idols of the nineteenth century.

DEVELOPMENT INTRODUCTION. The development introduction, like that of the work as a whole, consists of a variety of compressed themes. Here Nietzsche's "Arrows," however, are directed at specific characters. With the exception of the first five, who were culture heroes of the period, all are nineteenth-century figures and in Nietzsche's language thus idols of the age.

DEVELOPMENT EXPOSITION. There are three themes in the development exposition. The first is concerned with French literati, the second with Anglo-American thinkers, and the third with German and Greek philosophers.

THEME I. The first development theme consists of ten aphorisms (2–11) and, with the exception of George Eliot, is concerned exclusively with French literary culture. In the first section, Nietzsche attacks French literary decadence as a corruption of the noble taste of classical France. He points out in a letter to Köselitz of 10 November 1887 that these thinkers in many respects resemble him but that they all lack the main thing—"la force" (KGB III 5:192; see also *NL*, KGW VII 2:254–55, and VIII 2:253–57). Nietzsche thus seeks to dissociate himself from them. As he remarks (in 7), "One must know *who* one is."

In the second section of the theme (7), Nietzsche explains that these artists failed because they believed nature conformed to some rule and attempted to copy it. Since nature is essentially chaotic, however, art must not imitate it but give it order, as Nietzsche explains in the third section of the theme (8–9). The French artists, however, lack the necessary creative frenzy and hence are ultimately a manifestation of descending rather than ascending life. In the final section of the theme (10–11), Nietzsche characterizes the three types of true artists and the sorts of frenzy that motivate them: the Apollinian (frenzy of vision), the Dionysian (frenzy of affect), and the architect (frenzy of the great will). This characterization, as we shall see, presents the three sides of Nietzsche's own art: the imagistic, aphoristic vision of the Hyperborean; the musical frenzy of the disciple of Dionysus; and the overarching fatalistic will to power of the architect.

THEME 11. The second theme is a consideration of Anglo-American thought and connects French thought, the development tonic, to German thought, the development dominant. George Eliot serves as the bridge between the two themes. Carlyle, Emerson, and Darwin are close to Nietzsche but like the French lack his power (12–14) because, as Nietzsche points out in the second section of the theme (15–16), they want only little advantages over men, while the impersonal type, that is, Nietzsche himself (*TI*, KGW VI 3:123), wants to be beyond them (15). Despite this difference, Nietzsche believes that the Germans will inevitably confuse him with them, just as they confused Schiller and Goethe, Schopenhauer and Hartmann (16).

The third section of the theme explains the differences between him and them. The most spiritual human beings do not try to escape from their contradictory passions into faith but rather honor life because of these contradictions (17). Nietzsche here develops the theme of the contradiction or opposition of philosophic reason and the Dionysian art that arose in "Reason." In the exposition, this opposition was merely presented as a dissonance; here in the development, Nietzsche examines the grounds for a reconciliation or harmony by measuring both positions in terms of their responses to the passions.[36] The greatest men in Nietzsche's view necessarily experience the greatest tragedies because they are motivated by the greatest passions (17). The artist understands this, as Nietzsche argues in the fourth section of the theme (as in 8–11), because he knows that man alone is beautiful or ugly, beautiful when he represents ascending, passionate life, and ugly when he represents descending, reasonable life.

THEME III. The third development theme begins in the dominant (the Germans) and juxtaposes it to the tonic of the work as a whole (the Greeks). It thus expresses the fundamental harmonic problem of the work in its most severe form. Schopenhauer, Nietzsche argues in the first section of the theme, has treated all the greatest monuments of life and especially sexuality as monuments to nothingness. Indeed, Schopenhauer even understands beauty as man's *redemption* from will and sexuality. He thus directly contradicts Plato, who argued that sexuality was a prerequisite of both beauty and philosophy. Moreover, according to Nietzsche, both are in this respect irreconcilable with Spinoza. These three figures represent the three original exposition themes, and their mutual contradiction exposes the European tradition itself as fundamentally contradictory. That Nietzsche fastens upon sexuality is hardly accidental. His standard of evaluation is life itself, and the essence of life in his view is not self-preservation but the will to power, the will to overcome even oneself, and on the most rudimentary biological level this means procreation. The contradiction within the European tradition about the value of sexuality thus reveals its fundamentally contradictory and nihilistic character. With this articulation of the nihilistic essence of European culture, Nietzsche's sonata reaches the moment of utmost dissonance and tension; the implicit disharmony of the exposition here becomes explicit. This is the musical and philosophical problem that Nietzsche must solve: he must subordinate the fundamental contradiction or dissonance of European civilization concerning the basis of life within a more comprehensive harmonic unity that grasps and affirms sexuality as the essence of life itself.

The immediate source of the nihilism of the nineteenth century, which appears in Schopenhauer, is the attempt to do away with moral purposiveness in art (24). Since art, according to Nietzsche, is the source of all purpose, this attempt leads to nihilism. Nietzsche's alternative, the tragic artist, faces the terrible in nihilism and transforms it into humanity's greatest affirmation of life. Saying Yes to the most abysmal possibility, he redeems humanity from purposelessness.[37]

As in the previous two themes, Nietzsche's antagonists resemble him.[38] And insofar as he resembles them, he embodies the most basic contradictions of the European tradition. Thus, by overcoming this contradiction within himself, by saying yes to this nihilism (and to his own life), he believes he can give birth to a new tragic age. The contradiction of the European tradition as a whole culminates for Nietzsche in himself, and the harmonic tension of the work is brought to a peak as the tension of Nietzsche's own soul.[39]

The last two sections of the third theme indicate how Nietzsche lives with this tension. Just as noble hospitality is reserved for the greatest guests (25), Nietzsche's life is reserved for the greatest problems. The heavy burden they impose, however, can only be alleviated by humor. Thus Nietzsche satirizes himself as a "deaf-mute" who did not recognize the musical potentialities of language (26) and as a literary female who believed himself filled with spirit as a classicist (27). However, he overcame the impersonality of scholarship by developing personal traits (28), and, when he became ill, the philologist (29) traveled to Italy and Bayreuth, where *"pure foolishness restores"* (30). Finally, he concludes the theme with the assertion of the necessity of great health for the genius (31). Nietzsche here reconstitutes his life artistically to demonstrate how the most destructive passions can be affirmed and made beautiful. He sees himself as the tragic artist, the musical Socrates who lays out a way to the future, and thus as the solution to the problems of both the eternal idols and the idols of the age. In the development-development, this formula for the transformation of nihilism into the tragic age of the *Übermensch* becomes explicit.

DEVELOPMENT-DEVELOPMENT. The development-development consists of seventeen aphorisms divided into three themes. The first is a consideration of morality, the second of freedom, and the third of genius. These three present the necessary and sufficient conditions for the rebirth of tragedy and the great politics Nietzsche associates with a tragic culture and age.

THEME A. In the first theme, Nietzsche contrasts the morality of the weak "ideal" man with that of the strong "real" man and asserts that the latter is more valuable since it is conducive to a higher form of life (33).[40] The former "parasitic" morality (34–35) thus must be replaced by a morality that benefits the strong, based upon a tragic sense of life that unlike Christianity regards death as the highest moment of life (36). The greatest obstacle to such a morality in Nietzsche's view is his contemporaries' certainty of their moral superiority. This, however, is the mere consequence of their weakness (36). It is, however, too late to return to the stronger morality of the Renaissance (37)—humanity must first pass through decadence and the most abysmal human possibilities.

THEME B. In the second theme, Nietzsche distinguishes two different types of freedom, his freedom, the freedom of the warrior, which is predicated upon inequality and danger, and liberal freedom, which seeks the safety of universal equality. The truly free man is close to both tyranny and slavery and becomes free only by disciplining his passions to avoid both of them. Such freedom, however, is possible only in a passionate and dangerous age, but such a possibility is lacking today because "the entire West no longer has those instincts out of which institutions grow, out of which the future grows" (39). Our instincts should not be abandoned, however, simply because they are wrong (41). Instead a new hierarchy must be established by legislators who recognize the necessity of lying (42), for without such conscious hypocrisy they will not differ from the saints and theologians of the past— the unconscious hypocrites of "Skirmishes" (18). Thus, modern European civilization must first pass through decadence if this is to be attained (43). The conservatives, according to Nietzsche, believe the opposite, certain that they can restore the *ancien régime* or shore up existing institutions, but this downward movement cannot be checked; it can only be dammed up and made more sudden.

THEME C. In the two preceding themes, Nietzsche presented two parts of this program for the world of the future, a new morality and a new freedom. The third theme presents the final necessity, the great genius who exercises this freedom and imposes this morality. These three are the pillars of Nietzsche's great politics that will create a tragic European order. Nietzsche first contrasts his conception of genius with that of the decadents (such as Carlyle and Schopenhauer) considered in the development exposition (44). The great man for him is a finale, who creates a higher form of life and thus exhausts life's resources. His model here is Napoleon, the "*ens realissimum*" (49). Such geniuses, however, most often become criminals because there is no opportunity for them (45), and even those who succeed must pass through a Chandala existence.[41]

This higher type is in fact the *Übermensch*. His is a perspective beyond good and evil. "Here the view is free," Nietzsche asserts, quoting Goethe's Faust.[42] The genius has an unrestricted view because he is above man. Thus, like Heracleitus, he may contradict himself, he may lie, he may even sacrifice his humanity or indeed, like Christ, his divinity—not from weakness but from the height of strength and love. Genius like beauty, however, is not the product of a single individual but rather of a political community's long series of decisions about every aspect of life (47). The tragic culture of the Greeks, for example, was prepared by the decisions of previous generations. Socrates and Christianity were also the results of a long tradition, but of descending not ascending life.

In the final section of the theme, Nietzsche argues that Rousseau's conception of a return to nature is impossible, leading only to the depths of decadence, that is, to the doctrine of equality and the French Revolution. Neither Rousseau nor the conservatives realize that God is dead and that in his absence all truths, institutions, and everything else that was based upon him have become untenable. With Rousseau, however, Nietzsche returns to the development tonic, that is, to the French and thus signals the end of the development and the beginning of the recapitulation.

DEVELOPMENT RECAPITULATION. The recapitulation of a sonata returns to the exposition themes in their original order but harmonically modified by the development so they can all return in the tonic. According to Nietzsche, the result of the descent into decadence ushered in by Rousseau was Goethe, who represents the self-overcoming of the eighteenth century (48). Goethe, however, seems to be a return not to the development tonic, that is, to the French, but rather to the dominant, that is, to the Germans. Nietzsche resolves this problem and simultaneously indicates why Goethe is the recapitulation: "Goethe no German event, but a European one" (49).[43] Goethe embodies all the development themes: the French, English, and German and indeed all post-Socratic European culture. This unification of the various cultural moments of the exposition is achieved through the unification of the three themes of the development-development in Goethe's own character. Goethe embodied all the strongest instincts of the eighteenth century (49), overcame them, and created himself by adopting a higher *morality*, becoming *free*, through trust in fate (49), and striving for universality as the *genius* must (50).

The problem of the idols thus seems to have been solved by Goethe, but unfortunately "Goethe might have been merely an interlude, a beautiful 'in vain' not only for Germany but for the whole of Europe" (50), and the nineteenth century merely the brutalized eighteenth century. Goethe failed because he was unable to solve the problem of the eternal idols. The source of his inability becomes clearer when we consider his place in the musical structure of the work as a whole. Goethe is the recapitulation and resolution of contemporary European culture. The harmony that he represents is merely the harmony that arises from sounding out the idols of the age. Thus, the problem of eternal idols that begins with Socrates is left unresolved. Despite the universality of his genius, Goethe remains within the Socratic horizon. He is thus only the last and greatest precursor of Nietzsche himself.

DEVELOPMENT CODA. The coda is the concluding section of a sonata, which succinctly and dramatically restates the principal themes of the recapitulation and the work as a whole. Nietzsche's development coda fulfills all these tasks in pointing explicitly to the solution of the problem of the idols, that is, to Nietzsche himself. Nietzsche presents himself here as a higher and more profound Goethe, as the genius, the great artist, who will complete the transformation of European culture. He is thus also a good European.

As originally conceived, the work ended with this section (Nietzsche to Köselitz, 12 September 1888, KGB III 5:417). This original form apparently consisted of an introduction and exposition considering eternal idols, a development considering the idols of the age, and a recapitulation considering the necessities for the future—which culminated in Goethe and Nietzsche. Nietzsche's own solution, however, was not stated in the original draft of the work. Biographical data are helpful here. Nietzsche's late works were prompted in part by his publisher's request for some short works to prepare the public for the magnum opus. This apparently played some role in *Twilight*.[44] The original ending of "Skirmishes" (51) points to the coming magnum opus. The preface, as we saw above, is even dated to the day Nietzsche completed *The Antichrist*, then conceived as the first book of the magnum opus. Nietzsche, however, soon decided that *The Antichrist* would play a different role. It seems likely that the decision to expand *Twilight* arose in conjunction with this decision. If this is the case, then the expansion may be the result of Nietzsche's desire to make it a self-sufficient work that articulated both the fundamental problems of European civilization and, at least in a preliminary way, their solution.

RECAPITULATION

In the recapitulation, Nietzsche returns to the tonic, the Greeks. The recapitulation, however, is also a return to Nietzsche himself. The title of the section, "What I Owe to the Ancients," emphasizes both elements. The *Nachlass* also contains an early draft of *Ecce Homo*, four sections of which form the core of "Ancients" (KGW VIII 3:435–41). This draft is dated October–November 1888, that is, after Nietzsche had completed the original draft of *Twilight* and decided on the new title. Thus, this addition points to Nietzsche himself. This is also indicated by the fact that Nietzsche originally intended this section to be part of *Ecce Homo*.

The recapitulation consists of an introduction (1), a consideration of Greek philosophy (2), Greek morality (3), and Greek political life (4), and a conclusion which unites these three in Greek art (5). The recapitulation thus repeats the themes of the exposition in their original order, although now they are all in the tonic.

INTRODUCTION. The introduction is a discussion of the classical style that Nietzsche himself has adopted. *Twilight*, according to Nietzsche, is neither a Yes nor a No to everything it considers; in fact it says nothing at all; it does not judge (1). *Twilight* is rather a new approach to the ancient world that goes beyond *The Birth of Tragedy* and Wagnerian music drama to Nietzsche's own fusion of image, emotion, and form, a fusion of the Apollinian, the Dionysian, and the architectonic. According to Nietzsche, his style is Roman—a mosaic of words, "where each word streams out its strength as sound, as place, as concept, to the right and left and over the entirety" (1). Each word is thus music (sound), architecture (place), and philosophy (concept). This stylistic unity is the key to understanding Nietzsche's "return" to the Greeks and the tonic—it is a return through the art of the "*imperium Romanum*, until today no one ever built or dreamed of building on the same scale!" (KGW VI 3:243). It is this Roman architectural element, that is, the frenzy of the will of power, that was lacking in Nietzsche's account of the Greeks in *The Birth of Tragedy* as an independent element to unite the Apollinian and the Dionysian. There, architecture was treated as an aspect of the Apollinian. With this element as the basis of a unified style, Nietzsche is able to return to the Greeks and overcome Socrates, philosophy, morality, and nationalism by subordinating them as dissonant elements within the architectonic structure of the work as a whole.

Like Goethe, Nietzsche uses his art to create himself and a new aesthetic doctrine with which to overcome not merely the idols of the age but the eternal idols as well. This was made possible by the development. Through his "Skirmishes" with nineteenth-century writers, Nietzsche developed a notion of art based upon life. Thus, he is able to return to the eternal idols of the original exposition in the recapitulation and subordinate them within his musical form, which is itself the form of life. In *The Birth of Tragedy*, he argued that life was only justified as an aesthetic phenomenon; here he suggests that all art and aesthetics is justifiable only as an expression of ascending life.

THEME I*. In the recapitulation of the first theme, Nietzsche overcomes the contradiction between his way and that of Socrates by exposing Plato's style and hence the Platonic Socrates as decadent. Such a judgment is possible because of the identification of beauty with ascending life and ugliness with descending life in the development, which allows Nietzsche here to discover a decadent Plato in an ugly Platonic style. Circumventing the Socratic barrier, he can then return to an earlier writer, Thucydides, as an example of good style and ascending life. This return to the pre-Socratic or at least to the pre-Platonic tradition is in fact a return to the world of tragedy, made possible because Thucydides and Nietzsche are heirs of an older tradition, that of the Sophists, just as Napoleon was the "heir of a stronger, longer, older civilization" (KGW VI 3:139).

THEME II*. The second theme also returns in the tonic with its tension resolved. The dissonance of Christian morality finds its resolution and harmony in the original, moral instinct of the Greeks, the will to power. It is not through philosophy, morality, or politics, however, that the rebirth of tragic culture is possible, but through an art that comprehends and portrays the psychological essence of life. This is the basis for Nietzsche's return to the pre-Socratics and for his reinstitution of the tragic world.

THEME III*. The third exposition theme returns in the tonic as the consideration not of German but of Greek political life and its misinterpretation by the Germans. This way of life, according to Nietzsche, bears the name Dionysus and is characteristic "of the older, still richer and self-overflowing Hellenic instinct" (4). It is this instinct and way of life that Nietzsche seeks to foster.

The third exposition theme considered contemporary Germany and particularly the antagonism of *Kultur* and *Staat*. Nietzsche finds the resolution of this dissonance in the pre-Socratic polis. Hitherto, the Germans and even Goethe failed to understand this phenomenon because they did not understand Dionysus, the antithesis to Christ and Christianity (4). Goethe still lived within the horizon of Socrates and Christianity and did not realize that the Christian God was dead. Hence, he was unable truly to return to the political-religious life of the Greeks symbolized in Dionysus.

Dionysus for Nietzsche represents "eternal *life*, the eternal recurrence of life; . . . *true* life as the over-all continuation of life through procreation, through the mysteries of sexuality" (4). As such, however, Dionysus also means suffering, for the pain of the woman giving birth is a necessary aspect of the sexual essence of life. The orgiastic Dionysian faith that Nietzsche claims to have discovered in the Greeks is thus the preeminent representation of ascending life. It is, however, also fundamentally tragic because it necessarily entails suffering. To deny the necessity of this pain is a sign of descending life, which seeks to escape from suffering by denying the orgiastic. Thus, Nietzsche can argue that Christianity "made something impure out of sexuality; it threw *dung* on the beginning, on the presupposition of life" (4). As such, it is the most abysmal example of descending life.

The last section of "Ancients" is a recapitulation of the last section of the third development theme and indicates the synthesis within which these themes reside. In the last part of "Germans," Nietzsche explained why educators were necessary for genuine political life and concluded that his German contemporaries did not satisfy this need. This problem is resolved in the recapitulation: the tragic poet is the true educator and thus the alternative to the Socratic notion of education that culminates in German *Bildung*. The poet-philosopher can establish the basis for a new politics because he does not seek to extirpate the creative passions by means of dialectic and philosophy but harmonizes and glorifies them in his music. He thus makes it possible for humanity to bear the suffering of a new tragic age (5). The tragic poet can bear the contradiction of the passions because he is able to subordinate them as dissonances within a higher musical harmony. The poet-musician must speak and transmit his teaching to the public, teaching those free spirits among them how to become something greater than they are and convincing the masses to give up any hope of an amelioration of their state. This was the original Greek way, which the early Nietzsche spelled out in his essay "The Greek State," and it is the basis of Nietzsche's political prescription for the future.

The last section of the final aphorism substantiates this; Nietzsche returns to *Birth*, to his concern with the original birth of tragedy out of music and to the rebirth of tragedy in his own time, to both Aeschylus and Wagner. In *Birth*, Aeschylus was the poet-musician whose art expressed the basic Hellenic instinct and informed Greek political culture; Wagner with his music drama was to recreate a tragic political culture in Germany. In *Twilight*, however, it is not Wagner but Nietzsche himself who plays this role. As this educator and founder of a new tragic age, Nietzsche characterizes himself as the last disciple of the philosopher Dionysus (5).

His reference to "the philosopher Dionysus" is surprising in light of his assertion in *Birth* that philosophy destroyed Dionysian culture and tragedy. This apparent paradox, however, points to the solution, to the mutual necessity and mutual incompatibility of Dionysian poetry or music and Socratic/Apollinian philosophy that Nietzsche discovered in *Birth*. There, he suggested the rebirth of tragedy would require a Dionysian philosophy or a musical Socrates but did not explain how such a synthesis was possible (KGW III 1:98). He claims, however, that he himself is the first tragic philosopher, the first to convert Dionysian into philosophic pathos (*EH*, KGW VI

3:310). Nietzsche discloses the ground for this synthesis in *Twilight* as the architectural unity of his musical philosophizing.

The recognition of the independence of this architectural element, still considered part of the Apollinian in *Birth*, allows Nietzsche to reconcile music and philosophy. The *Nachlass* gives us an indication of the character of Nietzsche's architectonic art and its relationship to the "philosopher Dionysus." Nietzsche lists a title for a proposed work as "*Dionysos philosophos. Eine Satura Menippea*" (KGW VIII 1:228). The reference here is to Menippean satire, a combination of poetry and philosophy, invented by the Cynic Menippus of Gadara, continued by his Roman follower Varro, and completed by Petronius in his *Satyricon*, as Nietzsche notes (*NL*, KGW VIII 3:261). Apparently, the philosopher Dionysus is a cynic and satirist like Petronius who, according to Nietzsche, "more than any great musician hitherto, was the master of presto in inventions, notions, words" (KGW VI 2:43). It is this "grand style" that his disciple Nietzsche similarly employs to combine music and philosophy within an overarching architectonic unity.

Such a grand style has hitherto been lacking in music, according to Nietzsche (KGW VIII 3:38–39). *Twilight* and Nietzsche's late work in general employ such a style: "I was the first to discover the art of the *great* rhythm, the *great style* of the periodicity of the expression of a monstrous up and down of sublime, superhuman passion" (*EH*, KGW VI 3:302–3). This is the character of Nietzsche's music—music in the grand style that combines image and tone within the architecture of the sonata form.[45] It is in this sense that Nietzsche is the last disciple of Dionysus the philosopher and, as he characterizes himself in the last sentence of "Ancients," the teacher of the eternal recurrence.

The rebirth of tragedy and the tragic age, which Nietzsche seeks to engender, rests ultimately upon the recognition and acceptance of the doctrine of the eternal recurrence, which is the core of his final teaching. The beauty and meaning of the tragic view of life depends upon the recognition of necessary and irreconcilable contradictions within the cosmos as a whole. In establishing the necessity and completeness of the cosmos, the doctrine of the eternal recurrence constitutes the central thesis of Nietzsche's final teaching. It is thus surprising that he does not discuss the eternal recurrence in *Twilight* or for that matter in any of the published works except *Zarathustra*, where it appears only in dreams, visions, and songs, and from the mouths of animals—in short, only mythologically. Are we then to conclude that Nietzsche does *not* teach what he himself claims is his fundamental teaching?

As I have argued in other essays in this volume, Nietzsche sees the works of 1888 as a preparation for the proclamation of the doctrine of the eternal recurrence. After the failure of *Zarathustra*, it became clear to him that the public needed a much more thorough preparation to understand his thought. They needed to understand his profound differences with Wagner (*The Case of Wagner*), his uncompromising critique of Christianity and Christian moralism (*The Genealogy of Morals* and *The Antichrist*), his rejection of nationalism and anti-Semitism in favor of the good Europeanism of the coming free spirits (*Beyond Good and Evil*, the fifth book of *The Gay Science*, and *Twilight of the Idols*), how to read his earlier works (the new prefaces to the older works written in 1886), and his own fateful role as the teacher of the eternal recurrence (*Ecce Homo*). While all of these works were written as a preparation for the coming proclamation of his final teaching, they focus almost entirely only on two parts of what I called in the first essay in this volume his (anti-)metaphysics, that is, his new theology and his new anthropology. He apparently intended to present his new ontology, and his new cosmology, more fully in the coming magnum opus. What is missing here is any consideration of his new logic. We get some sense of what he has in mind, however, from the manner in which he composed *Twilight of the Idols* and (as we shall see) *Ecce Homo*.

In an outline for his proposed magnum opus, he specifies the subject of one section as "the teaching of the eternal recurrence as *hammer* in the hand of the most powerful man" (*NL*, KGW VII 2:295). The eternal recurrence is the hammer with which Nietzsche philosophizes, that is, with which he sounds out idols and demonstrates that they are hollow. It is thus the standard against which he measures them. Evaluation, however, is not rejection—the idols are not destroyed. Rather, Nietzsche demonstrates that each is a necessary moment of the structure of life as a whole, that is, of the eternal recurrence. The eternal recurrence is thus the standard insofar as it establishes the structure of the whole within which the idols have their tragic meaning.

We saw in our consideration of the title of *Twilight* how the hammer for Nietzsche formed a new sword and a new necessity, how it produced the lightning and the storm to dissolve the twilight and reveal the new tragic age. Here, we see explicitly how this is to be achieved. The doctrine of the eternal recurrence is the great tool with which the *Übermensch* and the tragic age he will bring into being are to be liberated from the stone within which they are imprisoned and the musical instrument that gives a tragic meaning to the contradictions or dissonances of the European tradition. In the continuation of *Zarathustra*, Nietzsche thus intended to have Zarathustra proclaim immediately after the recognition of the eternal recurrence, "*I have the hammer!*" (*NL*, KGW VI 1:516) and later, in proclaiming the advent

of the *Übermensch*, he was to have said, "Man is that which must be overcome. *Here I hold the hammer* that overcomes him" (*NL*, KGW VII 1:637;
see also VIII 1:130). The hammer of the recurrence with which Nietzsche
teaches and intends to call forth the *Übermensch* and tragedy is the musical
form, the grand style, of his work as a whole. Nietzsche's fundamental teaching is thus not explicitly presented in *Twilight*, but still shapes his thinking
and his expression of that thinking in and as the musical form of the work
as a whole. It is a demonstration of his new musical logic. It is in this sense
that the disciple of Dionysus the philosopher is also the teacher of the eternal recurrence. It is the architectonic combination of music and philosophy
that is the proper vehicle for the transmission of the doctrine of the eternal
recurrence. The coda of the work as a whole, entitled "The Hammer Speaks,"
makes this clear.

CODA

"Hammer" was added to the work after the body of the work was completed,
perhaps at the same time as "Ancients." It is a slightly altered version of section 29 of "On the Old and New Tablets" in the third part of *Zarathustra*.
Nietzsche apparently first intended to use it at the end of *Ecce Homo* but
sometime shortly after 4 November 1888, when *Ecce Homo* was completed,
attached it to the end of *Twilight of the Idols*.[46]

The section in *Zarathustra* is the penultimate section before Zarathustra's
recognition of his deepest and most abysmal thought, the thought of eternal
recurrence of the same, in "The Convalescent" (*Z*, KGW VI 1:264) Nietzsche
perhaps meant to draw attention to this section of *Zarathustra* when he
characterized *Twilight* in the preface as a convalescence. As the culmination
and summation of *Twilight*, "The Hammer Speaks" thus seems to present itself and the work as a whole as the penultimate moment in humankind's development leading up to the revelation of the eternal recurrence and hence
as the penultimate moment in the development of tragedy and a tragic culture. This is also suggested by the fact that Nietzsche decided to use the last
section of "On the Old and New Tablets" as the conclusion of *The Antichrist*,
the work following *Twilight*, after he decided it would not be the first book
of the magnum opus. The series of works was thus apparently meant to lead
the highest elements of humanity over the last two steps of the path to the
revelation of the eternal recurrence and the birth of the tragic age.[47]

Nietzsche may have given us a subtle indication that this is indeed the
case. Zarathustra argued that the human was a rope stretched between beast
and *Übermensch* and that he would reach his Great Noon, the moment of

decision, and the proclamation of the recognition of the eternal recurrence, when man stands precisely at the middle of his way. Is *Twilight* this middle? The first and last words of the text proper seem to indicate as much: "In the middle ... of the eternal recurrence." If this is the case, then the last words of the coda may articulate the necessity that Nietzsche discerns for the present: "Become hard!" Choose to be the sardonic jester rather than the man whose courage carries him only to the middle of the tightrope, and leave pity behind and be willing to leap over human beings who can go no further even though they will then perish.

MUSIC AND PHILOSOPHY

The goal of Nietzsche's project is nothing less than the transformation of European civilization, a renewal of European political culture and the overcoming of present-day humanity. In the words of Zarathustra, "God died: now *we* want the *Übermensch* to live" (KGW VI 1:353). The *Übermensch*, who lives beyond God and all idols, is the basis of this new tragic age. He grasps the doctrine of the eternal recurrence and hence understands the *necessity* of the highest and the most abysmal human possibilities, or, in the terminology of *Twilight*, of both ascending and descending life. The death of God is thus the necessary presupposition of the *Übermensch* and hence of tragedy and the great politics of the tragic age, but it is not in itself sufficient to engender them. Nihilism merely prepares the way for the musical transformation of European civilization.

As we have seen, Nietzsche's music is fundamentally bound up with philosophy in his architectonic synthesis. He suggests this in a letter of 20 October 1887 to Hermann Levi: "Perhaps there was never a philosopher who was a musician to the degree that I am" (KGB III 5:172). With this synthesis Nietzsche returns, however, not merely to the ancient tragedians but also to the pre-Socratic philosophers. Of first importance are the Pythagoreans.

The Pythagoreans in Nietzsche's view provided the basis for the reconciliation of philosophy and music, of Apollo the god of measure and Dionysus the god of ecstasy, by demonstrating the mathematical basis of tonality and the musical basis of mathematics. They were thus able to transform all qualitative differences, that is, all contradictions or dissonances, into quantitative differences and consequently could conceive of the world with all its contradictions and dissonances as a fundamentally rational and harmonious musical-mathematical composition. In their view, "The entire essence of the world whose image was music, although played on only one string, might be expressed purely in numbers" (*PP*, KGW II 4:343–44). However, this does not dispose of the contradictions. On the contrary—it is precisely the maintenance of the contradictions that is necessary to harmony. The world harmony is thus "the unity of the manifold and the harmony of conflicting dispositions." If contradiction is an element in everything, then harmony is in everything too; but, as Nietzsche continues, this is nothing other than the doctrine of Heracleitus (*PP*, KGW II 4:343–44).

Heracleitus, who saw the "eternal crash of waves and rhythm of things," understood nature as becoming, "which he comprehended in the form of polarity, as the separation of a force into two qualitatively different, antithetical activities that strive toward reunification" (*PTAG*, KGW III 2:316, 319).[48] This world of contradiction and becoming seems to ordinary human beings to dissolve into meaninglessness, but, for those who have ears to hear, "all opposition runs together into a harmony" (*PTAG*, KGW III 2:324). This is the essence of the tragic that the harmony and beauty of the world are impossible without contradiction, that is, without suffering. The meaning of music as the Dionysian art that expresses this world harmony thus resides in "the wonderful meaning of *musical dissonance* .... The Dionysian, with its original joy even in pain, is the common womb of music and tragic myth" (*BT*, KGW III 1:148; see also III 1:40). This insight is truly comprehended and given form only by the aesthetic man, who has learned from the artist and the genesis of an artwork how the conflict of multiplicity can bear in itself law and right, how the artist stands contemplatively above and efficaciously within the artwork, how necessity and play, opposition and harmony, must couple themselves in the procreation of art (*PTAG*, KGW III 2:325). Only through art and the artist can one grasp the character of the world harmony and hence of tragedy.

For Nietzsche, this conception of music as world harmony is the basis for the transformation of nihilism, which recognizes contradiction only as meaninglessness, into a tragic culture, which understands contradiction as characteristic of a harmonious cosmos. This harmonizing of contradictions, which Nietzsche attributes to music, is also called the will to power.

The will to power presupposes opposition but subordinates it within itself. This in Nietzsche's view is the essence of all that is, and it is this essence that music represents (*BT*, KGW III 1:46–47, 101–4; see also III 3:382, IV 1:43). Music is thus the most fundamental art and consequently the source of all other human arts, including speech (*BT*, KGW III 1:46; III 3:380). Since humans become the rational animal through speech, "man as a whole is a phenomenon of music" (*NL*, KGW III 3:329). Music as the representation of the will to power thus expresses the essential truth of man and the cosmos, of life itself in the most comprehensive sense.

The harmony of opposites that the will to power assumes and music represents, however, is insufficient and can sustain itself as a coherent account of the whole only if this harmony is itself a moment of a complete and sufficiently grounded melody. If each harmony is only in itself and not *fundamentally* related to every other harmony, it is merely contingent and accidental and hence unstable and ephemeral. If music represents the essence of what is, then it must encompass all existence. Every harmony, whether dissonant or perfect, must reside within the melody that this music constitutes. Sonata form for Nietzsche represents such a complete and comprehensive melody.

If Nietzsche's new anthropology and new cosmology find their best expression in music, then the new ontology embodied in the eternal recurrence finds its best representation in sonata form. Ontologically, the eternal recurrence of the same ensures the wholeness of the whole and hence the sufficient reason or ground of every event and therefore of every opposition in and through the circularity of the causal series. Sonata form is the representation of this circularity, of the eternal recurrence of the same, and as such an appropriate form for Nietzsche's work.

There are apparently two different teachings of the eternal recurrence in Nietzsche's thought, a metaphysical or scientific teaching that presents the eternal recurrence as a cosmological process and an existential teaching that presents it as the experience of the abyss, of the necessity of the most horrible human possibilities. The recognition of the musical structure of Nietzsche's work offers a clue to the resolution of this ambiguity. The teaching of the eternal recurrence is at heart neither a metaphysical nor an existential but rather a musical philosophical doctrine that unites the other elements of Nietzsche's (anti-)metaphysics. As the synthesis of progression or development and circularity or repetition, sonata form is a representation of the will to power as the eternal recurrence. The exposition themes recur in the recapitulation and hence constitute a circular *melodic* structure. The entire form, however, is a *harmonic* progression that aims at the resolution of the original harmonic tension or opposition between the exposition themes through a development of these themes. This development is the subordination of harmony to melody, that is, the transformation of the harmony to correspond to the original and recapitulated melody. In sonata form, as in the music of Greek tragedy, "*melody* is thus the first and most general" (*BT*, KGW III 1:44). This melody, however, is not the Wagnerian infinite melody but an architectonic concatenation of melodic phrases into a circular whole.

The musical expression of the will to power that underlies both Nietzsche's new cosmology and his new anthropology thus finds its logical representation in sonata form. The cosmological teaching is reflected in the architectonic *circularity* of the form as a whole, and the anthropological (and existential) teaching in the assertion that pain and suffering are essential to life and can never be overcome. This is made bearable by the recognition of the *progression* from dissonance to harmony, from the tension in the exposition of descending and ascending life, of Socrates and Nietzsche, of Christianity and tragedy to the harmony of the highest and lowest moments of life in the tragic age portrayed in the recapitulation.[49]

The distinction between the philosophical and the musical in *Twilight* is thus resolved. Of course, it has long been recognized that Nietzsche sought such a reconciliation, but most scholars have doubted that he actually attained it. Nietzsche recognized, however, more clearly than many of his successors that the greatest obstacle to the attainment of this goal was the thought of Socrates-Plato. Plato expresses the problem succinctly and dramatically in book 10 of the *Republic* when Socrates tells Glaucon of an old quarrel between philosophy and poetry and admits that, while he feels poetry must be banned from the city they have constructed in speech, he hopes that it can find an argument for its readmission since he is so charmed by its beauty. Nietzsche produces such an argument. It is an argument, however, not for the admission of poetry to Plato's philosophical republic but for the unity of philosophy and poetry/music in a Nietzschean regime that harks back to the tragic character of Greek political actuality and yet looks forward beyond the twilight of the present nihilistic age and its idols, indeed beyond European civilization itself, to the tragic culture and great politics of the *Übermensch*, to a future Kallipolis, but a Kallipolis ruled not by a philosopher-king but by an artist-tyrant.

Life as Music: Nietzsche's Ecce Homo

Ecce Homo: How One Becomes What One Is. A strange title for a stranger work. Nietzsche began writing the book on his forty-fourth birthday apparently as a present to himself.[1] It is often characterized as his autobiography, but scholars have long recognized that if it is an autobiography in any ordinary sense of the term, it is a manifest failure.[2] Others see it as an attempt to provide a new model for human life.[3] And yet Nietzsche himself suggested that whatever the work's protagonist has done, it cannot not be replicated, learned, or repeated, at least not by anyone other than himself. For others the work is the creation of a literary persona, a ghostly double that replaces the actual human being, presenting to the reader not an actual man but a literary character who is not only extraordinarily wise and clever but also an extremely gifted writer and, modestly, "destiny." Such apparently megalomaniacal claims have led still other readers to conclude that the work is beclouded by the looming insanity that was soon to engulf its author.[4] A strange book indeed.

The phrase *ecce homo* is generally translated as "Behold the man." It is the Latin translation of the biblical Greek of John 19:5, *idou ho anthropos.* This passage is the phrase spoken by Pontius Pilate as his soldiers thrust Christ out before the Jewish mob on the *via dolorosa.* The meaning and purport of his statement remain unclear. In one sense Pilate is clearly telling the crowd to behold the man who has been rendered up to him for judgment. Pilate, after all, believed Christ to be innocent and let the people choose between Christ and a known criminal, Barabbas, intending to wash his hands of the guilt of killing an innocent man. In another sense, however, the phrase may mean "Behold the *man*," that is, *not* the *god* or the *king.* The Jewish leaders told Pilate that the source of their anger was the fact that Christ had claimed to be the son of God and king of the Jews. When Pilate asks Christ if this is true, he refuses to answer directly, asserting that his kingdom is not of this world. Pilate apparently takes this avoidance of a direct answer to be a quasi-confession of something that he believes he can understand, something dangerous both as a challenge to Caesarian rule (particularly the collection of taxes) and as an affront to the gods, both politically unsettling and theologically dangerous. When he presents Christ again for crucifixion, he thus says, "Behold your king." Behold, see, recognize the external form or idea of the thing, understand *what* it is. Of course, here the phrase is used ironically and as a means of reasserting Roman dominance since Christ is crowned with thorns, and weighted down with the cross on which he will die.

In choosing this phrase as the title for the work, Nietzsche presents himself to the world as a latter-day Christ.[5] Given what he says in the first line of the work, the analogy is perhaps not so surprising: "Seeing that before long I must confront humanity with the most difficult demand ever made of it, it seems indispensable to me to say *who I am*." He must tell them who he is because his identity is apparently no clearer or better known to most people than was the identity of Christ. To continue the analogy, he too presumably expects to be tormented, rejected, denied, cast out, and crucified.[6] And to extend the analogy even further, he also thereby hints that he too is the son of a god and king of a world yet to come, someone in fact as important as Christ himself. The analogy to Christ, however, only goes so far. Indeed, Nietzsche states unequivocally that he does not want to be declared holy, or to become the founder of a religion. On closer examination, many things thus appear even stranger than at first glance. What then are we to make of this strange book and its author?

Some context may help. The manuscript was written in 1888 and was the last work Nietzsche finished in the period of his thinking that began with his realization of the doctrine of the eternal recurrence in 1881 and that was intended to culminate in his never-completed magnum opus as we have discussed in previous essays. This phase of his thought began with the great Yes-saying of *Thus Spoke Zarathustra*, which was then followed by what Nietzsche called the No-saying task of *Beyond Good and Evil, The Genealogy of Morals, The Case of Wagner, The Antichrist*, and *Twilight of the Idols*. The last three were written in 1888 at the same time as *Ecce Homo*, and aimed at the critique of contemporary art (*Case of Wagner*), Christian religion (*Antichrist*), and European philosophy (*Twilight*), the three great realms of what Hegel called absolute spirit. Together these five No-saying works thus represent a comprehensive critique of contemporary European culture.

Insofar as *Ecce Homo* appears in this context with its obvious Christian allusions, it must be understood as part of this critical task, and thus as connected to *The Antichrist*. Of course, Nietzsche's Antichrist is not the Antichrist of *Revelations*, which he saw as a Christian attempt to blacken the radiance of Dionysus, the god of life itself, by portraying him as Satan. Nietzsche's anti-Christianity in this sense is part of an effort to rehabilitate Dionysus and the vision of life he represents.

Seen in this light, Nietzsche's title becomes somewhat clearer. Nietzsche claims to be the last disciple of Dionysus. Like Christ he proclaims the coming kingdom of his god, but it is not the God of Christianity but the anti-God, Dionysus, that he proclaims.[7] Nietzsche thereby presents himself as the antipode to Christ, and hence as the Antichrist.[8] Understood in the context of his other works of 1888, *Ecce Homo* thus seems to have been intended as a complete reversal of Christian values, as a rejection of both the Christian God and Christ, as well as everything that Christianity established in its binary opposition to ancient piety.[9] This point is driven home explicitly in the final line in the work: "Have I been understood?—*Dionysus versus the Crucified.*—"

But what does Nietzsche mean by presenting himself in connection with Dionysus? Surely, this is meant on one level to be the reversal of a reversal. But what is being reversed here? And where does this reversal leave us? Nietzsche gives us a clue to the meaning of this connection at the very beginning of the work. *Ecce homo*, "Behold the man," Pilate says of Christ. "Look at him." Nietzsche seems to repeat this in his title, but we do not actually see him. There is no man to behold. At best we see only the letters and words that make up the sentences that describe his corpus, that is, his works, his embodied doings, the tracks he passed over in becoming what he is. We thus do not actually see Nietzsche, the existing human being, who in this work as in all others eludes us. In fact, he directs us in an alternate direction in the italicized last sentence of the first section of the preface: "*Hear me! For I am such and such a person. Above all, do not mistake me for someone else.*" Hear me, not *see* me. Listen, don't look, presumably because in looking we will be deceived and mistake him for someone he is not, while listening to him we will perceive more clearly who he is. But what does this mean? How can listening and hearing avoid the mistakes that seeing produces? Why can we hear what we cannot see?

In what follows I will argue that we can only understand *Ecce Homo* if we do in fact listen to Nietzsche, that is, only if we use our ears to understand what our eyes mistakenly focus upon and misconstrue. In doing so, I will try to explain the decisive musical character of Nietzsche's presentation of himself in *Ecce Homo*, of his attempt to characterize his life and indeed life itself as music, to show that in presenting himself as the last disciple of

Dionysus he is claiming to be the voice of the god himself, asserting that he is the god's "prophet" calling humanity back from the nihilistic abyss that Christianity has opened up and directing man onto an extraordinarily difficult and dangerous path that leads to the *Übermensch*. In doing so, I will argue that it is only possible in Nietzsche's view to *hear* this call because Dionysus is the god of music who speaks not in words but through them in a way quite different than the logic that more visually oriented readers follow. To understand Nietzsche's life as music is therefore to understand life itself as music, not as being but as becoming.

To begin to understand these claims, we will first need to understand more clearly not who but what Nietzsche claims to be, that is, what role he sees himself playing in the unfolding of becoming. Second, we need to examine what he understands music to be, and then, third, how his self-presentation in *Ecce Homo* reflects this musico-philosophical project of preparing his readers to hear his call for the revaluation of all values.

WHAT DOES NIETZSCHE CONCEIVE HIMSELF TO BE?

In the preface of *The Genealogy of Morals*, published in 1887, Nietzsche asserts that, "We are unknown to ourselves, we men of knowledge—and with good reason. We have never sought ourselves—how could it happen that we should ever find ourselves?" He concludes with the admission that "we are necessarily strangers to ourselves, we do not comprehend ourselves, we have to misunderstand ourselves, for us the law 'Each is furthest from himself' applies to all eternity—we are not 'men of knowledge' with respect to ourselves" (KGW VI 2:259). Nietzsche here admits that he does not and indeed cannot understand himself. This stance hardly seems to provide a basis for an explanation of who he is. In *Ecce Homo*, however, Nietzsche does not attempt to tell us who he is. This work is not autobiographical or confessional. Nietzsche does not attempt to tell us about himself as an individual or as a member of the human species. His goal is rather to tell us *how* he became *what* he is, that is, what role he has come to play in the unfolding of events.[10]

But what does this mean? Dionysus is the god of ecstasy, of the orgiastic, of the dance; the god of tragedy and of music; the god of mania, of frenzy; the god of nighttime wisdom, of the abyss; the god who is born again every spring and repeatedly torn to pieces by his maenadic worshipers. He is thus the god of fecundity, and the inexhaustibility of life. But this god was already described in great detail in Nietzsche's first work, *The Birth of Tragedy*. Does Nietzsche then imagine a simple rebirth of this god and of ancient piety here in his final work? This hardly seems likely and is actually belied by Nietzsche's characterization of the god. In *The Birth of Tragedy*, Dionysus was conjoined with Apollo as the most potent of the two natural impulses at the basis of Greek art, which found its highest expression in Greek tragedy. Dionysus represented the contradictory primordial will, the infinite world-self, the deep abyss out of which, as Hesiod explained, the world came into being, but also the infinite pain of the great in vain that paralyzed the wills of Oedipus, Hamlet, and others, the impulse that found relief only in orgiastic festivals, and dwelled always behind masks. Apollo by contrast was the *principium individuationis*, the image of a single individual dissociated from the whole, the principle of order and form, and in tragedy the individualistic mask through which ordinary human beings were able to see and tolerate the Dionysian abyss.

In *The Birth of Tragedy*, both Apollo and Dionysus were contrasted to Socrates. Indeed, the death of tragedy and the disappearance of the spirit of music were attributed in large part to the advent of Socratic (and Euripidean) dialectic. This dialectical approach turned from the earlier reliance upon instinct to reason as the tool with which to understand existence and plumb its darkest depths. Suffering in this context was not understood to be the consequence of a primordial contradiction at the heart of existence but as the result of ignorance. It was thus not ineluctable but remediable. In Nietzsche's view it was this Socratic dialectic (incorporated and given world-historical importance by Plato) that set up the notion of a true or real world in opposition to an apparent world, that is, the world we generally inhabit. This living world is only the moving (and thus imperfect) *image* of eternity, as Plato put it in the *Timaeus*. The real world, according to Plato, is the world of unchanging presence, of what he called ever-being (*aei on*).

Nietzsche believed that this other, "real" world, as it appeared in the thought of Socrates and Plato, was a psychological remedy for the disgregation of the Greek instincts, but in contrast to art, which turned these conflicting instincts into something higher, dialectic worked as a narcotic to ease the pain of the contradiction by putting them to sleep. Perhaps more importantly, this distinction of the real and apparent worlds opened up the space within which Christianity was able to organize its revolt against the master values of antiquity. Philosophy, as the younger Nietzsche conceived it, was thus antagonistic to art and especially to the Dionysian.

The philosopher Dionysus that Nietzsche claims to follow in *Ecce Homo* is hard to reconcile with his earlier vision of Dionysus. Nietzsche gives us some inkling of a possible connection in his passing reference near the end of *The Birth of Tragedy* to the possibility of a musical Socrates or a Socrates who practices music (KGW III 1:98). This was clearly a role that he imagined at the time he himself might play in connection with the Wagnerian project of cultural renewal.

What I want to suggest is that Nietzsche's claim in *Ecce Homo* to be the last disciple of the philosopher Dionysus is a claim to play just such a role, although with several important caveats. First, Nietzsche no longer sees the role of such a figure as a supplement to the musical genius he describes in *The Birth of Tragedy*. Indeed, he argues in *The Case of Wagner* that the Wagnerian music he had earlier imagined giving birth to a new tragic age was merely a decadent form of playacting. Second and following from the first, he no longer thinks of this figure as a philosopher who practices music but as a disciple and indeed vessel of the god of music whose music is itself philosophical. The role that he describes for himself in *Ecce Homo* in this sense derives from the role he foresaw in *The Birth of Tragedy*, but is not identical with it.

Ecce Homo is thus not an autobiography of Friedrich Nietzsche but an account of how he became the disciple and herald of the philosopher Dionysus. This is already apparent in the subtitle to the work, *How One Becomes What One Is*. As many scholars have noted, this subtitle is derived from or at least closely related to Pindar's famous imperative, "Become what you are!" Exactly what Nietzsche intends with this imperative, however, is less clear. One might read the phrase in an Aristotelian manner as demanding one strive to actualize one's own potential. Such a reading, however, imagines that there is an eternal *telos*, or end to things that one must recognize, an ideal shape or form concealed in the thing that comes to its natural end through growth and development. For Nietzsche, however, there is no eternal reality or "what" that stands over against the endless flux of becoming. Indeed, all such "whats" are merely the creation of conceptual boundaries that conceal the truth of Heracleitean change. At the core of Nietzsche's deepest thought is the recognition that the only real "thing" is the eternal recurrence of becoming itself, the titanic "how" of the whole, the never-ending motion that eternally repeats itself, the closest approximation of becoming to being (*NL*, KGW VIII 1:320). It is in this context that we need to understand the subtitle of *Ecce Homo*. It describes *how* one becomes what one is, that is, it is an account of the becoming, the how of the what that defines who Nietzsche is, that is, the role that he plays in the midst of the eternal recurrence of the same.

What then is this role? He claims in *Ecce Homo* to be the teacher of the idea of the eternal recurrence, the role he earlier attributed to Zarathustra.[11] This is his ultimate Dionysian wisdom. Or to put it another way, as the disciple of the philosopher Dionysus, he proclaims Dionysus as the whole of becoming, the great circle of becoming, the "how" that only becomes a "what" when taken as a whole. Such an explanation, however, does not go far enough. As Nietzsche admitted already in *The Birth of Tragedy*, the name "Dionysus" is finally only an Apollinian image for something more profound and abysmal, what Nietzsche there calls "primordial music." His description of himself as the herald of this Dionysian wisdom in *Ecce Homo* is thus the proclamation of the primordial music that is the eternal becoming and eternal repetition of all things. He is thus the singer of the song of self where the self is nothing other than the musical heart of becoming.[12]

As the teacher or singer of the eternal recurrence, Nietzsche confronts humanity with the most difficult demand ever made of it. As we have seen in the preceding essays, this demand grows out of the need to choose between the *Übermensch* and the last man at the moment Nietzsche calls the Great Noon when humans stand midway between beast and *Übermensch*. In the language of *Zarathustra*, it is the choice to become lion-spirited, that is, an active nihilist or destroyer, or to become the hedonistic last man. The necessity that drives this choice and thus confronts humanity at the Great Noon is brought about by the proclamation of the doctrine of the eternal recurrence of the same that Nietzsche believes will have a cataclysmic effect, washing clean the philosophical and moral horizon that has been dominant for the last two thousand years. For a few free spirits this will be a great liberation, but for most it will be an unmitigated disaster. Nietzsche thus tells us in the first paragraph of the last section of *Ecce Homo*, "Why I Am a Destiny," that his name will be associated with a "crisis without equal on earth, the most profound collision of conscience, a decision that was conjured up against everything that had been believed, demanded, hallowed so far" (KGW VI 3:363). This is the "revaluation of all values: that is my formula for an act of supreme self-examination on the part of humanity, become flesh and genius in me." In describing how he has become what he is, the disciple of the philosopher Dionysus, he also describes the coming destiny of humanity as the teacher of the eternal recurrence.

Ecce Homo is thus not an autobiography, the creation of a literary character, or a model for a new human possibility, but the account of how Nietzsche came to be the last disciple of and speaker for this god, and thus how he came to be the repository of the wisdom that will bring about the cataclysmic Great Noon. The Friedrich Nietzsche described in *Ecce Homo* is then not a writer or philosopher but the herald of an apocalyptic transformation. He is the anti-Christ as the disciple/consubstantial son of the anti-God, Dionysus.

This account, however, cannot be adequately told in mere words. Words, as Zarathustra asserted, are merely dream bridges among things that remain eternally apart. They are abstractions from and falsifications of becoming, snapshots of a world that is eternally moving. The words of Nietzsche's self-presentation are thus fictions that are necessary for beings like us who are incapable of seeing the truth of the whole and remaining sane. They are the conceptual scrim, playing a role analogous to the role he previously ascribed to Apollinian dream images, which makes it possible for us to bear the truth. This truth is presented not in the words themselves but in the linking together of the words, in the process of becoming that they mark out. Traditionally, this linking together of words has been understood as logos or logic. Nietzsche believed that Kant had demonstrated that the traditional rationalistic understanding of logic had become untenable as a means for understanding the whole. *Ecce Homo* is representative of Nietzsche's new logic rooted not in reason but in music. The truth of *Ecce Homo* thus lies not in the content of the words in the text but in the text as a performance, as the musical unfolding of the god of music performed by his disciple Friedrich Nietzsche.

NIETZSCHE'S LIFE IN MUSIC

As we noted in the previous essay, it would be hard to exaggerate the importance of music for Nietzsche. Nietzsche himself described his most profound moments as musical. His principal memories of his father's funeral as a five-year-old were associated with the ringing of bells and the solemn organ hymns. He recounts how moved he was in 1857 by a performance in Naumburg of Mozart's *Requiem*, Handel's *Messiah* and *Judas Maccabeus*, and Hayden's *Creation*.[13] He was already a prolific pianist and improvisationist by the time he was twelve and taught himself composition soon thereafter. He began composing as a teenager and continued to work on compositions until his breakdown in 1889. While his musical works are often regarded as pedestrian, they show a real grasp of the principles of composition and are also characterized by an effort to emulate some of the effects he discovered in ancient Greek meter and rhythm.[14] Leaving the question of the quality of his composition aside, there is no doubt of the impact of his musical activities on his written work, and it is equally clear that his musical efforts were shaped by his studies and thinking.

His life and work were deeply enmeshed in music in many different forms, as we discussed in the previous essay. His initial concern with music was expressed in his first work, *The Birth of Tragedy*, and while he parted company with Wagner, he never gave up on his notion of the necessity of a musical Socrates to renew European culture. This was equally true of *Zarathustra*, which Nietzsche described as musical.[15] Even though Nietzsche abandoned the *Zarathustra* project, he did not abandon his determination to write musically, although he intended henceforth to speak (or sing) in his own name.

His crucial goal in this context was not merely to communicate philosophical ideas, but to express and shape what he calls "inward states" in *Ecce Homo*. In fact he considers this the essence of style:

> To communicate a state, an inward tension of pathos, by means of signs, including the tempo of these signs—that is the meaning of every style, and considering that the multiplicity of inward states is exceptionally large in my case, I have many stylistic possibilities—the most multifarious art of style that has ever been at the disposal of one man. Good is any style that really communicates an inward state, that makes no mistake about the signs, the tempo of the signs, the gestures—all the laws about long periods are concerned with the art of gestures. Here my instinct is infallible. . . . The art of the great rhythm, the great style of long periods to express a tremendous up and down of sublime, of superhuman passion, was discovered only by me. (KGW VI 3:302–3)

Inward states—what we more typically call emotions, feelings, moods, or passions—are only tangentially open to self-examination. However, while they cannot be directly known, they can be accessed, expressed, communicated, and evoked through art and music. This use of art as a means of communication, evocation, and provocation is at the core of Nietzsche's works from 1881 until his breakdown in 1889. The origin of this understanding of art, however, goes back much earlier. Indeed, the particular notion of the role and importance of style is already present in Schopenhauer's theory of art that Nietzsche drew upon in formulating his account of Dionysian art in general and music in particular in *The Birth of Tragedy*. In his late work, Nietzsche returns again to Dionysus, but here it is not to a Dionysus conjoined with Apollo but a Dionysus conjoined with Socrates. The view into the Dionysian abyss is thus no longer filtered by images but by concepts.

The artist is able to develop such a style, according to Nietzsche, not through reason but only through instinct. The artist thus writes *what* he does and *as* he does not because he *knows* it is right but because it *feels* or *sounds* right. Nietzsche explained the anthropological or psychological basis of this claim in *Zarathustra*. A human being, he tells us there, is at bottom not an I or an ego. The conscious self exists, but it is merely the tip of a psychic iceberg that is moved and shaped by forces hidden beneath the surface of awareness. This deeper and more concealed part of our being Zarathustra calls the self or the body. The body in his account is made up of passions, which act in a certain sense like force vectors, each pulling in its own direction. The passions themselves reflect the deeper drives and instincts that characterize our species as a whole. And these instincts are a manifestation of the basic drive of life itself that Nietzsche calls the will to power.

This hidden reality beneath the surface of consciousness is thus not placid or peaceful. Indeed, the passions that constitute the body all long to be expressed and satisfied, and are consequently always at war with one another if they have not been trained and redirected. We are thus shaped and torn by instinctual forces in ways that we generally do not and in most cases cannot recognize or comprehend. For Nietzsche, our principal way of being in the world is thus not as conscious beings but as affective beings. What we are in the fullest sense is bound up with our feelings, passions, or moods. These shape our becoming. Moreover, these forces cannot be controlled by thinking, which remains at the surface of consciousness, but they can be redirected by forces that impact the deeper rhythm of affective life. The expression of an inward state, which Nietzsche sees as essential to art, is thus the expression of the particular rhythm of the flow of time, of becoming itself. The rhythm of this flow and its intensity is what art in particular makes perceptible to us. Music translates the inner flow of time that we experience in our moods, our feelings, and our passions into the flow of musical notes.

Indeed, Nietzsche believes that such a possibility may only be available to music. "Language," he argued already in *The Birth of Tragedy*, "can never adequately render the cosmic symbolism of music, because music stands in symbolic relation to the primordial contradiction, and primordial pain in the heart of the primordial unity, and therefore symbolizes a sphere which is beyond and prior to all phenomena" (*BT*, KGW III 1:47). Music makes the rhythmic unfolding of the self in time perceptible as a succession of notes that constitute a melody. All possible effects, excitements, manifestations of the will, all feelings, according to Nietzsche, can then be expressed by the infinite number of melodies (*BT*, KGW III 1:101; cf. *GS*, KGW V 2:111–24, and *NL*, KGW VIII 2:159). Music in this sense precedes and has already shaped the world that we grasp with Apollinian images and Socratic concepts.

Music also offers us a means of bringing some harmony to this psychic world that is torn by conflicting passions. In ancient times, according to Nietzsche, men believed that rhythm was a magical power that could be employed to control even the gods, by fostering orgiastic states of excitement that satiated the demons who possessed human beings (*GS*, KGW V 2:115–18; *BGE*, KGW VI 2:92). More characteristically, in Plato and Aristotle, music was imagined to aim not at pathos but ethos, at the formation of character.[16] Like Plato and Aristotle, but also like many Baroque (and other modern) music theorists, Nietzsche was convinced that particular musical modes had distinctly different effects upon the passions, turning the listener in one direction or another. Music can be used to train us to march or dance in step and thus can make us into members of a group or community.

Through musical compositions we thus can establish order not only in our own psyche but also in those of others. The psyche normally is characterized by struggle and contradiction. In the healthy psyche, one passion comes to dominate and turns the other affects to its ends. It thus forms an orderly, reinforcing whole in which the passions all move in a single direction. Such rank ordering of the passions creates a powerful will that can transfigure the chaos and contradictions of existence into a new harmony first within the individual and then within others (*PTAG*, KGW III 2:316, 319, 324; cf. *NL*, KGW III 3:63). In this way a powerful and dominating passion can shape the flow of time to its own ends using music to move itself and others from dissonance and contradiction to consonance and harmony. Nietzsche thus concludes that "the will and its symbolism—harmony—are in the final analysis pure logic! . . . Harmony is the symbol of the pure essence of the will" (*NL*, KGW III 2:66; cf. 4:23).

The present age in his view is characterized by a collapse in the prevailing order of values that has characterized the world since the advent of Christianity. The death of God produces a breakdown of order in the individual psyche since there is no longer an unchanging moral lodestar to guide human actions. There is thus no means to guide the unfolding of the affects in time and consequently no unifying direction to coordinate and harmonize the passions. They again are unfettered and at war with one another. Wagnerian music, as Nietzsche came to understand it, does not seek to organize these passions into a new whole but indulges them, allowing listeners to wallow in their feelings of suffering and pity with only a vague hope of redemption. Wagner's famous infinite melody is thus not really melody at all because it does not regularize and harmonize becoming. Wagner, Nietzsche concludes, did not create a musical form but formlessness. He made music swim, not dance, and his music therefore does not make us healthy but sick. It is expressive but expresses only the primordial chaos of a decadent psyche. It is thus not the product of healthy instincts but only a form of playacting.[17]

Nietzsche believes that such music cannot deal with the coming nihilistic catastrophe. He pins his hopes instead on musical philosophers who have disciplined psyches, guided by healthy, life-affirming instincts. They alone have a chance of developing a Dionysian music that can master chaos, a music that resolves cacophonous contradictions into new harmonies.

THE MUSIC OF *ECCE HOMO*

Nietzsche claims to be such a musical philosopher and seeks to demonstrate this with *Ecce Homo* itself. His account is philosophical but also musical, not in the Romantic style of Wagner but more in the manner of Hayden, Mozart, Beethoven, and Schumann. In this way Nietzsche presents his life as music. His goal is to demonstrate that in his becoming he is already a manifestation of the powers of the god of music Dionysus, and to show through the carefully orchestrated structure of his work how the discipline of music is able to weld the most discordant contradictions into a harmonious whole.

Nietzsche structures *Ecce Homo* in sonata form.[18] Sonata form has three main sections: an exposition, a development, and a recapitulation, which are sometimes preceded by an introduction and occasionally followed by a coda. Typically, each section is thought to perform a specific function in the musical argument.[19] An introduction is optional before the main musical argument. The exposition presents the principal material for the piece in one to three themes often in contrasting styles and in opposing keys connected by a transition that modulates from the tonic or home key to the dominant, typically a perfect fifth removed from the tonic. The musical problem of the piece is set by the contrast between these two keys, a contrast that must be harmonized to resolve the problem. The exposition is followed by the development in which the music explores the harmonic and textural possibilities of the exposition themes.[20] This work in the development then makes possible a transition back to the original themes of the exposition in the recapitulation with all of the themes in the tonic key and with the musical problem thus resolved. The sonata thus begins in dissonance and reworks this dissonance into a new harmony. This is often the end of the sonata, although at times a flourish is added in the form of a coda.

With this brief sketch of sonata structure, it is fairly easy to see how Nietzsche employs it in writing *Ecce Homo*.[21] The overall structure of the work is clear in the section titles:

Introduction
  Preface[22]
  Exposition
    Theme 1: Why I Am So Wise
    Theme 2: Why I Am So Clever
    Theme 3: Why I Write Such Good Books
  Development
    The Birth of Tragedy–The Case of Wagner[23]
  Recapitulation
    Why I Am a Destiny

In *Ecce Homo*, Nietzsche tells the story or perhaps more accurately sings the song of how he came to be what he is. It is not only the song of the self but the presentation of the self as the singer of the world-song.[24] Who then can sing the song of the world, that is, present the doctrine of the eternal recurrence of all things? As Nietzsche tells us in *Ecce Homo*, "nobody can get more out of things . . . than he already knows. For what one lacks access to from experience one will have no ear" (KGW VI 3:297–98). The wisest thus must have the greatest depth and range of experience. But for Nietzsche experience is always intimately associated with the affective bodily character of our lives. Thus the wisest will have to embody the greatest range of affective human possibilities. In *Ecce Homo* Nietzsche presents himself as just such a man. His life, he claims, is no ordinary life but encompasses all things. The implicit claim that he makes here was made explicitly a few months later when on the verge of madness he proclaimed himself to be "all names in history."[25]

As wild and megalomaniacal as this claim may at first appear, Nietzsche gives plausible reasons why we should accept it in the first theme of the exposition. Contrary to everything we might expect from the title of the section, he does not discuss the qualities of his mind or the nature of his education but focuses instead on his body, that is, the passions, instincts, and drives that have combined to make him what he is. His "wisdom" is thus not a conscious wisdom but something instinctual that is concealed from reflection, something only evident in the retrospective examination of his own actions.[26]

The good fortune of my existence, its uniqueness perhaps, lies in its fatality: I am, to express it in the form of a riddle, already dead as my father, while as my mother I am still living and becoming old. This dual descent, as it were, both from the highest and the lowest rung on the ladder of life, at the same time a *decadent* and a *beginning*—this, if anything, explains that neutrality, that freedom from all partiality in relation to the total problem of life, that perhaps distinguishes me. I have a subtler sense of smell for the signs of ascent and decline than any other human being before me; I am the teacher *par excellence* of this—I know both, I am both.

He thus begins with the assertion that his life, which he has inherited in a bodily sense from his parents, is rent by the deepest contradictions. He has experienced or better suffered the extremes of life. He is both sick to death and also alive and thriving, and while these profound contradictions have sickened him, his instincts have also found a way to a healthy psychic harmony. His wisdom thus derives from his basic biology. He combines in his body the greatest possible contradictions, and thus has plumbed the limits of human possibilities. The song of the self that he sings thus has little to do with thinking or reflection and much more to do with the chaos and contradiction in his own body that he has not merely endured but come to love and affirm.[27]

The proof of his wisdom in his view lies in the fact that he has survived these contradictions and turned them from weaknesses into strengths. He chose the healthy path, not knowingly but instinctively, ceasing to be a pessimist when his vitality was at its lowest, thus rejecting decadence and turning to a path of health and strength. What did not kill him, he claims, made him stronger. Furthermore, this path led him away from everything decadent, that is, from everything German, and especially away from Wagner's excessive indulgence of the passions and pity.[28] He became instead a good European (which even here he suggests may be physiological, pointing to the possibility that his ancestors were not German but Polish). He also thereby freed himself from all resentment, from what he called the spirit of revenge in *Zarathustra*. Thus while he lives by *amor fati*, he is not a fatalist, but has come to feel gratitude for everything. As he puts it: "Accepting oneself as if fated, not wishing oneself 'different'—that is in such cases *great reason* itself" (KGW VI 3:271).[29] The ultimate foundation for this attitude, as we discussed above, is the doctrine of the eternal recurrence.

While the first theme details the *pathos/phusis* that is the source of Nietzsche's wisdom, the second theme turns to a consideration of the *ethos* or habits that explain his cleverness. What he actually knows, he tells us, is that the salvation of the human race depends not upon faith or works, but upon the right instinct for food, climate, and recreation. In his case this manifests itself as a taste for the Italian or the Mediterranean diet rather than that of the Germans or the English, and a southern versus a northern climate. As for recreation, he favors the classical European culture that grew out of the Italian Renaissance as opposed to the Romantic culture that grew out of the Reformation and that is currently centered in Germany and manifest in Wagner. Here too he describes himself as a healthy good European in contrast to a decadent German.

All of these matters on the surface seem to be objects of knowledge and choice, but Nietzsche suggests here, as in the first theme, that he is driven to live in the way he does by his own body, which will tolerate no alternative. "Sickness brought me to reason," as he puts it. All these matters—nutrition, place, climate, recreation—are matters of the instinct for self-preservation and self-enhancement. Together they constitute what he calls prudence or taste, a taste for ascending versus descending life, and for the art and culture that support it.

The second theme with its emphasis on the southern and classical thus stands diametrically opposed to the first theme that is rooted in the northern world of Germany and Poland. Nietzsche's song of the self is thus torn by contradiction and dissonance from the outset, and this contradiction presents the musical problem the work has to solve.

Summing up the first two themes Nietzsche asserts that selfishness is the answer to the question of how one becomes what one is, but by this he does not mean a conscious doctrine like that of Mandeville or of anyone else we are familiar with. Indeed the reverse. The selfishness he has in mind is the selfishness of the body, something instinctual not epistemic; something that our constitution forces upon us, not something we choose. Indeed, he even asserts that to become what one is, one must not have the faintest idea of what one is. The whole surface of consciousness must be kept clear of great imperatives, because such imperatives or ideals are really nothing other than commands given to us by others to follow their paths rather than our own. To be guided by conscious choices is thus to lose oneself in others and to serve their purposes. Nietzsche is well aware that there are many incentives to follow socially acceptable and laudable pathways. For this reason he argues that it is necessary to cultivate an indifference to honors, women, and money. As he puts it, "My formula for greatness in a human being is *amor fati*: that one wants nothing to be different, not forward, not backward, not in all eternity. Not merely bear what is necessary, still less conceal it—all idealism is mendaciousness in the face of what is necessary—but *love* it" (KGW VI 3:295). This theme ends again with the doctrine of the eternal recurrence just beneath the surface.

Nietzsche begins the third theme with the unequivocal statement that "I am one thing, my writings are another matter" (KGW VI 3:296).[30] The discussion in this theme and in the descriptions of the individual works that follow are thus not about the substance of Nietzsche's books, but about him, his character, and specifically how he became the teacher of the eternal recurrence and the disciple of the philosopher Dionysus. His explanation of why he writes such books again is rooted in the instinctual basis of his and indeed all life. His books, he claims, cannot be put down. Like everything else he has written, they are absurdly dramatic. He also claims to say things no one else will say because he strives not for the ordinary and acceptable but for what is forbidden. Indeed, he identifies himself here as the Antichrist. Perhaps even more importantly, however, he claims that his style employs the art of "the great rhythm" (KGW VI 3:302). He also claims that he is a peerless psychologist who understands and reveals the hidden motives that drive human behavior. In this respect he is one with "the genius of the heart," who is mentioned in *Beyond Good and Evil* and who has been variously identified as both Dionysus and Socrates (KGW VI 2:247–48). Or to pull all of these remarks together, he writes such good books because he is a musical Socrates and the disciple of the philosopher Dionysus.

The problem set up in the exposition is to explain how someone like Nietzsche, filled with so many contradictions, living in a time and place that contradicted everything necessary for him in terms of diet, climate, and culture, could find a path to health and affirmation, or to what he calls *amor fati*. The answer to this question is laid out in the detailed history of the composition of his works. Thus the development section of the work is in fact an account of Nietzsche's development, not intellectually but psychologically, or anthropologically, or even characterologically, that is, the subterranean or instinctual development that is evident retrospectively in his books. The path detailed here describes the development of a new psychic order and a new way of life, so that his inner contradictions discussed in the first theme and his manner of life discussed in the second theme can be harmonized with one another. Without going into great detail, this is essentially the story of his wayward path through decadence, from perspectivism to lasciviousness to relativism to nihilism to the recognition of the doctrine of the eternal recurrence and the production of *Zarathustra* as the teacher of the eternal recurrence, the failure of *Zarathustra* to find hearers in the present age, and the critique of modernity and contemporary European life as a preparation for its destruction and the revaluation of all values in a great work yet to come.[31] Or to put it another way, it is the story of someone who came to understand the meaning of a god, who proclaimed the coming of the *Reich* of this god, who was not heard, and who now stands just before the Great Noon, that is, before the apocalyptic transformation that will bring this god and his *Reich* into existence, although only after years of war and immense suffering. In this section Nietzsche thus describes his transformation from a mere mortal human being into a destiny. *Ecce homo* indeed.

This account of his development then makes possible a return to the original themes in the recapitulation. The first theme focused on the contradictions in Nietzsche's character. In explaining why he is a destiny, he asserts, "I contradict as has never been contradicted before and am yet the opposite of a No-saying spirit. I am a bringer of glad tidings like no one before me. . . . For all that, I am necessarily also the man of calamity" (KGW VI 3:364). He believes that he will consequently be associated with something tremendous, a crisis without equal. This is because he is the teacher of the death of the Christian God, the collapse of European morality, and the doctrine of the eternal recurrence that will bring about the "revaluation of all values." This revaluation, as he sees it, "is my formula for an act of supreme self-examination on the part of humanity, become flesh and genius in me" (KGW VI 3:363). The result of this proclamation will be convulsions the like of which humanity has never known, wars of unprecedented destructiveness, and the advent of great politics. He thus concludes that "I am by far the most terrible human being that has existed so far; this does not preclude the possibility that I shall be the most beneficial" (KGW VI 3:364). He explains that what he means by this is that he is the first immoralist, a role he first played behind the mask of Zarathustra but now plays openly. He negates and destroys in order to be able to say Yes in the most profound way possible.

He concludes the piece with a crescendo in three aphorisms, all beginning with the phrase, "Have I been understood?" that is, has the reader understood what I am? He tells us that what sets him apart from the whole of humanity is the fact that he was the first to uncover Christian morality as a source of corruption, as an antinatural teaching that taught men to despise life. Christian morality is decadent and unselfs man. All theologians in particular—and here Nietzsche especially means his father—were decadents. This discovery, which was first announced in *Zarathustra*, breaks history in two, according to Nietzsche. Its proclamation will lead to a catastrophe.

To return to the first theme of the exposition, Nietzsche claimed there that what distinguished him was that he was both his father and his mother, that he both understood decadence and the mortal sickness it entailed as well as the way out of decadence. Life in Germany, he told us in the second theme, was impossible for him. As a healthy man, he thus could live only as a pariah. The solution to this problem is clear from the recapitulation, and it is encapsulated in the final line of the book, *"Dionysus versus the Cruci-*

fied."[32] Only the exposure of Christianity for what it is and the inevitable collapse of everything that is built upon it, including all of European morality, offers a way out and up. And the teaching that leads in the ascending direction is that of Dionysus, the doctrine of the eternal recurrence of the same that makes possible the absolute affirmation of life and *amor fati*. The Great Noon is the moment of revelation that stands between these two ages, the moment when the truth of both is apparent and in which there are no shadows.[33]

In *Ecce Homo* he reveals that he is the singer of this song, which is the song of Dionysus and the song of life ascendant. Nietzsche thus claims that he is a destiny not because he wants to be but because as part of the unfolding of all things he is the moment in which the whole affirms and wills itself, the moment of the appearance of the god who in his eternal birth and death wills the constant renewal of the whole. Nietzsche in this sense portrays his role as the herald of the god who must come, the one who will redeem humanity from nihilism and institute a new tragic age, and establish a thousand-year Dionysian *Reich* (*NL*, KGW VIII, 2:41, 313, 431).

But it is not the story of the thinking or reflection that produced this great idea. Rather it is a story of what he now in retrospect believes was going on beneath the level of consciousness in his body or with his passions and instincts that has brought him to be what he is. *Ecce Homo* is in this sense not only a book of self-presentation but of self-discovery, a demonstration of the workings of fate and the will to power that has brought him to this terrible idea, that lives itself out through him. In this sense it is about divine possession and the hidden direction given to him from birth by the Dionysian world-will. It is the story of his shaping as the vessel for the epiphany of the god, the way in which he became the voice of this god. Hence *Ecce Homo.*

The last thing Nietzsche presumably wrote in *Ecce Homo* was the short note he places between the preface and the first part. It is in musical terms and not only in musical terms a rest:

> On this perfect day, when everything is ripening and not only the grape turns brown, the eye of the sun just fell upon my life: I looked back, I looked forward, and never saw so many and such good things at once. It was not for nothing that I buried my forty-fourth year today; I had a *right* to bury it; whatever was life in it has been saved, is immortal. . . . *How could I fail to be grateful for my whole life?*—and so I tell my life to myself.

Ecce Homo is Nietzsche's musical exploration and affirmation of his life and of all things. It is his great Yes to the eternal recurrence as it completes itself and sings itself in and through him. It is in this sense his epiphany as the disciple/son of the god of music Dionysus.[34] And like the god, beyond this point he could not go, torn to pieces in a few months not by his maenadic followers but by his own psyche, not a crucified individual who would rise again, but the one who became "all names in history."

Ecce Homo may indeed be a work of madness, but if so, it was not the result of the madness that eventually overcame Nietzsche. It was rather the divine madness of the idea of the eternal recurrence that possessed him from 1881 on, a madness rooted in his thinking and life from his earliest years, an idea rooted in German thought and culture at least since Luther that God is active in the world through select individuals, through what Goethe called demonic individuals and what Nietzsche typically referred to as the genius. Nietzsche's god was the god of music, and his life thus finally could only appear to him as music. *Ecce Homo*—behold the man—at its core asks the reader to behold the god or better yet to hear the divine music.[35]

Nietzsche and Dostoevsky on Nihilism and the Superhuman

Nietzsche's intellectual development was decisively shaped by his accidental discovery of three books:[1] Schopenhauer's *World as Will and Representation* when he was twenty-one, Stendhal's *The Red and the Black* at thirty-five, and Dostoevsky's *Notes from the Underground* at forty-three.[2] The impact of Schopenhauer has long been recognized, and the importance of Stendhal is similarly clear to most Nietzsche scholars. The role that Dostoevsky played, however, is less obvious in large part because Nietzsche discovered his work only a little more than a year before the collapse that ended his productive life. Yet in that short time, he read as many of Dostoevsky's works as he could find including *The Landlady, Notes from the Underground, The House of the Dead, Crime and Punishment, The Demons*, and perhaps *The Idiot*.[3] There thus can be little doubt that in his last feverish year of philosophical activity, Dostoevsky was a nearly constant presence in Nietzsche's thought. In what follows I will try to describe the way in which this encounter shaped Nietzsche's thinking, and particularly Dostoevsky's impact on Nietzsche's exploration of the death of God, nihilism, and the possibility of the superhuman.

NIETZSCHE'S FINAL TEACHING

As we have seen, Nietzsche's thought, by his own account, falls into three periods. His early work aimed at cultural renewal. During his middle period, he became pessimistic about the possibility of such renewal and turned his efforts toward the exploration of alternative ways of life and to the analysis and praise of the decisive role of distinctive individuals who as firstlings he believed were invariably opposed to prevailing cultural norms, criminals in thought if not in deed. This project gave way after 1881 to the new (and ultimately final) project we have been discussing.

In Nietzsche's view, this teaching aims at the proclamation of the idea of the eternal recurrence, which must be accepted or rejected as a whole. Schopenhauer had followed the path of absolute negation and renunciation; Nietzsche wants to affirm the whole, willing everything that has ever been or ever will be.[4]

Nietzsche initially presented this idea as the teaching of Zarathustra in an effort to give the doctrine a mythic significance it would otherwise have lacked. His intended audience was not the scientific or scholarly community of his time but a moral and cultural elite. *Zarathustra* in this sense was a counter-Gospel that Nietzsche hoped would appeal not only to the reason but also to the hearts and wills of the best of his contemporaries, those Nietzsche called free spirits or higher men.[5] Nietzsche's Zarathustra in this context plays the role of an Antichrist, not a God who becomes a human but a human being who becomes godlike, not a Christlike figure who evokes great pathos but a playful and generous character, even if at times he appears to be inhuman and pitiless. And perhaps most importantly, Zarathustra does not preach a doctrine of sin and the need for repentance or redemption but a doctrine of innocence and self-overcoming.

Nietzsche believed that this doctrine would ultimately produce a new order, but he recognized, as we have seen, that in the short term its effect would be cataclysmic. Nietzsche himself hesitated in the face of such an apocalyptic vision, but not for the reasons one might imagine. The fact that many ordinary human beings would be swallowed up in this transformation did not trouble him a great deal. Nietzsche was much more concerned about the suffering and fate of those Zarathustra calls "higher men," the intellectuals and artists of his time who recognized that God was dead but who were unable to find a way out of the abyss opened up by that event. The final barrier to proclaiming this teaching was thus what Zarathustra refers to as "pity for the higher man." While these "higher men" were high and thus potential companions for Nietzsche, in his view they were not high enough, not truly above man. They too thus would have to perish in order for the *Übermensch* to come into being.

THE IMPACT OF DOSTOEVSKY ON NIETZSCHE

It was in the context of his struggle to overcome nihilism that Dostoevsky came to play an important role for Nietzsche and a comparison of the two can give us important insights into Nietzsche's final teaching. Nietzsche considered Dostoevsky to be a preeminent example of Christian faith and of slave morality, as he admitted in a letter to Brandes of 20 November 1888, but he admired Dostoevsky because of his psychological insight into the nihilists (KGB III 5:483). Dostoevsky's portrayals of such characters as the underground man, Raskolnikov, and Kirillov confirmed and deepened Nietzsche's understanding of such men. Like Nietzsche, Dostoevsky recognized that these men were daring enough to try to become something more than their contemporaries, and like Nietzsche, he also recognized that they were not strong enough to achieve their ultimate goal. In contrast to Nietzsche, however, Dostoevsky thought that their failures marked out the limits of human striving, thus demonstrating the futility of pursuing a superhuman god-manhood, and consequently the need to return to God and the man-God, Christ. Nietzsche, by contrast, concluded that their failures were due to the residue of Christianity that informed their moral sensibilities, leaving them paralyzed with feelings of pity and guilt. Like the tightrope walker in *Zarathustra*, they were stuck at the midpoint of the line between beast and *Übermensch*, on the verge of the Great Noon, but unable to take the step from believer to destroyer because they could not bear the suffering it would bring to their fellow human beings. They thus had to perish.

While Nietzsche first laid out this project in *Zarathustra*, the book did not have the impact he anticipated. The biblical and mythic imagery, the epigrammatic and parablistic style simply made it too strange and alien not merely for the average reader, but also for Nietzsche's friends and admirers. However, while he was profoundly disappointed with the work's reception, Nietzsche did not lose faith in the teaching that lay at its heart. Instead, he concluded that the work was "untimely," that the public was so mired in positivism, utilitarianism, and Christianity that they simply could not see the truth. He realized he needed to better prepare them for the task he had set before them and change the way they perceived him. His previous work had led his readers to assume he was a disciple of Schopenhauer and Wagner, a pessimist, a Romantic nationalist, a dyspeptic cultural critic, or a hero worshiper like Carlyle or Stendhal. From 1881 on, however, he came to think of himself as first and foremost the teacher of the eternal recurrence. As part of an effort to change the public's misperception, he republished his earlier works with new prefaces as we saw above.

It was in the midst of writing these prefaces that he discovered Dostoevsky. Dostoevsky's impact was immediate and strong, as is evident in the new preface to *Dawn*, in which, as we have seen, draws on Dostoevsky's portrayal of the underground man.[6] This allusion is a clue to the nature of his reception and use of Dostoevsky. The purpose of the new prefaces was to describe the stages of Nietzsche's passage through decadence and nihilism to a new health. In tying the author of *Dawn* to Dostoevsky's underground man, Nietzsche portrays himself as formerly mired in the same sickness that characterized Dostoevsky's protagonist. This was a form of life that Nietzsche believed he had overcome. Dostoevsky's mole thus represents one of the stages in the development of nihilism, one form of the "higher man."

Nietzsche thought that Dostoevsky had given a masterful account of this kind of human being in *Notes from the Underground*. He particularly admired Dostoevsky's analysis of what he calls "the psychology of the psychologist," as he mentioned in a letter to Köselitz of 7 March 1887 (KGB III 5:41–42). With this phrase Nietzsche refers to what we might call the psychology of modern self-consciousness or subjectivity. Modernity rests upon the belief that self-consciousness reveals the truth of what we are, providing us with the solid foundation (an "Archimedean point" to use Descartes' famous phrase) for science and the mastery of nature. Even in his earliest works, Nietzsche rejected this view. What Dostoevsky investigates and portrays more fully than anyone else, according to Nietzsche, is the psychology of this form of self-consciousness, the unconscious or subconscious foundation of such self-consciousness and the notion of truth that is founded upon it.[7] He thereby also reveals the emptiness of modern philosophy and the culture upon which it is built.

The problem with this form of thinking for Dostoevsky lies in the fact that while the Cartesian notion of self-consciousness liberates the individual from divine deception and gives him the capacity to set his own course through life, this godless self-consciousness is an empty shell or solipsistic universe without moral directions. Dostoevsky's literary examples thus reinforced Nietzsche's notion that the spiritual problems facing Europe were insoluble within the parameters of the modern notion of consciousness. Without God, self-consciousness reveals only a looming abyss, the absolute aloneness of the self without any goals or purposes other than those revealed by one's momentary desires. Within self-consciousness, the atheist thus cannot understand himself or find his way in life.[8] All of the efforts to better the human condition through science and the hopes of progress are thus in vain because at its foundation this scientific enterprise is the source of aimlessness. The unreflective masses (Nietzsche's last men) may find solace in the notion of progress preached by the utilitarians and displayed in monuments such as the Crystal Palace, but the higher men cannot. For them the material pleasures of such a life cannot make up for the lack of spiritual direction. Such a life is profoundly dissatisfying and leads nihilist intellectuals not merely to boredom and despair but to murder, madness, and suicide.[9] In such characters as Raskolnikov, Kirillov, and Stavrogin, Nietzsche believed that Dostoevsky had revealed the psychopathology of this hypersensitive self-consciousness. Dostoevsky for him thus provided the clearest and most compelling account of the inner life and ultimate fate of the nihilist.[10]

While Nietzsche accepted Dostoevsky's portrayal of the nihilist, he rejected his conclusions about what should be done. Dostoevsky believed that self-reflection and modern science were rooted in the systematic doubt of Cartesian skepticism that undermined faith that alone could give direction and meaning to life. He hoped for a revival of this faith by urging Russians to return to their Slavic tradition and abandon European rationalism.[11] In this way he believed that it would be possible to escape from the mirrored box of self-consciousness.

Although Nietzsche shared many of Dostoevsky's concerns about the debilitating character of Cartesian egoism, he drew different conclusions about the ultimate source of the problem. For him the return to any form of Christian faith would fail, because the inwardness of such hyper-self-conscious individuals was not the consequence of a turn away from Christianity, but the product of Christianity itself.[12] Nietzsche was thus convinced that all of Europe would eventually be engulfed by the same nihilism he had passed through and that afflicted Dostoevsky's nihilistic protagonists. For Nietzsche the solution to nihilism lay in going where Dostoevsky was unwilling to go, where Dostoevsky believed no human could go. Dostoevsky's nihilists can find no way out of the aporia of self-consciousness. They are defeated by guilt, by pity, and by despair. Nietzsche concluded that these "higher men" were not strong, hard, or high enough. Overcoming nihilism thus depended upon the formation of a harder people, tempered, as we have seen in the preceding essays, by years of brutal conflict, a people who in contrast to Dostoevsky's nihilists would be able to move beyond this impasse and forge a stronger European civilization.

Here too the encounter with Dostoevsky aided Nietzsche in formulating his solution, although contrary to Dostoevsky's intentions. What particularly struck Nietzsche in this regard were not Dostoevsky's peasants and holy men, but the sturdy, fatalistic criminals he had encountered during his exile in Siberia and described in *The House of the Dead*. The fact that the strong often found themselves at odds with prevailing mores was clear to Nietzsche as we discussed above. Dostoevsky's Siberian criminals, however, added a final element because they exemplified a fatalism that was often missing in their Western European counterparts. This fatalism apparently played a role in the development of what Nietzsche came to call *amor fati*, which he closely associated with the doctrine of the eternal recurrence. It was from such men and not out of the hyper-self-conscious, nihilist intellectuals that the *Übermensch* in Nietzsche's view would be born.[13]

DOSTOEVSKY'S VISION OF THE NIHILIST

Dostoevsky, of course, was not the first to portray the nihilist. Turgenev's Bazarov (1862) and Chernyshevsky's Rakhmetov (1863) antedate all of Dostoevsky's nihilistic characters. However, in all previous literary examples, the nihilist hero is described from the outside looking in, more as a rare and incomprehensible phenomenon than as a living, thinking, and above all self-reflective human being.[14] The greatness of Bazarov, for example, is only visible in his effects on others. We never see the inner workings of his mind. Rakhmetov is a strange and mysterious being who stands apart and is held in awe by those around him. Dostoevsky's portrayal of the nihilists' internal struggles is new and offers deeply revealing insights into the psychology of the nihilists that were missing in much of the earlier literature.

As we saw above, Nietzsche distinguishes incomplete and complete nihilism. Incomplete nihilism stretches back to Plato and includes all of Christian thought and modern philosophy up to Hegel. Complete nihilism begins in the nineteenth century and recognizes the death of God and the essential aimlessness of human life. This form of nihilism is either passive or active. Passive nihilism includes Schopenhauer and his followers. Within this category Nietzsche includes most Russian nihilists, whom he wrongly believed were fundamentally influenced by Schopenhauer.[15] Active nihilists, according to Nietzsche, do not merely renounce the world but seek to destroy it, to assert their freedom through negation. In this category he includes revolutionary nihilists such as Bakunin and Nechayev who use violence to disrupt and destroy the existing order. Dostoevsky's nihilists such as Stavrogin and Kirillov stand on the border between active and passive nihilism. Stavrogin rejects the moral order of his time but cannot bring himself to destroy it. He violates its norms, but is unwilling to participate in the revolutionary movement. In the end, for him there is nothing to do except hang himself.

Kirillov was the most extreme nihilist that Nietzsche encountered in Dostoevsky's works. He is a positivistic atheist akin to Turgenev's Bazarov.[16] He is horrified by the "stupid, blind, insane and problematical" reality of a world deprived of God. His nihilism is total and all-engrossing. It is also not a merely passive despair that leads to ascetic renunciation but a form of active nihilism. However, he directs the negative energy of his will not against the prevailing order. Indeed, he is unwilling to inflict pain and suffering on others. This contradiction leads him to suicide.[17] Everything in his view depends upon humanity rising above the fear of death because the idea of God is given force and reality by this fear. To kill oneself simply in order to demonstrate that one does not fear death will, he believes, enable him (and through him the rest of humanity) to become god-men.[18] By killing himself he thus hopes to redeem humanity.[19] However, he does not and cannot attain the liberation he longs for, and remains trapped by his ideas and his fellow nihilist conspirators. While he kills himself, he is thus not able to affirm life and remains rooted in negation.

None of Dostoevsky's characters ever moves beyond such active nihilism to what Nietzsche calls radical or Dionysian nihilism. This form of nihilism in Nietzsche's view accepts and affirms the idea of the eternal recurrence. It thus requires a harder, more fatalistic and more affirmative human being. Taken to its end, Nietzsche thus believes that nihilism need not end in murder, madness, or suicide, but opens up the possibility of an exuberant, joyful, and potentially superhuman existence.

IVAN KARAMAZOV

Dostoevsky's most comprehensive exploration of the nihilist mentality was his portrayal of Ivan Karamazov in *The Brothers Karamazov*. While Nietzsche never read this work, Dostoevsky's Ivan poses the greatest challenge to Nietzsche's reading of nihilism and reveals in a particularly vivid fashion the gulf that separates the two thinkers. Moreover, the demands of the radical nihilism that Nietzsche describes in his final teaching become more concrete in the light of Ivan's response to the death of God, the recognition of human mortality, and the meaninglessness of human striving.

Like many students of his generation, Ivan in Dostoevsky's story falls under the spell of modern European ideas while at the university. Positivism, utilitarianism, and natural science lead him to question the existence of God and the possibility of life after death. Like Turgenev's Bazarov and unlike Chernyshevsky's Rakhmetov and Dostoevsky's own Kirillov, Ivan is not obviously involved in revolutionary political activity. Nihilism for him is principally a moral/theological problem only tangentially related to politics. His studies have led him to believe there is no natural impulse or law of nature that men should love one another and thus no natural ground for communal life. All such love, he concludes, must therefore be due to a belief in immortality. Hence, if belief in Christianity with its promise of a final judgment dries up, there will no longer be any restraint on egoism, for if nothing is immoral, everything including cannibalism will be lawful.

Ivan expresses such opinions brashly and without regard to their consequences. Despite the apparent daring with which he proclaims these ideas, however, they impose real psychological costs on him. In this respect he is a much more serious character than Pyotr Verkhovensky, the leader of the nihilist group in *The Demons* who plays at being a nihilist revolutionary but never suffers the spiritual torments that beset Dostoevsky's other nihilistic protagonists. Dostoevsky gives us a graphic indication of the burdens such thinking imposes on Ivan in three chapters of *The Brothers Karamazov*, "On Rebellion," "The Grand Inquisitor," and "The Devil: Ivan's Nightmare." The first two are part of a lengthy discussion between Ivan and his pious younger brother, Alyosha. The third is a dialogue between Ivan and the devil when Ivan is suffering from a brain fever. The three chapters taken as a whole spell out with great force the nihilist position that Dostoevsky rejects.

In the chapter "On Rebellion," Ivan suggests that either there is no God and then nothing is evil or there is a God and he is utterly complicit in evil. The example he uses to prove this thesis is the torture and murder of innocent children, those who have not "eaten of the apple," and are thus without sin. The fact that such crimes occur indicates to Ivan that God does not exist or that he is not just or merciful. In either case existence is meaningless.

Ivan is aware that there is a traditional Christian answer to this charge, that such evil is only apparent and not real because as finite beings we cannot understand God's infinite purposes. Humans thus cannot understand how the justice and goodness of the whole may require the apparent injustice of specific parts. Moreover, scripture indicates that at the end of time God's justice will be made evident and everyone will be reconciled with one another in him. Ivan, however, asserts that even if there is a final revelation of the necessity of the suffering of the innocent, it cannot justify that suffering, nor the God that allowed it. No future knowledge or event can undo the suffering of innocent children or reconcile them with their tormentors. Such actions are simply unjustifiable. There is no theodicy. Thus Ivan declares that he "gives back his ticket." Either there is no God and the world is simply a set of random events in which everything is permitted, including the torture and murder of innocent children, or there is a God who created and rules the world, and he is evil. In either case, Ivan wants no part of it. He renounces existence.

Ivan is convinced that if God exists he is guilty of allowing such abominations. Like Kirillov he rejects the notion that there could be a utilitarian justification for such suffering, pointing out that the happiness of all cannot be purchased by the sacrifice of even one innocent. In contrast to Kirillov, however, he loves life more than the meaning of it. As he puts it, "I have a longing for life, and I go on living in spite of logic. Though I may not believe in the order of the universe, yet I love the sticky little leaves as they open in spring. I love the blue sky, I love some people, whom one loves sometimes without knowing why. I love some great deeds done by men, though I've long since ceased perhaps to have faith in them, yet from old habit one's heart prizes them."[20] As a result and in contrast to Kirillov, Ivan is not defeated by his nihilistic ideas.[21] He is sustained by his sensuality (by what he calls his Karamazov baseness). In this respect he is closer to Nietzsche than to the hyperrational Kirillov. Reason and a desire for justice and an end to evil are important for him, but there is a deep wellspring of love that sustains him.

Ivan's second argument is developed in "The Grand Inquisitor," which extends the argument in "On Rebellion" by showing that not only God the creator but also God the redeemer is complicit in human suffering. It is thus directed not against the idea of an omnipotent and omni-benevolent Father but against the gnostic or Manichean notion of a divine Son who can redeem the evil Father's errors. The argument is presented through a story set during the Spanish Inquisition in Seville. The city is dominated by a Grand Inquisitor, a hardened old man who rules through a mixture of religious awe and terrifying violence. Just a day after an auto-da-fé in which almost one hundred heretics were burned alive, Christ appears in the midst of a crowd. Although he is there only for a short visit, he is immediately recognized and adored by the people. The Grand Inquisitor has him taken into custody and imprisoned within a cell where the Inquisitor visits him in the middle of the night. The rest of the story is a monologue in which the Inquisitor explains and attempts to justify his life to Christ. It is a defense of his own actions and a condemnation of Christ for failing to alleviate human suffering.

The Inquisitor's basic accusation against Christ is that God granted all human beings free will but granted only a tiny number of them the ability to make good use of it. Freedom thus causes suffering for most human beings. Only a few benefit from it by entering into paradise while all of the rest are condemned to eternal damnation. The Inquisitor suggests that Christ could have saved all of humanity from such suffering but chose not to do so. Drawing on the account of Satan's temptation of Christ in the wilderness, he argues that Christ rejected the three keys to human happiness and well-being, all of which were revealed to him in Satan's three temptations. What is crucial to human happiness, he argues, is miracle, mystery, and authority; the miracle (of converting stones to bread) because it satisfies the basic human instinct for survival, mystery because it provides human beings with something to live for, and authority because it removes the burden of freedom and choice that most men cannot bear. Christ, according to the Inquisitor, knew how necessary all three of these were to human well-being, but rejected them, leaving human beings with an absolute freedom so that a small number could prove themselves worthy of salvation.

The Inquisitor asserts that he and those like him took a more humane path, entering into league with Satan against Christ in the interest of the vast majority of humanity, taking the burden of freedom upon themselves, providing the masses with bread, and a comforting belief in salvation, thus relieving them from the terrible necessity of a choice that they could not make or endure. It is wrong, the Inquisitor tells Christ, to blame the weak for what they can never do, and it would be wrong to blame him and his fellows for deceiving and ruling over them for their own good. They, he claims, love men more than Christ does, and thus should not be blamed for what they have done because it was done not for personal gain but for the love of humanity. To put the argument in theological terms, the Inquisitor argues that it is not possible to love both God and one's neighbor, and that his choice of the latter was more "Christian" than Christ's choice of the former. Christ does not answer but simply kisses the Inquisitor on the lips, and the Inquisitor then lets him depart.[22]

When Ivan finishes, Alyosha realizes that the entire story was only a reflection of the struggle going on in Ivan's soul. This terrifies him. He argues that no one can live with such notions in one's heart. This also seems to be Dostoevsky's opinion since in the end Ivan is driven mad when confronted with the realization of his ideas. The precipitating cause of Ivan's collapse is his discovery that his arguments have persuaded his half brother Smerdyakov that all things are lawful and, as a result, Smerdyakov has killed their father and let the blame fall on their fourth brother, Dmitri. Ivan comes to believe that he is responsible for his father's murder and cannot bear his guilt. He berates Smerdyakov for misunderstanding him and leaves. This pulls the moral rug out from under Smerdyakov's feet, and with no further way to justify his actions, he hangs himself. Back in his room, Ivan falls into a fever and in his delirium has a discussion with the devil.

Throughout this feverish dialogue, Ivan is never sure whether the devil is an independent being or his alter ego, some darker part of himself.[23] Ultimately, however, this does not matter, since the devil has all of the limitations of human beings, and thus has no knowledge that transcends human experience. Like Ivan he exists in doubt, certain only of the "I think, therefore I am" of Descartes but uncertain whether anything outside of him, including God, exists. The devil is thus as trapped in the same prison of self-consciousness as Ivan himself is.

In his dialogue with the devil, Ivan is brought face-to-face with the consequences of his earlier arguments against faith. If there is no God, then man is god, as Kirillov recognized, but, if so, then this man-god is indistinguishable from the devil, and thus incapable of doing good, whatever his intentions. Without God, man or the man-god is lost without hope on the empty sea of self-consciousness.

At the core of modern self-consciousness is a will to know and to command that seeks certainty and security. The path to such knowledge and power, however, depends upon the negative force of methodological doubt. To know for modernity is not to rely on authority, however sacred or august, but to grasp the truth oneself. This truth, as Descartes put it, must be confirmed by one's own mind as indubitable. The test of knowledge for modernity is thus methodological doubt that calls everything into question and seeks to ground knowledge on a *fundamentum inconcussum absolutum veritatis*, on an absolutely immoveable foundational truth. It is for this reason that the critical spirit, which calls everything into question, is the basis of European rationalism. As Hegel and his successors recognized, self-consciousness is thus negativity. Goethe personified this element in Mephistopheles, who describes himself as "the spirit that always negates."[24] Ivan's devil is only another in a long line of these demonic, critical spirits. His negativity, however, is ultimately greater than that of Mephistopheles. Mephistopheles tries to do evil but always ends up doing good because God has ordered the world so that all actions have a happy ending. Kant shared this teleological assumption. Ivan's devil, by contrast, wants to do good but always ends up doing evil. The world as the Grand Inquisitor correctly made clear is out of joint, and everything as a result inevitably ends in tragedy.[25] Thus, even the most powerful man-god-devil lives in unhappiness and dreams like Ivan himself of being a simple merchant's wife who is able to believe and live happily in ignorance. The fate of the devil in this sense is no different than the fate of anyone who lives without faith.

Ivan's devil understands that this negativity also has a political dimension, but he discounts its importance. He knows that the "new men," the nihilist revolutionaries, are bent on destroying everything. He argues, however, that such revolutionary measures are unnecessary. When men deny God, he asserts, the old conception of the universe and the prevailing moral order will come to an end without the need of the cannibalism these revolutionaries want to practice. The universal rule of God, according to Ivan's devil, will then be replaced by the reign of the man-god who will infinitely extend humanity's power over nature.[26]

Dostoevsky does not deny that this process will eventually make life better here on earth. In this respect the utilitarian dream of progress is not vacuous. What he suggests is that in the absence of God and immortality no one will have any reason to love one another or act in concert with one another. Indeed, each person who realizes the truth and thus becomes a man-god will have every reason to act on purely egoistic principles as Smerdyakov did. Such a life, however, is not worth living even if one can live in a Crystal Palace. The path that rests on doubt and negation rather than love thus leads only to madness, murder, and suicide. With nothing to give man direction, he will wander over the earth without a home, without a destination, and without anyone to accompany him on his journey.

DOSTOEVSKY AND NIETZSCHE'S FINAL TEACHING

Nietzsche learned a great deal from Dostoevsky's account of the nihilist psyche but was not convinced that Dostoevsky had finally understood nihilism or that he had adequately grasped the possibility of finding a way through nihilism to a higher form of existence. He knew from his reading of *The Demons* that Dostoevsky had considered such a possibility but had rejected it as an impossible attempt to transcend the limits of human nature. Viewed against the backdrop of this daunting account of nihilism, we can begin to glimpse the daring character of Nietzsche's final teaching, which charts a path into and through the abyss that swallows up Dostoevsky's heroes. Nietzsche realizes that following this path is extraordinarily dangerous, but he believes it is the only alternative to the pessimism and despair of passive nihilism and the desire for revenge that characterizes revolutionary nihilism.

Both Kirillov and Ivan exemplify the moral and psychological burden of nihilism. Both seek to live without God, but the effort to do so drives them to madness and suicide. Affirming the doctrine of the eternal recurrence, however, demands that one live an even more demanding atheistic life. It does not mean just saying that one does not believe in God, as Kirillov and Ivan do, but willingly living without God, as they are unable to do. Moreover, this willing is not simply the willing of what one finds pleasing or entertaining or even "most beautiful," but, as we have seen, willing *everything*, that is, everything that is beautiful, everything that is ugly, and everything that is horrible. Ivan argued that one could not believe in or affirm a God who allowed the innocent to be tortured. Such a world was either ruled by blind chance or an evil demon. Kirillov more or less agrees but thinks that the world can be redeemed by his suicide. Nietzsche's teaching of the eternal recurrence is an effort to force men to confront just such a purposeless universe. In Nietzsche's view his teaching is a hammer that will shatter even such higher men as Ivan and Kirillov because it demands that they affirm the torture of the innocent, not as the act of a malicious deity or the product of blind chance, but as what they want, as what they will, and as what they do. Ivan is shattered by the discovery that Smerdyakov murdered their father because Smerdyakov followed Ivan's ideas to their logical conclusion. When faced with this fact, Ivan (like Raskolnikov) is plunged into guilt and wants to be punished.[27] Nietzsche argues that the Ivans and Kirillovs of the world who want to overcome nihilism must affirm not merely such deeds done in their name or in the name of their ideas but must actually *want* to do such things themselves. This extreme affirmation is crucial for escaping from the spirit of revenge and living joyfully in the face of suffering. The guilt that Dosto-evsky's nihilists feel in Nietzsche's view is a reflection of their weakness, a consequence of their pity, and thus a reflection of the continued dominance of Christian values even in the absence of God. This weakness is not shared by Dostoevsky's Siberian criminals whom Nietzsche so admires, and in this sense these criminals are better models for the type of human beings who can deal with nihilism than the intellectuals Dostoevsky portrays. What is needed is not a guilty conscience but a hard fatalism, *amor fati*. Such men not only do not flinch from affirming such deeds, they actual draw strength and joy from such an affirmation. For Nietzsche such men as Kirillov and Ivan are decadents, sick and weak, and thus unable to pass through nihilism, unable to move beyond the midpoint between beast and *Übermensch* at which the believer must become a destroyer. They therefore must perish in order to make room for a stronger, healthier human being, the true man-god who is beyond good and evil but still the foremost proponent of life itself.

Such an affirmation carries Nietzsche beyond Kirillov, Ivan, and even the Grand Inquisitor.[28] The Grand Inquisitor like Kirillov seeks to take the burden of guilt upon himself, to rule human beings, to provide them with their daily bread, give some purpose to their lives, and subordinate their rebellious instincts to authority. Despite his obvious strength and power, he is driven not by a desire for self-overcoming or a desire to create something greater than himself but by pity. He had the strength to be one of the elect but apparently concluded (as Ivan did) that a God who allows suffering when he can alleviate it is not worthy of his worship. The Inquisitor is thus the image of a paternalistic authoritarian ruling humanity for its own good, perhaps modeled on Hegel's notion of a universal class of philosophically educated bureaucrats or Plato's philosopher-king. Nietzsche believes that such rule would only perpetuate the weakness at the heart of contemporary human beings who seek solace in the dream of a better world.

The construction of such an imaginary world may seem to be an act of charity, but for Nietzsche it is an act of weakness, an attempt by the slaves to realize an imaginary revenge on their masters by creating a place that is everything this world is not, an eternal realm in place of the actual world of becoming, a place where the strong cannot do what they want and where the meek do in fact inherit the earth. As we have seen, the preeminent source of the desire for revenge in Nietzsche's view is the inexorable character of becoming, the "it was" against which the will itself shatters. The lust for revenge, however, is an entirely reactive passion, and as long as we are driven by it, we are incapable of acting freely or actually willing or creating anything at all.

As we have seen, Nietzsche believes that his doctrine of the eternal recurrence allows us to overcome the spirit of revenge.[29] But the idea of the eternal recurrence is just an idea, a possibility that may or may not be true. Why then does Nietzsche take it so seriously? Many scholars have pointed out that while the eternal recurrence is possible, it is not necessary or demonstrable. It thus seems a slender reed upon which to set such a titanic undertaking. Nietzsche was not unaware of this fact. As an account of the whole, it can have no demonstration. However, whether or not it is true, the idea is a test, an experiment in which one attempts to live one's life as if the idea were true. To affirm the idea of the eternal recurrence in this sense is not just to accept the possibility of the worst but its actuality, to will it, to believe in it. For Nietzsche, in contrast to Dostoevsky, it is thus important to imagine a world in which innocent children are tortured and killed in order to be able to say not "I give back my ticket," but "Once more," to want to be the author of such deeds, to want to be eternally both the pain and the joy of becoming.

For Nietzsche, only someone who can will in this way can overcome the pessimism and despair that destroyed Kirillov and Ivan. The *Übermensch* that Nietzsche imagines is the Grand Inquisitor freed from pity and his desire for revenge, the Grand Inquisitor (or as Nietzsche put it Caesar) with the soul of Christ, an active rather than a reactive being who guides and shapes humanity not as a result of pity or out of charity but according to his own aesthetic sensibilities and desires. He is supremely alive and does not seek to ease his own burden or that of his fellow human beings but to increase both. He is an artist and a tyrant. This *Übermensch*, in Nietzsche's view, however, does not yet exist and can only come into being as the result of a long process of breeding tougher, more pitiless human beings. He is convinced, however, that such beings will come to be through a long process of tempering under the harshest conditions.[30] Only then, when the last vestiges of Christianity have been eliminated will the *Übermensch* be possible.

Nietzsche did not complete the task of spelling out this final teaching.

What form it would have taken remains unknowable. That he imagined it would provoke the Great Noon, an apocalyptic day of decision for European civilization, however, seems incontestable. Here too the parallel to Dostoevsky is enlightening. Dostoevsky imagined that it was the Russian national destiny to bring about the advent of the kingdom of God as the consummation of human history.[31] Moreover, he was convinced that the critical turning point in human history was near at hand. The appearance of the man-god in his view was an indication that the Antichrist had arrived. He was convinced that the reappearance of the man-God could not be far behind, and that his return would redeem not merely humanity but nature itself. Nietzsche adopted a position that was radically opposed to that of Dostoevsky, which for him was the epitome of decadence and Christianity. The new world would be brought into being in his view not by the appearance of the God-man but by the coming to power of the true man-god, the *Übermensch*. For Nietzsche, however, this event lies on the far side of centuries of war. The true enemy for him in the present is Christianity and Christian values. This fact is spelled out clearly in the phrase Nietzsche places at the end of *Ecce Homo*: "*Dionysus versus the Crucified.*"

NIETZSCHE CONTRA DOSTOEVSKY

Despite their shared analysis of the origins of nihilism, Dostoevsky and Nietzsche diverge profoundly when it comes to the appropriate response to this problem. For both the central question turns on man's relationship to God within the broader context of Christianity. They both recognized that Cartesian skepticism and modern science have undermined faith in Christianity. They also recognized the looming disaster that the loss of faith entails. This disaster in their view was evident above all in the careers and fates of the nihilist intellectuals. Both Nietzsche and Dostoevsky felt a profound kinship with such men. Both, however, believed that they had found a way out of the nihilistic abyss these nihilists encountered. Their paths out of nihilism and their prescriptions for dealing with it, however, were quite different.

Dostoevsky believed that the path that humanity has to follow is the path of faith, a path rooted in the love of God and his creation. This relationship in his view is made possible through the mediation of Christ, the man-God, whose incarnation is the demonstration of the divinity of all created things. Dostoevsky identifies such a religious stance with the traditional faith of the Russian peasant, exemplified in Father Zosima in *The Brothers Karamazov*. Zosima's faith fills him with a love for all things that gives meaning and purpose to his life.[32] By contrast, Nietzsche believes what is needed is not a return to Christian faith, but a hardening and culling of humanity by a struggle for preeminence. In his view the ultimate source of nihilism lies in Christianity and hence a return to it would be pointless. War in any case is inevitable given the irreversible decline in faith. The consequent hardening of humanity will then produce not Dostoevsky's imaginary man-God but an elite out of which the *Übermensch* will arise. This *Übermensch* will be able to overcome the spirit of revenge by affirming the doctrine of the eternal recurrence of the same, which will allow him to become truly active and creative and thus able to give human beings new values and purposes for their lives. This *Übermensch* is clearly related to the man-God whom Dostoevsky sees as the epitome of all that is wrong with modern life. Dostoevsky rejects the path of willfulness in favor of faith, and Nietzsche rejects the path of faith in favor of will.[33]

All this said, it would be a mistake to conclude that their differences can simply be described as a disagreement between a believer and a nonbeliever. Both Dostoevsky and Nietzsche stand within the larger penumbra of Christianity. Christianity has always been a syncretistic religion that combines many different streams of thought.[34] From the beginning Christians have debated the nature of their God, and this question was resolved in favor of Trinitarianism (as opposed to Arianism) only by imperial power. Even after the settlement of this fundamental question, the relationship between the three persons of the godhead remained a continuing point of dispute that erupted time and time again. Moreover, even when Christians agreed about the nature of God, they often disagreed about the nature and weight of his attributes. On this question Nietzsche and Dostoevsky clearly part company.

Both Nietzsche and Dostoevsky reject the scholastic view of a preeminently rational God, just as they both reject the Enlightenment notion of a rational humanity and a rational cosmos.[35] Their differences seem to turn more around their view of the other two principal attributes of the divine: omni-benevolence and omnipotence, that is, love and power. For Dostoevsky the principal attribute of God and his creation is love, while for Nietzsche the central principle that governs the cosmos is the will to power. Dostoevsky sees such willfulness as the key element in nihilism that leads to the man-god. Nietzsche sees a reliance upon a transcendent love in the face of the manifestly tragic circumstances of life as a debilitating self-deception. For Dostoevsky the only way to escape nihilism is faith in the coming God-man. For Nietzsche it is only by means of an affirmation of the doctrine of the eternal recurrence of all things that the *Übermensch* can come to be.[36]

Both Dostoevsky and Nietzsche see human beings playing a decisive role in overcoming nihilism. For Dostoevsky the people is the fount of all salvation. The particular people Dostoevsky has in mind is the Russian peasantry, who in his view are the true repository of Orthodox faith, which alone has sustained an authentic Christianity in the face of modern European rationalism. Salvation is only possible if the intellectuals and rulers bow down to the people and follow their pious lead. Poets and other artists like Pushkin who hearken to the people's sensibility give this spirituality form. Indeed, Dostoevsky sees himself playing a similar role in demonstrating concretely the possibility of an authentic Christian life of love.

Nietzsche discounts the importance of the existing people but recognizes the need for the formation of a new people in order to bring about the transformation he longs for. This people will be formed, however, not by love or a reliance on existing traditions but by war and struggle that will obliterate the old faith and create a new people capable of instituting a new faith in a new god. Nietzsche's vision of the future is thus much more aristocratic and less communitarian than Dostoevsky's. It is also much less nationalistic. For Dostoevsky it is the Russians and particularly those who have clung to Slavic traditions who are the way into the future. Nietzsche rests his hopes not on Germans, Frenchmen, or Italians but on "good Europeans." It is from among this cosmopolitan group tempered by war and by the affirmation of the eternal recurrence that a superhuman artist-tyrant-poet-legislator will arise. This "genius of the heart" as Nietzsche refers to him in *Beyond Good and Evil* will give men new values and new goals (KGW VI 2:247–49).

While on the surface Nietzsche's prescription may seem atheistic and the epitome of secular humanism, there are many reasons to see it as deeply connected to a vision of God that focuses almost exclusively on divine will to the exclusion of all other characteristics and attributes. Nietzsche points us in this direction with his references to Dionysus and to "the golden wonder" "for whom only future songs will find names," as he puts it in *Zarathustra* (KGW VI, 1:276). For him the artist plays a crucial role in unveiling this new god and founding this new faith. It is, however, finally a faith for the valiant and the powerful rather than the meek and pious. While Nietzsche learned a great deal from Dostoevsky, he parts company with him on basic moral questions. While Dostoevsky believed that the death of God leads to madness, murder, and suicide, Nietzsche was convinced that at least for the few it opened up the possibility of a new cheerfulness and a tragic nobility.

Given Nietzsche's own descent into insanity and the circumstances that surrounded it, it would be easy to conclude that Dostoevsky was correct. But even if the legend that Nietzsche collapsed clinging to the neck of a horse to keep it from being beaten by its master is true, an individual example, and especially the act of someone as beset by medical problems as Nietzsche, proves nothing. Moreover, Nietzsche did not imagine that he would be able to reach the heights that would be possible for those who had been hardened by the experience of the coming wars. An examination of Nietzsche's thought against the background of Dostoevsky, however, does give us some idea of the immense demands he places upon human nature and thus some greater perspective on the likelihood of the success of his final teaching.

Nietzsche and Plato on the Formation of a Warrior Aristocracy

Friedrich Nietzsche is one of the most inspiring and most troubling thinkers of our time.[1] He calls humanity to awe-inspiring heights, but argues that these heights can only be attained by a few extraordinary human beings. He despises equality, denies that freedom is anything but a relative superiority in power, and sees the desire for peace and prosperity at odds with nobility and human thriving. He thus points us toward the superhuman, but the path to this superhumanity is one that most today find unacceptable. While many have admired and drawn on his critique of liberalism and have recognized the powerful appeal of his hope for a new nobility, his unstinting elitism and his claim that violence is essential to human well-being have proven anathema for liberals and democrats alike.

In an effort to separate the awe-inspiring from the frightening and use his thought to strengthen or ennoble contemporary liberalism, many scholars (often following Walter Kaufmann) have argued that Nietzsche's antiegalitarianism and praise of violence are merely literary tropes, and that when he speaks of war and warriors he is only talking about a struggle of ideas, not real combat. After two world wars and the horrors of Nazism blackened Nietzsche's reputation, such efforts are perhaps understandable as a means of reawakening attention to the challenge he poses for the Anglo-American tradition. There can be no doubt that Nietzsche would have been appalled by the Fascists and Nazis who were driven almost entirely by a desire for revenge, and outraged that his thought was used to support the German nationalism and anti-Semitism that he had so vociferously criticized.[2]

That said, the evidence from Nietzsche's notes and letters demonstrates overwhelmingly that at least during the last eight years of his life in sanity when he formulated his final teaching he was convinced that war and widespread destruction were inevitable, but hoped that this period of struggle might make possible the development of a martial aristocracy out of which his *Übermensch* might arise. Opponents of liberalism such as Deleuze and Foucault accept the fact that Nietzsche is a bellicose critic of liberalism, but they see his longing for the destruction of liberal society as akin to their own. However, they reject his critique of democracy and support for aristocracy. Or rather they argue that the ironic, self-undermining character of Nietzsche's thought makes it possible to reinterpret his advocacy of a vertical order of rank as a horizontal order of difference that is at its core essentially democratic and agonistic. While this deconstructed and reconstructed Nietzsche might be preferable to the actual Nietzsche, and more useful to us today, we have to recognize that this view of an agonistic, proto-democratic Nietzsche is at odds with the evidence we have for what the historical Nietzsche actually believed.[3]

This essay begins with an examination of the role of violence in political life through an analysis of the problem of Achilles, the archetypal hero of the Greek tragic age. It then focuses on the Platonic solution to this problem that played such an important role in almost all later thinking about politics. This framework provides us means to evaluate Nietzsche's advocacy of violence, war, and a warrior elite as essential steps to the realization of his *Übermensch* and a new tragic age.

VIOLENCE AND THE POLITICAL: THE NECESSITY AND DANGER OF WARRIORS

Mao Tse-tung, whose early teacher was the first to translate Nietzsche into Chinese, famously remarked that political power grows out of the barrel of a gun. While this dramatic claim was certainly hyperbolic, it was not merely rhetorical. Indeed, in some sense it is simply true. Even if violence is not always necessary to gaining power, it often is. Moreover, the ability to deploy violence is essential to the preservation of all regimes, and obviously plays a decisive role in the relations between states. This fact has been recognized by nearly everyone who has seriously reflected on political life. Violent force, however, is not merely needed to defend the state from foreign invasion; it is also necessary for the maintenance of internal order. Thus John Locke famously defines political power as "a right of making laws with penalties of death, and consequently all lesser penalties for the regulating and preserving of property, and of employing the force of the community, in the execution of such laws, and in the defence of the commonwealth from foreign injury; and all this only for the public good."[4]

While violence may be necessary, the regime itself is not merely the rule of force. In fact, it rests on the *legitimate* use of force.[5] For the use of violence to be legitimate, it must be authorized, and it must be for the general good rather than the good of any particular group or individual. Violence thus can only be an element of the political if it serves something higher, that is, if it is subject to an authority that arises out of a bond of affiliation that makes the political realm a community rather than a collection of disparate individuals struggling for power. This said, it is clear that an ever-recurring need for force endangers the political. The force that is necessary to preserve the regime can also be used to destroy it, transforming a community into an imperium governed not by agreement but by violence and other forms of co-ercion. Those who use force on behalf of the regime thus are a constant and unavoidable threat to the political realm. Indeed, the preeminent political problem is how to limit, control, and direct the use of violence.

The creation and preservation of the political realm thus require the restraint of those who use violence, that is, the restraint of the warriors whether we call them the military or the police. The first question we need to ask then is who a warrior is and how he differs from other citizens. In the simplest sense, the warrior is a person who is willing to kill or be killed, someone who is both courageous and cruel. The "and" here is of consid-erable importance. There are obviously those who are courageous but not cruel, just as there are those who are cruel but not courageous. Neither of these are warriors. The former are saints or moral heroes; the latter, crimi-nals or sociopaths. Both types are rare, and their combination is even rarer.

The archetypal warrior in the European tradition is Achilles. He is a nat-urally ferocious man—a lover of discord, as Agamemnon correctly describes him—who longs above all else for glory on the battlefield.[6] He believes he will attain immortal fame by being foremost in slaughtering enemies. While we are likely to see him as a psychopath, the Greeks saw him as something superhuman, the manifestation of a primal cosmological power.

What distinguishes Achilles from other humans is the character of his *eros*, his love or drive. Humans as they appear in the *Iliad* are pulled toward one of the three human goods: power, honor, or pleasure. The story of the *Il-iad* focuses on Achilles' monomaniacal pursuit of honor, which is contrasted to Agamemnon's pursuit of power and Paris' pursuit of sensual pleasure. The warrior, as seen through this lens, is possessed by the desire for honor and driven mad, overcome by rage, when it is denied him. This is no accident. Rage is a particular danger for the warrior because it is rage that makes him ferocious, and that is thus the source of his prowess. In this respect Achilles is quite different than Hector who "learned to be courageous." One cannot learn to be cruel, hard, or unrelenting without a natural ferocity. Hector thus can never equal Achilles. Such ferocity, however, is a great danger because it can turn into rage with one's fellows. While the warrior is necessary, he is thus also a constant danger to the community. Indeed, in the *Iliad* the misdirected ferocity of Achilles is the source of the disaster that shatters the community, bringing "countless ills upon the Achaeans."[7]

While the warrior is necessary to political life, he is thus also a source of instability. Indeed, political life can only be sustained when the warrior is convinced that he has been properly recognized. He then is willing to subordinate himself to political authority. The preservation of the political realm thus depends on the warrior recognizing that unless he puts the well-being of his friends or fellow citizens above his own honor, he is merely "a useless weight on the good earth," as a grieving Achilles puts it.[8] The political realm can only come into existence if the warrior uses violence in the service of his friends, family, and fellow citizens, and it is only through his continued support that it can be sustained. The ferocious warrior who turns against the community of friends, family, and fellow citizens destroys the political. He is willing to do whatever is necessary to secure his mastery and recognition as lord. This warrior wants not merely to be recognized as best, but to rule absolutely, that is, to be tyrant, and to gather to himself not merely the supreme honors he deserves but also everything else he desires.

THE LURE OF TYRANNY: PLATO VERSUS THE SOPHISTS FOR THE SOUL OF THE WARRIOR

Perhaps more than any other ancient thinker, Plato recognized the need to restrain the warriors' penchant to use violence to obtain absolute power. He tried to deflect them from this endeavor by convincing them that it was incompatible with their own well-being. He was particularly concerned with this problem because he believed that the excessive freedom of Athenian life produced immoderation and corruption that were the breeding ground of tyranny. Instead of simply pursuing glory, ambitious Athenian warriors would, he feared, be drawn to power and pleasure as well. He was concerned that such men, under the influence of the sophists, would seek to become tyrants.

The *Republic* is centrally focused on the problem posed by the warrior in an open society such as Athens. The dialogue begins with the attempt by Polemarchus (whose name means "war leader") and his roving band of young men/warriors to "capture" Socrates and Glaucon and have them do their bidding by accompanying them to the house of Polemarchus' father Cephalus. Polemarchus tells Socrates that he must either prove stronger or do as they say. This beginning is clearly reminiscent of Thucydides' Melian dialogue in which the Athenians tell the council of Melos that the city must submit to them because it is a law of nature that the strong do as they wish and the weak do as they must. In this respect the problem of the rule of force in the *Republic* is presented as the result of the internalization of the desire for imperium that characterized Athenian foreign policy.

In response to the demand that he prove stronger or obey, Socrates suggests that there is another possibility, that he might persuade them to let him go, but Polemarchus answers that this won't work because they won't listen. This sets the problem that the rest of the dialogue is meant to address—how to convince warriors to act civilly rather than tyrannically, and thus how to make them loyal citizens of the polis rather than wild beasts that want to destroy it. The initial problem in the *Republic* is how to get the warriors to listen, to participate in dialogue with their fellow citizens rather than simply using force to get what they want. One answer to this question is contained in the opening scene when Adeimantus, who is a member of Polemarchus' band but also the brother of Glaucon and the student of Socrates, takes Socrates' remark as a suggestion and seeks to persuade (rather than force) them to come along. Consanguinity and friendship clearly play a role in moderating the warrior's demands or at least in changing his methods, just as they did in the *Iliad*.

While the contending parties reach a modus vivendi as a result of Adeimantus' intervention, this peace is upset when they reach the house of Cephalus by the sophist Thrasymachus (whose name means "wild beast"), who seeks to convince the young men that as warriors they should not just stand with their friends against their enemies but use power to shape the laws to their own advantage. In other words, he claims that warriors should be tyrants. The rest of the *Republic* is essentially Socrates' attempt to convince these young men/warriors that they should not want to be tyrants but instead to voluntarily subject themselves to the rule of reason in the person of a philosopher-king. Plato tries to show in books 2–9 that in the best regime they and all of their fellow warriors would be brought up to accept this notion as a matter of course, but that even if such a regime does not come to be, they can and should still live according to its laws, avoiding the lure of tyranny, and following a philosopher such as Socrates if one is available, or if not at least following his precepts.[9]

The argument in the *Republic* is twofold. The major argument responds to the claim that the life of the thoroughly unjust man, that is, the tyrant, is superior to the life of the just man. To refute this position, Socrates has to show that the life of the just man even when he is thought to be a perfect villain is more choice-worthy than the life of the tyrant when he is mistakenly honored as the city's greatest benefactor. The second argument, presented as an analogy supporting the first, lays out the structures of the best regime, a true comm*unity* in which the people as a whole and the warriors in particular are happier than in any other city.

This argument assumes that there are three goods humans strive for—pleasure, honor, and wisdom. Plato knows that many men strive for power and wealth but treats them as merely instrumental to the pursuit of the primary goods. Thrasymachus, Glaucon, and Adeimantus suggest that spirited men should strive for power so that they can enjoy all the goods. In countering this argument, Socrates has to show that spirited men do not want all the goods but only those that will make them happy. He thus argues, perhaps with Achilles in mind, that spirited men/warriors need honor above all other things, friendship in the community of like-minded individuals, plus a modicum of wisdom and pleasure added in order to be happy. He also demonstrates that power is not choice-worthy because it is a burden rather than a benefit. He thus believes he has proven that the warriors' happiness will be better served by being ruled by philosophy rather than being tyrants.

This argument in the *Republic* rests on a number of problematic assumptions. The first is the notion that each human being has a specific natural ability and consequently a specific nature that is preeminently satisfied by just one of the primary goods. This becomes the basis for the caste system in the ideal city (rooted in or at least reinforced by the noble lie). The second is the idea that it is possible to determine what an individual's nature is at a relatively young age. The third is that the rulers of the city can master and direct *eros* in ways that will avoid the conflict over specific sexual objects such as that in the *Iliad*. The fourth is that the rulers can organize reproduction to overcome the love of and preference for one's own offspring. The fifth is that the warriors will be content with being housed and fed at public expense and will not try to accumulate private wealth. And finally, the sixth is that the philosopher will be able to determine who must marry whom in order to sustain the caste system, and to produce other philosophers who can do the same.

Plato recognizes that these assumptions are at best problematic. This is evident in the account Socrates gives of the decline of the regime in books 8 and 9, where it becomes clear that the warriors are not naturally attracted to a single good but choose an ever greater assortment of goods including excessive honor, unlimited wealth, every available pleasure, and finally all good things whatsoever. Hidden in this account is the recognition that the attraction to tyranny is powerful among the warriors and can only be overcome by equally powerful restraints. There are, of course, multiple structural constraints upon the warriors, but the success of the regime depends finally on its system of education.

The goal of the educational system in the *Republic* is to soften the warrior class. It is true that warriors are chosen because they are spirited, but being spirited does not mean that they have to be ferocious, and thus liable to the kind of rage that burst forth so disastrously in Achilles. Plato's warriors do not fight merely because they are filled with an unbearable passion that seeks release in battle but because they have the right opinion about what is terrible, fearing shame more than death, and desiring fame or glory more than pleasure or wisdom. Their courage is thus preeminently rational and not passionate. In this respect they are an amalgam of Achilles who was made strong and hard by "Zeus's ordinance" and Hector who "learned to be courageous." Plato's warriors are thus chosen because of their disposition, but they are formed and constrained by their education.

The *Iliad* sought to demonstrate that the warrior is caught in a contradiction between the love of his friends and his demand to be honored above them. Achilles thus inevitably comes to a tragic end. In the long run, he cannot sustain friendships and thus cannot be a fellow citizen. Plato agrees this is a problem, but argues that a regime can be constructed that will allow warriors to attain honor and enjoy perfect friendship with their fellows, if they give up political power, wealth, the exclusive right to particular sexual partners, and offspring that they recognize as their own, that is, if they give up all of the goods that were the source of conflict in the *Iliad*.

Within the *Republic* this choice is made more likely by the educational system that produces not freely thinking individuals but "noble dogs," who do good to friends and harm to enemies, and are indifferent to their sexual partners, wealth, and offspring. This educational system is supplemented by a social system that makes the accumulation of wealth, women, and offspring impossible. In contrast to the Spartan system, the system of education in the *Republic* emphasizes training in music and de-emphasizes physical training or gymnastic. The goal is not to heighten ferocity but to temper it. The warrior in this sense will not be driven by the need to vent his innate ferocity but by a rational desire for his own happiness. This is markedly in contrast to the Spartan goal of making the citizen as ferocious (and yet as obedient) as possible.

The model of a warrior is presented to children in poetic depictions of the gods, the demigods, and human heroes, sanitized to constrain and direct the imagination of the proto-warrior to the proper objects. In contrast to the work of Homer and Hesiod, these new works are to portray the world not as tragically broken but as harmonious, governed not by a dark and incomprehensible fate but by a (single) good and rational god who rewards meritorious behavior and punishes evil. In this world the warrior is not the epitome of the cosmological tragedy but a particular type of human being who has a role to play in a harmonious political order. At the core of this order is the belief that each individual has a character that falls in one of three classes and that each has an employment and reward suitable to his or her nature. That all of these teachings are intended to resist the natural tendency of the warrior to desire and appropriate all things is evident in the fact that the ultimate rule for the censors is that they never allow anyone to depict a tyrant as happy.

Importantly, the *Republic* suggests that the philosopher-king is drawn from the warrior class, although he only becomes a philosopher by means of a higher education in mathematics, astronomy, antistrophe, and above all dialectic. In contrast to any ruler in the *Iliad* or in earlier Greek tragedy, the philosopher-king can thus serve as a true pilot for the ship of state avoiding all of the rocks and obstacles that might send the ship down. Or to use the language of the *Statesman*, he is the master weaver who combines all of the threads of society into one single if elaborate fabric.

The possibility of founding and maintaining the best regime thus depends on the existence of the philosopher-king. However, the philosopher-king must die, and as hard as he may try to produce a successor out of the available human material, he will not always succeed. The best regime thus remains subject to the laws of time and must perish, giving rise to a series of regimes that tend ever more toward tyranny.

As disheartening as the inevitable decline of the best regime may be, it is the failure of this utopian project that underpins the practical moral project that is the immediate goal of the *Republic*. Plato knew that there could be no decent politics in Athens without warriors who were willing to resist the degeneration of democracy into tyranny. The goal of the *Republic* and of the Academy was thus not just to produce the best regime—a difficult task heavily dependent on accident or divine intervention. Rather Plato hoped to sustain the political community by preventing its further decline into tyranny. Plato's efforts (recounted in the *Seventh Letter*) to turn Dionysus of Syracuse in a less tyrannical direction, and the efforts of Plato's student Dion to overthrow Dionysus (recounted in Plutarch's *Life of Dion*) testify to these purposes.

In his efforts to convince the warrior classes to avoid tyranny, Plato never suggests that war or warriors could or should be eliminated. Indeed, while he seeks to reduce the likelihood of war by reducing excessive consumption and production, and by limiting contact with other cities, he recognizes that warriors will be needed even in the best regime, and the account of the development of the philosopher in book 7 suggests that he comes out of the warrior class and is intimately acquainted with war-making. Finally, insofar as the philosopher also serves as king and has to manage the state, he must lead the army as well. Thus, for Plato the philosopher must be harder than we might imagine, experienced in war and war-making, and able to use and command the use of violent force.

NIETZSCHE'S INTERPRETATION OF PLATO

Nietzsche was engaged with Plato throughout his creative life. In the early 1870s, he gave a course on Plato and the Platonic dialogues, and also dealt with Plato in a course on Greek literature. In his published works and *Nachlass*, there are more than 350 references to Plato. In fact it would not be an exaggeration to say that among philosophers Plato is Nietzsche's chief antagonist. He admits as much near the end of his productive life, referring in a note to his "old antipathy to Plato," whom he sees as a modern soul corrupting the thought of antiquity (*NL*, KGW VII 2:19).

In the midst of ancient philosophy, he sees Plato as the first syncretistic thinker, combining his early attraction to Heracleiteanism with Socratism, and in his later studies both with Parmenides and the Eleatics. His bookish syncretism is in stark contrast to the earlier philosophers who all exemplified a particular type of life (*PP*, KGW II 4:212–14; 4:43). For this reason he characteristically speaks of pre-Platonic philosophy rather than pre-Socratic thought. Indeed, he is clear that Plato is not a pure Socratic, contrary to the predominant view of his (and our) time (*Pl*, KGW II 4:45). Plato in his view was driven by two impulses: the first was a fear of death (rather than tyranny, which he seemed willing to tolerate), and the second the desire to be a lawgiver like Solon or Lycurgus (*Pl*, KGW II 4:45–48, 54).[10] Here Nietzsche makes a great deal out of Plato's visits to Syracuse and of the political activity originating from the Academy, particularly that of Dion and his followers. Nietzsche even declares that Plato was first and foremost a political agitator (*Pl*, KGW II 4:9).

Plato's written work in Nietzsche's view was prosaic. He believes that the dramatic qualities of the dialogues have been vastly overrated in modern times (*Pl*, KGW II 4:161). In fact, in his view the dialogues are inferior to and principally a propaedeutic for Plato's oral teaching in the Academy. The focus of Plato's teaching was not systematic but dialectical (*GL*, KGW II 5:198) and aimed only at a rational education. He denigrated the study of art and culture, including Homer and the cultic life of the ancient world that Nietzsche saw as the ground of human community (*NL*, KGW II 4:55, 76, 141, 151, 179; *NL*, KGW VII 2:17). Indeed, Plato in Nietzsche's view sought to drive artists out of the state (*NL*, KGW III 3:8–17). He relied entirely on dialectic to promote what is essentially a moral and not a political teaching (*PP*, KGW II 4:354). He thus puts the idea of the good above being, and sees the beautiful, which otherwise was so predominant for the Greeks, as merely a reflection of the good (*Pl*, KGW II 4:162–63). That said, Nietzsche sees Plato's statesman as a practical artist who aims at the harmony of the state, but he does so only by a strict separation of castes that eliminates the tension and agonism that was essential to Greek political life (*Pl*, KGW II 4:137). At his core, Plato like his Christian successors hated the actual, sensual world, its passions, and antagonisms and preferred the transcendent world of the ideas (*Pl*, KGW II 4:152, 155). He was thus more interested in morality and theology than in art and politics and had the creation of a caste of the good and the just who would preserve this morality as his ultimate political aim (*NL*, KGW VII 2:35).

Nietzsche's own thought, which resembles that of Plato in many ways, seeks to undo the changes that Plato initiated that sought to resolve the contradictions in tragic culture. Nietzsche's goal, as we have seen above, is an amalgamation of the conceptualism of Socrates and Plato with the poetic musical thought of the dramatists and philosophers of the tragic age.

OF LIONS AND SUPERMEN: NIETZSCHE'S WARRIORS

In contrast to Plato, who lived in a period of constant warfare, Nietzsche lived during an extended period of European peace. Like Plato (and unlike almost all other philosophers from the death of Marcus Aurelius to his own time), he served in the military.[11] While he bemoaned the waste of human life in combat, he was perhaps more concerned that the Prussian victory had left Germany culturally destitute (*UM*, KGW III 1:155–60; *TI*, KGW VI 3:100–104). He saw the victory as the result of technical superiority in the organization of men and material and not as the result of a higher, more heroic culture that would help to rejuvenate the German spirit.

As we have seen above, from his earliest days, Nietzsche was concerned with German cultural decline. The outward forms of this decline included a preference for democracy over aristocracy, the spread of the belief that work had value, a longing for world peace, the degeneration of art and music into disingenuous spectacle, the increasing dominance of a morality of pity, and a hypersensitivity to suffering. He was convinced that this decline, which had begun with Plato and that found its foremost expression in Christianity, had brought Europe to the verge of total collapse.

As desperate as he believed things were, Nietzsche was not without hope. Indeed, he believed that the coming collapse would also wipe clean the cultural horizon so that a new beginning would be possible (*GS*, KGW V 2:253–56). The role of war and the warrior in Nietzsche's thought is bound up with this development. In order to understand this, however, we need to examine the grounds for Nietzsche's conviction that such a crisis was at hand, the nature of this crisis, and what he believed was necessary to overcome it.

As we have seen, for Nietzsche man is a willing being, not a mind or a soul but a self or body consisting of a multiplicity of conflicting passions, which are expressions of drives or instincts that are at the bottom all moments of a world-will or cosmological force that Nietzsche calls the will to power. This world-will is the constant struggle among all things for dominance and for self-overcoming. Humans experience this will as the inner struggle of competing passions, and become more powerful as their particular passions are all organized toward a specific goal, that is, when directed by a dominant passion. Being powerful thus is the result of organizing oneself hierarchically.

Weakness and degeneration by contrast are the result of the disintegration and collapse of such a hierarchy. Nietzsche believed that the crisis that he saw afflicting European civilization was the result of the breakdown of the long-standing psychic and social order that had shaped European humanity. He believed that the highest values, which derived from the Platonic and Christian vision of a good and rational God, were devaluing themselves, and as a result, the entire moral and political system would thus inevitably collapse.

With the destruction of the prevailing hierarchy, humans both individually and collectively would be pulled in conflicting directions by competing desires. Nietzsche believed such a decline was reflected in the development of liberal democracy and commercial society that legitimated and sought to satisfy every conceivable desire. Freedom in this context means the absence of any external or internal impediment to one's momentary desires. Humans in democratic and commercial societies recognize nothing as intrinsically more valuable than anything else, and are thus increasingly unable to subordinate *any* passion or desire. Since power and strength arise from such subordination, humanity becomes decisively weaker, producing in the end the last man.

The other possibility, which Nietzsche himself espouses, is an ascent from present-day decadence to the *Übermensch*, the titanic figure that haunts his later works. This possibility, however, is distant and can only be achieved by arduous struggle. With the advent of nihilism, human beings are left in limbo, no longer believers but also unable to believe in themselves or in a superhuman possibility. In *Zarathustra* Nietzsche describes a path through a series of stages, with the camel transformed first into a lion, the lion into a child, and the child finally into the *Übermensch*. According to Nietzsche, this is the only way to this goal. No leap of the imagination or faith can traverse the great gulf that separates us from the *Übermensch*. While it is only a short way from the camel to the last man, the path to the *Übermensch* requires not just a new way of thinking but a new way of being, and that means the reformation of the body, or the self and the passions.

Each new stage of human existence is possible only on the basis of the establishment of a different hierarchy of the passions and drives, that is, only on the basis of a *physiological* change in the nature of the human. A new hierarchy thus can only be established as the result of a new disciplining of the passions, and this in Nietzsche's view requires violence and war.[12] The path to the *Übermensch* for Nietzsche is thus open only to warriors.

The first step on this path is thus the emergence of leonine spirits who reject and negate the old values that sustain the existing world. While many might find this prospect horrifying, Nietzsche is less concerned about the coming carnage and looks instead to the future with a new cheerfulness that grows out of his sense of liberation (*GS*, KGW V 2:253–56). His disgust with late nineteenth-century Europe, with the idea of human dignity and the value of labor—forms of slave morality—is profound, and he sees its destruction and the resulting chaos as the basis for a new manliness, which will produce a humanity hardened mentally, physically, and morally. In reflecting on the character on which he believes these new higher men should model themselves, he specifically points to the heroes of the Norse sagas, whom he praises for their hard-heartedness (*BGE*, KGW VI 2:220). Out of these warriors will grow a new aristocracy, repeating a process Nietzsche believes has occurred many times before.

How this process will unfold and transform these warriors into an aristocracy is not something that Nietzsche (in contrast to Plato) considers in any detail. He does not develop a system of education or training for this elite although he assumes they will be transformed and acculturated in some manner. That music and perhaps dramatic festivals will play a role seems certain but what this role will be and how it will be concretely achieved is not something that Nietzsche laid out or to be fair even considered. He was much more interested in convincing his contemporaries to choose the path that he believed led to such an aristocracy rather than with detailing how this aristocracy should be forged, trained, and ennobled.

It is out of this aristocracy that Nietzsche believes first the child and then the *Übermensch* will arise (Z, KGW VI 1:98), but even here he remains quite vague about the nature of the process. The first stage in this process is some kind of forgetfulness in which the lion spirit (or perhaps his descendants?) regains the innocence of the child, his psychological freedom from the past. As we have seen, such forgetfulness, however, is not enough. Forgetfulness frees us from the psychological burden of the past and allows us to act *as if* we were willing spontaneously and creatively. Despite the attractiveness of such a restored innocence, Nietzsche came to realize that the hope for such a forgetting is illusory, and that a more profound solution was needed. To free oneself from the past and the spirit of revenge, it was necessary that it be *affirmed*. As we have seen, this is the goal of Nietzsche's doctrine of the eternal recurrence. To affirm this doctrine, it is necessary to will all things. This is what Nietzsche calls *amor fati*. But how this doctrine will be imparted and willed to produce such an *amor fati* remains quite vague.

Moreover, while the end of Nietzsche's project is the *Übermensch*, he never describes this Promethean being. The *Übermensch*, he claims, will be to man as man is to the ape (Z, KGW VI 1:8). The implication is that we can no more imagine the character of his existence than the ape could imagine ours. Nietzsche thus describes him only obliquely and allusively. In *Zarathustra* he is called the vintager with the diamond knife for whom only future songs will find names (Z, KGW VI 1:276). In *Beyond Good and Evil*, he is the genius of the heart who wants man stronger, more evil, more profound, and more beautiful (KGW VI 2:247–49). In the works of 1888, he is Dionysus or *Dionysos Philosophos*. In his late notes, he is characterized as an artist and a tyrant and Caesar with the soul of Christ (*NL*, KGW VII 2:289). What distinguishes the *Übermensch* is that he is able and willing to create and thus also to destroy on a monumental scale. He can and does use violence but does so only positively and creatively. He is free from the spirit of revenge and loves all that has been or will be. He is hard and pitiless but not intentionally cruel. He is a warrior but also an artist, who will lead humanity not toward some abstract or universal good but toward a goal determined by his dominate passion. The explicit character of his relation to others and to the warrior aristocracy in particular is never spelled out. He remains a distant promise, and the image of this being serves in part as a siren song calling to those who despair in the midst of bourgeois society to throw themselves into the stream and risk death in pursuit of something higher. And there is, of course, no guarantee that such a goal can actually be achieved or that it is even possible.

NIETZSCHE CONTRA PLATO

In his late thought, Nietzsche repeatedly describes himself as an implacable enemy of Christianity, which he calls "Platonism for the people." Many Nietzsche scholars and postmodernists accept this claim unquestioningly. There is reason to doubt, however, that it is true. Nietzsche recognizes that there are crucial differences between the thought of Plato and Christianity. He claims that Plato was a noble young Greek seduced by Socrates into questioning and criticizing the master morality of his time. Even if this were true, it would not prove that Plato (or Socrates) was a manifestation of the slave revolt in morals Nietzsche sees at the heart of Christianity. Plato may seek to soften or temper the warrior or master morality exemplified in the *Iliad* and manifest in the Peloponnesian War, but tempering the warrior culture is not the same as abandoning, reversing, or overthrowing it. Warriors play a decisive role in Plato's ideal regime and the philosopher-king himself comes from the warrior class and not from a class of priests, craftsmen, or farmers. In the *Republic*, the meek do not inherit the earth. To be sure, the meek are not viciously abused and indeed are reasonably well off by comparison to the actual regimes of Plato's time, but they do not rule and they are not models for a virtuous or pious life. Plato's ideal regime may be less tyrannical and more paternalistic than typical Greek states, but it is still well within the parameters of what Nietzsche calls master morality. Even if one assumes that Plato's real goal was not to realize the ideal regime but only to prevent a slide into the worst regime, that is, into tyranny, he still cannot be counted as favoring the slaves or lower classes. He does not call upon craftsmen and farmers to rise up in revolution or to martyr themselves nor does he suggest that the warriors should feel guilty for their actions. Moreover, while he suggests Greeks ought not be enslaved, he does not suggest that slavery be abolished. He does not try to convince the young men/warriors that tyranny is morally wrong because of the harm it does to others but suggests it is bad choice because of the harm it does to tyrants. Tyranny thus will not make them happy in this world and may be punished in the afterlife.

Nietzsche's critique is thus distorted by his conflation of Plato's moral teaching and Christianity. His characterization of Christianity as "Platonism for the people" is true as far as it goes, but he also tries to reverse this claim, effectively arguing that Platonism is Christianity for the elite or at least for intellectuals. Even if we accept Nietzsche's portrayal of Socrates in *Twilight* as someone for whom life was a disease for which death was a cure, there is no indication that Nietzsche thought that Socrates or Plato were seeking revenge against the warrior class (*TI*, KGW VI 3:67). It is not the strong who are punished and the weak who are rewarded in the Myth of Er. Rather, the strong who are philosophic are rewarded, and the strong who are tyrannical are punished.

Beneath the apparent differences between Plato and Nietzsche on the question of the role of war and warriors, there are surprising convergences that become visible when we focus on the context of their arguments. In a world dominated by war and warriors, in pursuit of empire and tyranny, Plato sought to soften and civilize warriors in order to produce an aristocracy and incorporate them within the community. His goal was not to turn them into pacifists but into a ruling class of dependable citizens led by the philosopher-king, a man of genius. Nietzsche, by contrast, argues we must encourage martial passions and harden the strongest to produce a warrior class. He believes that only war can bring this about. He does not love violence but sees it as inevitable and believes it will make it possible to avoid the degeneration of humanity into a herd of consumers seeking the immediate satisfaction of their momentary desires. While this seems to be diametrically opposed to Plato, Nietzsche is not speaking to fourth-century Greeks but to nineteenth-century Europeans, not to a Hellenistic world dominated by hardened warriors whose deepest desire was to dominate others but to a still largely Christian Europe dominated by producers and consumers who dream of peace, prosperity, and commodious living. Thus, while there would undoubtedly be many differences between Nietzsche's new warrior aristocracy and the humanized warrior elite of Plato, these differences might not be as profound as we commonly assume.

Nietzsche does not simply want to produce a race of warriors on the model of Achilles. Such warriors are necessary, but he imagines that they will ultimately be civilized. However, what is missing in his thought is any account of how this will occur, that is, an account of the institutional structures and system of education to civilize these "blond beasts."[13] He is overwhelmingly concerned with convincing young men to become warriors rather than clerks or shopkeepers, but says very little about what should happen to them after that. He is hopeful for the future because he believes the warriors who it brings into being will be the source of a new aristocracy. What he does not do is explain how this transition will take place. Even this aristocracy, however, is not his ultimate goal. It too is merely a means. His ultimate goal is to create an *Übermensch* who is free from the spirit of revenge, whose violence will not be merely reactive, but he does not explain how violence can become creative. He sets out an awe-inspiring goal for humanity, but it is surprisingly lacking in particulars. Moreover, he does not even begin to explain concretely how humanity can reach this goal, or even whether it can.

Nietzsche does expect his warriors to sacrifice themselves to produce the *Übermensch*, but are they likely to do so? Nietzsche tries to inspire his readers, and to impart to their task a missionary zeal, but is there any reason to think that such motivation can be successful in the long run? Moral, religious, or aesthetic appeals can have immense short-term effects, but they have never ultimately been successful unless they are institutionalized and strengthened by a system of training and education that gives people more immediate incentives to pursue long-term goals. In the absence of these, even the most magnificent goals are soon set aside. Are Nietzsche's warriors then likely to pursue the distant *Übermensch* in the absence of such incentives, or will they follow the path almost all warrior aristocracies have followed in the past toward self-aggrandizement, the accumulation of property and sexual objects, the insistence on honor, and the preferential treatment of their offspring? There are certainly no institutional structures that Nietzsche considers to prevent such a development, and very little in his minimalist account of a future educational system that would offer any hope of redirecting traditional aristocratic behavior.

For these purposes Nietzsche seems to rely almost entirely on the coercive and persuasive force of his *Übermensch*, the artist-tyrant of the future, much as Plato does on his philosopher-king. As part Caesar, part Christ, something of Goethe, a bit of Napoleon, a piece of Aeschylus, a sprinkling of Pericles, and last but certainly not least a dash of Socrates or Heracleitus, the *Übermensch* is certainly magnificent. Indeed, the picture of this figure that Nietzsche paints has engaged the imagination of readers for more than a century, but is such a being possible? And even if such a being is possible, is he likely to come into existence? And if he does, is such an event ever likely to be repeated? Is Nietzsche's *Übermensch* any more likely than Plato's philosopher-king?

Nietzsche asserted in an early, unpublished work, "The Greek State," that the sole reason ordinary humanity is justified is the production of the genius. While in his middle period he seems to have adopted a stance more favorable to the many, in his late thought he seems to have been willing to sacrifice everything in the hope that such a genius might be produced. Nietzsche foresaw an age of war and hope for a hardened warrior elite. Plato lived in such a world and believed that a warrior elite left to its own devices produced only the brutal tyranny spelled out in the Melian dialogue and evident in many cities of his time. Plato, like Nietzsche, hoped to produce a genius and hoped that he would rule over a city, but he recognized, as Nietzsche perhaps did not, that hortatory rhetoric alone would not make this happen. Indeed, such rhetoric was likely only to produce the rule of violence as warriors became tyrants rather than forming a political community in which they could play a leading role. While Nietzsche saw the parallels between Plato's *Republic* and his own ideas, he seems so closely to have identified Plato with Christianity that he was unable to learn the lessons that Plato had to teach. Nietzsche thus never formulated a notion of the political and remained like many of his followers wedded to the notion that all social interaction is merely the exercise of power and domination.[14]

Nietzsche is certainly not useless to those who would like to use his thought in an effort to bolster liberal or democratic theory, but in attempting to do so, it is crucial to recognize that he was not a friend of liberalism or democracy and that especially in his late thought he increasingly turned toward a more apocalyptic vision of the future that was surprisingly vague in its details and willing to tolerate unprecedented war and destruction in the hope of overcoming nihilism and establishing a more exalted form of existence.

CONCLUSION

What Remains

The great work that Nietzsche imagined would encapsulate and complete his final teaching and would bring about an apocalyptic revaluation of all values was never completed. In early January of 1889, after at least a month of warning signs in both his letters and behavior, Nietzsche suffered at catastrophic psychic break from which he never recovered. The cause of this break and his increasing descent into the mental darkness and physical paralysis that led to his death in 1900 has never been definitively determined. Initially there was a suspicion that the cause was syphilitic. However, this diagnosis, which was championed in the early twentieth century by the notorious Dr. Paul Julius Möbius, has been called into question and other more plausible diagnoses suggested. Perhaps the most convincing is the suspicion that Nietzsche suffered from a slowly growing right-sided retro-orbital meningioma, which would not only explain his break and subsequent decline, but also his long-standing migraines and right-eye blindness.[1] All of these diagnoses, however, are speculations based on reported symptoms and not physical evidence. Some have speculated that there may have been a congenital condition involved since his father also suffered a similar although more sudden collapse, but such a connection is unlikely since his father almost certainly died of a stroke. If the cause of his collapse was a medical condition, then the only question of interest is when his decline began and how it impacted his thinking. In particular one would then have to ask what portion of his later work should be counted as the product of an unbalanced mind, and how this affects our notion of his final teaching. Few doubts on this score have been raised about *Zarathustra*, *Beyond Good and Evil*, or *The Genealogy of Morals*. Those who want to discount his works as the products of incipient madness are much more likely to focus on the works of 1888. However, despite Nietzsche's at times extravagant claims in these last works, there are good reasons to believe that his thinking in these works was generally sound. In my reading, for example, there is a surprising disparity between Nietzsche's published works of this period, which seem well reasoned, and a number of his letters, which at times seem excessive and unbalanced. The published work in which his mental stability seems most in doubt is *Ecce Homo*. After all, he does suggest there that he is destiny and compares himself to Christ. While this undoubtedly seems extravagant to the contemporary reader, viewed in the context of the nineteenth century, such claims are less surprising. Indeed Napoleon and Wagner made similar claims, and Nietzsche's claims were at least partially borne out by his impact on the twentieth century.[2] I do not mean to assert that Nietzsche was correct in his claims, only to suggest that they should not be dismissed as the ravings of a madman.

Many of Nietzsche's friends felt that his letters during the last half of 1888 reflected a vastly inflated sense of his own worth. In the last weeks before his breakdown, he even began to suggest that he occupied a quasi-divine status, and in his last letters, he signed himself either Dionysus or the Crucified. While many have seen these behaviors as signs of a clinical megalomania, Klossowski, among others, confronts us with a much more troubling possibility, deriving from his observation that Nietzsche's "delirium" is very difficult to distinguish from an extraordinary lucidity about his own actual importance in the history of the West.[3] Thus, while we must not overlook the signs of Nietzsche's growing imbalance, his work is so brilliant and so shockingly prescient that it is hard to escape the suspicion that perhaps his "madness" was in fact the lucidity of an ultimate genius peering fearlessly into an abysmal reality that the rest of us happily paper over with our illusions.

If for a moment we set aside the question of contingent reasons that may explain why Nietzsche did not finish the magnum opus that was to be the capstone of his final teaching, we can confront a philosophically more interesting question: Could Nietzsche, or for that matter anyone, have completed this work and/or have definitively spelled out his final teaching?

There can be no doubt that for a number of years Nietzsche was convinced that he could and indeed would produce such a work. Moreover, there can also be no doubt that in the midst of extraordinary pain, suffering, and isolation he put himself under tremendous pressure to actually do so. He speaks of this not merely in his late published works but repeatedly in his letters and notes. This pressure is clearly bound up with his sense of responsibility for what he took to be his Promethean task as the teacher of the doctrine of the eternal recurrence, a teaching that he was convinced would initiate an apocalyptic transformation of the existing world order.

He also clearly recognized the difficulties and dangers of this task. As we have seen, he knew, for example, that Dostoevsky, whose insights as a psychologist he never doubted, believed that such a burden was simply intolerable for human beings. Nietzsche recognized that there were profound psychological obstacles to overcome in order to complete his task, and he knew that many of these were operative in his own case as well. It was for this reason that he characterized pity as Zarathustra's final sin, the last obstacle that he had to overcome in order to proclaim his doctrine of the eternal recurrence.⁴ Nietzsche's studies, especially of the ancient world, however, had led him to believe that pity was not an intrinsic human characteristic (as thinkers from Rousseau to Schopenhauer had suggested) but merely a product of the slave morality propagated by Christianity. He thus believed that it could be overcome by a restoration of something like the master morality of antiquity, or some superhuman hybrid of ancient and Christian morality. Such a new morality, however, could not spring into existence out of nothing but would only come to be as a result of centuries of warfare. While Nietzsche himself may have been too weak, too weighed down by his Christian upbringing, and thus too decadent to bear all of the suffering this entailed, his own failure should not be taken as a dispositive proof that no one could bear it. And if we have learned anything since Nietzsche's descent into madness, it is that cruelty is at least as intrinsic to human beings as pity, and that vast populations can be subordinated to the rule of a pitiless elite hardened by war and revolution.⁵

While the tremendous burden of Nietzsche's task may have prevented his bringing it to a conclusion, there are other more mundane reasons that also might explain his difficulties. Nietzsche himself recognized, for example, that he needed a much better preparation in the natural sciences to explain his ideas of the will to power and the eternal recurrence. Indeed, as Löwith notes, in attempting "to justify his teaching scientifically, Nietzsche dealt with Dühring, Julius Robert Mayer, Boscovich, and probably also Helmholtz, and weighed a plan to study physics and mathematics at the University of Vienna or the University of Paris."⁶ While many have argued that Nietzsche was essentially an existential thinker and that he never intended to give a scientific foundation to his theories, such claims simply are not corroborated by his own actions and plans. Moreover, it is reasonably clear that this lack of scientific training impeded his completion of the magnum opus. Nietzsche's consideration of the will to power in his published works and notes, for example, is cursory and missing almost all of the detail that is so obvious in the sections of his work dealing with antiquity, Christianity, and music where his scholarly training is obvious and extensive. Nietzsche speculates about possibilities but marshals little evidence to back up his claims and does not even develop a plausible account that ties together his often quite brilliant insights and observations. It thus seems possible that while Nietzsche was unable to complete his task, he might have been able to do so if he had had more time to obtain the training he knew that he needed.

This failure to explore the scientific basis of his theories was also in part the result of his decision to devote his time after *Zarathustra* to a critique of the existing order.[7] Indeed, the principal focus of Nietzsche's late work— what he called the No-saying part of his project—was a critique of morality, art, religion, and philosophy, or what Nietzsche more generally referred to as culture. All of this clearly had a practical purpose in preparing for his proclamation of the eternal recurrence and the Great Noon.

Since Nietzsche's immediate goal was to call forth the No-saying and No-doing spirits he believed were immediately necessary, it also may simply be the case that he believed that a more comprehensive articulation of his (anti-)metaphysics could wait until a later time and did not need to be included in his magnum opus. If this was the case, then an actual account of the ontological or cosmological meaning of the will to power and the eternal recurrence might be superfluous and distracting from the task at hand. Thus, Nietzsche may have imagined that he would lay out a fuller account of his final teaching at a later time, or that it would be completed by his "children," who would be better suited to see and develop it. Here it is difficult to separate the philosophical/psychological component of Nietzsche's thought from the rhetorical/practical elements. However, if *The Antichrist* is any indication of what he actually intended for the magnum opus, the rhetorical/practical/destructive element certainly seemed to have moved to the forefront as he worked through the project.

While this may have been the case, it only explains why Nietzsche may have decided not to spell out his final teaching in detail in the magnum opus. What it does not do is show us that such an explanation was impossible. A more powerful reason to question whether Nietzsche could have completed this task has been raised by those, beginning with Heidegger, who have claimed that Nietzsche could never overcome nihilism or metaphysics because his thought was so deeply and irrevocably mired in subjectivity, the final form of metaphysics. Whether this critique hits home, however, depends on what one means by subjectivity.

It is certainly true that Nietzsche's late thought, especially after *Zarathustra*, often seems to be rooted in a psychological subjectivism. In fact, Nietzsche more often characterizes himself as a psychologist than as a philosopher in the works of 1888. This subjectivism is also evident in his multiple autobiographical investigations during this period. On the surface, his thought thus seems to be subjectivistic in a narrow sense, apparently relying on reflection to come to terms with the self and through the self with the world. It thus might seem that he operates within the horizon of the Cartesian notion of the self as a *res cogitans* although perhaps deepened by investigation of the subconscious realm by earlier Romantics. If this is the way one conceives of subjectivity, however, Nietzsche cannot properly be characterized as falling within its horizons. Nietzsche rejects the insubstantial Cartesian self and the later modern notion that manifests itself most fully in Hegel's claim that perfect self-knowledge is possible through a retrospective introspection. As we saw above, Nietzsche begins *The Genealogy of Morals* with the assertion that men of knowledge are essentially unknown to themselves. Subjectivity in this narrow sense is an illusion for Nietzsche. We can know very little by looking into ourselves, since most of our being is inaccessible to introspection and most of what we do see is illusory. Reflection and consciousness for Nietzsche are thus generally limited sources of knowledge and are prey to self-deception.

When Nietzsche describes himself as a psychologist, what he claims to be practicing is more akin to what we would call anthropology, that is, to an investigation of the body or self, which he imagines to be a conflicting struggle of passions and affects for dominance set in an ethnographic context. In this respect, he is much more closely tied to the thinking of the more empirical tradition of modern thought that begins with Bacon and Hobbes and that focuses less on the thinking self than on the body that thinks, less on reflection than on a reading of the struggle of one's own passions, and less on free will or action and more on the ways in which our behavior is determined by specific passions, drives, and instincts. It is thus not surprising that he focuses on English psychologists at the beginning of *The Genealogy of Morals*. Even here though, the similarities go only so far. He emphasizes, for example, the enormous difficulty we have in completing the task that Hobbes sets out that each individual read himself. In his view this is always extremely difficult and depends on the practice of the *Entlarvungspsychologie* that he developed over a long period of time in his middle period and that he was only able to develop, he claims, as a result of the intense pain and suffering he had to endure that forced him to abandon all of his illusions about himself.

While this more objective approach to self-understanding may free Nietzsche from the suspicion of being ensnared in a narrow notion of subjectivity, it does not mean that his thought is not subjectivistic in a larger sense, which, beginning with Heidegger, is imagined to include both subject and object and to be bound up with the larger modern effort to make humanity master and possessor of nature through the development of technology. What is crucial to subjectivity understood in this way is establishing human being (and not God) as the ground of all things. From this perspective Nietzsche does fall within the horizon of a metaphysics of subjectivity that is rooted in the notion of a self-positing or self-making self or will. As I have shown elsewhere, Nietzsche stands in a tradition that extends back from Schopenhauer and Fichte to Descartes, and nominalist theology.[8] Humans in this sense are not *res cogitans* but *res volens*, not thinking things but willing things, and they establish themselves not by the self-knowledge but by self-positing, or self-willing. While Nietzsche's thought may fall within this broader notion of subjectivity, even here it is important to distinguish the respect in which this is true. Nietzsche certainly does not believe in the will in the sense that most of us use the term in ordinary language. He denies, for example, that a free or autonomous will exists. The will that is causal in his view is the world-will or will to power that is one with the motion of all things as determined and delimited by the eternal recurrence. To will is then to be one with this process, to be as Nietzsche characterized himself, the last disciple of the god of the eternal recurrence, Dionysus, and live according to the doctrine of *amor fati*. Now, insofar as Nietzsche actually imagines the author of this will to be a who, that is, an anthropomorphic god, he is still thinking in subjectivistic and anthropomorphic terms, that is, he is imagining the entire motion of the cosmos to be the consequence of a free divine will akin to the divine will that nominalist and voluntarist Christians (including Luther) imagined to characterize their God. Of course, it is not at all clear how we should understand his references to Dionysus. In *The Birth of Tragedy*, the name Dionysus is only an illusory Apollinian image for what he there sometimes calls the contradictory primordial one or primordial music. Later he concludes that this primordial heart of things can have no name. We may need to give it a name to endure our insight into it, but it is ultimately overpowering, akin to what Kant called the sublime or what Heidegger (commenting on Sophocles) later called *to deinon* (the uncanny or overpowering) or *to deinataton* (the most uncanny or overpowering). Thus while Nietzsche may fall within the metaphysics of subjectivity in the broadest sense, this is not typically what scholars have in mind who seek to criticize him on this score. What is clear if one accepts this interpretation, however, is that Nietzsche's alternative to the nihilism he sees as the product of a rationalist Christianity is itself deeply immersed in an alternative version of Christianity, as I have argued at great length in my *Nihilism before Nietzsche*.[9] While Nietzsche thus may not be able to offer as radical an alternative to metaphysics (or to Christianity) as many of his successors believe is necessary, it does not follow that his final teaching is necessarily either incoherent or inconsistent. And it thus does not mean that his final teaching could not have been completed.

What is immensely apparent from the examination of Nietzsche's notes and plans, however, is that Nietzsche himself was having great difficulties in settling on a plan for the magnum opus that made sense to him. The complexity and the variety of his ideas, his concerns about style and literary/poetic/musical form, his hopes to avoid his previous failure to find an audience, his doubts that he could speak definitively about some of the most important topics he needed to treat, his worries that the work would fall prey to the censors, and above all his concern about the practical effects of his teaching—all impeded the completion of the work. With great joy he announced the completion of *The Antichrist* to his publisher and friends as the first book of the *Revaluation* in the fall of 1888, to be soon followed, he assured them, by the remaining books, but as he further considered the matter in the last few days of 1888 or early January 1889, he seems to have decided that *The Antichrist* was the *Revaluation* in its entirety and thus to have abandoned the project altogether.

What are we to make of this fact? This is a complicated question. The proximity of this decision to his collapse makes it very difficult to determine whether this decision was the product of a rational mind or of his growing mental instability. During this very late period, his behavior and letters were extremely erratic. Even if we discount mental instability, it may still be the case that in the back and forth of his plans he actually did decide to give up on the project, but might very well have changed his mind had he had the time and the capacity to reconsider his decision. He had certainly changed his mind on such issues many times before. He also may have decided to conclude the magnum opus with *The Antichrist* and intended to present this teaching of the eternal recurrence in a different form. Indeed, even if he had given up on his magnum opus, his letters and notes clearly indicate that he had not given up on this final teaching or the (anti-)metaphysics at its heart.

QUESTIONS

For all of its magnificence, what remained of Nietzsche's final teaching after he plunged into insanity in early January 1889 was unequal to the overpowering vision that inspired him that August day in 1881 by the shores of Lake Silvaplana. That said, we cannot overlook the fact that even in its unfinished state his teaching has been one of the most compelling intellectual forces in the modern world during the last 125 years. Ironically, the very incompleteness of the project may have contributed to its impact. His stunning insights have inspired many of his readers, but the incompleteness of the project has also allowed them to use his ideas for their own ends, to carry out projects that were often at odds with Nietzsche's own goals. This helps to explain the fact that he has been an inspiration and a guide to amazingly diverse thinkers and movements including modernists, antimodernists, postmodernists, imperialists, postcolonialists, anarchists, socialists, Fascists, nationalists, Nazis, Zionists, futurists, critical theorists, Dadaists, libertarians, and existentialists. It is understandable that all of these different groups and movements have made use of Nietzsche to help them develop their own worldviews, and it would also be absurd to condemn them or accuse them of misusing his thought. Once the products of thought enter the public sphere they cease to belong to their author and can and will be made use of by others for their own purposes. Unfortunately, Nietzsche was betrayed before much of his work reached the public sphere and afterward by a sister who sought to turn him into something he was not, much more in keeping with her anti-Semitism and her own desire for fame.

What I have tried to show, however, is that Nietzsche had his own vision for what his completed final teaching would look like, in part visible in his existing works, and in part drawn from his notes and letters. I have suggested that this teaching constituted something like an (anti-)metaphysics that sought to found a new ontology with the doctrine of the eternal recurrence, a new logic with his notion of music, a new cosmology of the will to power, a new theology that rejected Christianity in favor of Dionysianism, and a new anthropology rooted in his vision of the *Übermensch* and the last man. Some parts of this new (anti-)metaphysics were clearly more fully articulated than others. The least well developed section was ironically the one for which he is perhaps best known, the will to power. I have suggested this was in part because he lacked and did not have time to obtain the scientific training he recognized was necessary to develop this portion of his teaching more fully.[10] The eternal recurrence as well remains underexplained, in large part, because Nietzsche was convinced its proclamation would be so important and so devastating that it would shake Europe to its core and bring about a revaluation of all values. It thus was meant to be the final chapter of the never-completed magnum opus, lighting a spark that he believed would transform the modern world.

In sketching out this final teaching, I certainly do not mean to endorse it, for despite all its magnificence and the incomparable artistry with which Nietzsche develops his arguments, the teaching rests on a number of problematic assumptions and urges us to follow an extraordinarily dangerous path to what well might be a merely illusory destination.

The fundamental assumption of Nietzsche's final teaching is that God is dead. When Nietzsche first broaches this idea in *The Gay Science*, a madman appears seeking God and the bystanders jokingly ask if God has emigrated or gone into hiding. These responses, of course, are meant as sarcasm, but they in fact conceal other possibilities that are relevant to evaluating Nietzsche's claims. Christianity does in a sense seem to have emigrated. While it has declined precipitously in Europe, Christianity has continued to thrive, for example, in America and has expanded its reach in much of the world outside of Europe. Even within Europe many thinkers deeply impacted by Nietzsche have pointed to alternative theological possibilities. Heidegger, for example, suggested that nihilism and the death of God were not the consequence of the diminution of man as Nietzsche argued but of the withdrawal of Being.[11] Heidegger draws here on the Christian notion of a hidden god, or *deus absconditus*, that goes back to late medieval nominalism and the mysticism of thinkers such as Meister Eckhart. Seen in this way, the suggestion that God has gone into hiding seems less far-fetched. Similar theological positions that take into account the death or withdrawal of God have also been defended by Thomas Altizer and Jean-Luc Marion among others.[12] Even within the secular and apparently atheistic realm, nonbelievers continue to believe in notions of human rights and human dignity that are drawn from Christianity and that are entirely at odds with the teachings of modern science. We thus cannot unquestioningly accept Nietzsche's proclamation of the death of God and the imminent collapse of everything based upon this God as if it were a sociological fact.

Nietzsche's assertion that the death of God leaves humanity with only two choices, the last man or the *Übermensch*, is also problematic. He imagined that the death of God would disrupt not only the external values that govern social and political life but also the internal psychic order of the self by obliterating the rank order of the passions. The death of God in his view would thus produce a disgregation of the passions that would end in a collapse of the self and throw society into the war of all against all. In his view there are only two ways to escape from this situation. The first is simply to weaken all of the passions, thus diminishing the conflict and tension among them by satisfying whichever passion is momentarily the strongest. This is the path of the last man. The other path allows the coming war to play itself out in the belief that it will lead to a new rank order of passions and a new code of values under the direction of superhuman artist-tyrants.

Nietzsche doesn't consider the possibility that there may be other ways in which society and the psyche can be organized. Everything for him depends upon the triumph of one dominant passion over all of the others and one superhuman ruler or ruling class in the state. However, this view overlooks a variety of other possibilities including, for example, the possibility of a psyche and a society rooted in friendship of the sort Aristotle praised and that characterized the relationships between most of the citizens in the Greek states that Nietzsche admired. In his early unpublished essay "The Greek State," Nietzsche discounts such friendship in favor of the domination of the genius and the enslavement of the masses (*NL*, KGW III 2:258–71). In his late work, he reiterates this claim and points to the need for domination with his claim that it is necessary to emulate the *imperium Romanum*, "the greatest form of organization under difficult circumstances hitherto attained" (*AC*, KGW VI 3:243). Moreover, this is only one example of an alternative that Nietzsche overlooks or rejects without argument. Other forms of organization for the self and the state are certainly possible, and one has to wonder whether he does not intentionally obscure this fact in an effort to convince his contemporaries to pursue the dangerous and uncertain path he prefers.

At a deeper level, however, Nietzsche's claim here rests on his view that conflict and the universal and unending struggle for power are the driving force in all things, and his general dismissal of love and friendship as motive forces in human affairs. We see this reflected in his analysis of the Greeks, where he focuses on agonistic competition in his early essay "Homer's Contest," and in his preference for Heracleitus (who declares that *polemos*, or war, is the father of all things) in contrast to Empedocles (who sees the world as a mixture of *philia* and *seiko*, or love and hate); on tragedies that end in death and disaster (*Oedipus Tyrannus* and *Prometheus Bound*) rather than tragedies that end in reconciliation (*Oedipus at Colonus* and *The Eumenides*); and on Thucydides' account of the hubris and collapse of Athenian democracy rather than Aristotle's focus on establishing enduring civic friendship and unity in all the different forms of regimes. Similarly, Nietzsche's praise of the Renaissance (under the influence of Jacob Burckhardt) rests on his belief that it is an essentially anti-Christian rebirth of antiquity driven by an elite group of artists and political strongmen struggling for power and influence rather than an outgrowth of Christianity rooted in the civic humanism of the Italian republicans. Nietzsche (like his follower Foucault) thus sees everything as a competition for power that depends either on the use of force or rhetoric. All relationships and all forms of order for him are thus merely the momentary crystallizations of existing power hierarchies. Nietzsche's Zarathustra spells out this authoritarian vision quite clearly when he proclaims, "Where I found the living, there I found the will to power; and even in the will of those who serve, I found the will to be master. That the weaker should serve the stronger, to that it is persuaded by its own will, which would be master over what is weaker still" (KGW VI 1:143–44).

While one might find this portrayal of human life one-sided and thus unconvincing, Nietzsche does at times present an account of human nature that is less bellicose, suggesting that there were (and presumably still are) really two kinds of humans based on their twofold biological nature. In his discussion of early human societies, he argues that while most humans were herd animals (who cooperated and generally lived in harmony with others), a few were predators. It was these predators, he believed, who dominated and organized the herd. He pays scant attention, however, to the ways in which herds organize themselves, and surprisingly even less to the way in which the predators organize themselves and cooperate with one another. Voluntary association thus plays little or no role in his thought, and he consequently sees no possibility for the herd animals to master themselves.[13] Without a master, he believed that the herd would be dominated by their immediate desires and that they would become mere consumers, last men.[14]

Like John Stuart Mill, whom he carefully read, Nietzsche thus assumes that almost everything of value in human life is the product of extraordinary individuals, although in contrast to Mill, he argues they are all driven by a desire to dominate and subordinate others. These extraordinary individuals are the creators of culture as well as of the social and political orders within which the rest of humanity lives. Through his reading of Emerson as well as his own observations, Nietzsche was well aware that the modern world was based upon division of labor and specialization, but unlike Mill and many of his contemporaries, he did not conclude that liberal democracy was the political form most commensurate with this fact or that the free market was the best way to maximize human well-being. Both in his view were forms of organization that facilitated the herd's desires for immediate gratification rather than the creative impulses of the genius, forms designed for the production and satisfaction of last men, not the production of supermen. Nietzsche thus sees the reduction of workers in industrial society to slaves or willing tools in the hands of powerful supermen as a great advantage and the possible foundation for a new morality that combines elements of master and slave morality (HAH, KGW VI 2:297). He is not interested in maximizing human happiness, achieving justice, or enhancing the lives of ordinary human beings, but in the production and increased power of the genius or Übermensch. In the words of Zarathustra, the only relevant political question is, thus, "Who will be lord of the earth?" (KGW VI 1:394).

Nietzsche assumed that the struggle for power that would ensue with the death of God would bring about the destruction of European civilization, and that it was his fate to set off this struggle by proclaiming the doctrine of the eternal recurrence. The world wars and revolutions of the first half of the twentieth century seem to have been a fulfillment of this prophecy and thus to confirm Nietzsche's prescience. Nietzsche also correctly described the pitiless elite that carried out this destruction. What he did not anticipate and, given his dismissal of the democratic mentality, what he perhaps could not understand was the compelling strength of the liberal democratic worldview and political system dedicated to human dignity and the dignity of work that he repeatedly denigrated and dismissed. He imagined that the industrial society that was coming into being around him would produce not citizens but drones who could be manipulated and dominated by a new aristocratic elite, drones who in any case would be incapable of self-government, driven as they were by their desire for immediate gratification. While in our darker moments we are prone to believe Nietzsche was correct, liberal democracies in times of trouble have proven to be remarkably resilient.

Nietzsche's failure to understand the strength of democratic society almost certainly rested in part on his misestimation of the continuing power of the Christian ethos in the liberal democratic (and particularly Anglo-American) regimes, even in the face of the death of God. In contrast to the German and Russian worlds, Christianity in England and the United States had been deeply infused during the radical Reformation with a humanistic secularism that attributed dignity to individual human beings, and taught them that they could and should make their own decisions about how to live their individual and collective lives. While this secularism in part had a non-Trinitarian origin, it was still essentially Christian. Nietzsche underestimated the extent to which this worldview could withstand the death of the Christian God. He also did not foresee that new, more democratic (and evangelical) forms of Calvinism rooted immediately in scripture would survive and thrive after the death of the rationalist God. Thus, while German and Russian Christianity did in fact suffer a collapse at least arguably of the sort Nietzsche imagined, this was less true elsewhere. Moreover, even in Germany and Russia, the collapse of Christian ideals did not lead to the atheism Nietzsche hoped for but to the rise and ultimate triumph of new political religions and the new messiahs to lead them. These new political religions (Nazism and Bolshevism in particular), however, remained almost entirely religions of negation, of death and destruction, led by revenge-seeking tyrants and their followers. These parties did in fact destroy the existing order, but they never became or fostered the aristocratic elite Nietzsche longed for, and as a result were never able to construct a tragic or Dionysian culture that could compete with the culture produced by secular humanism. As we saw in our comparison of Nietzsche and Plato, however, this last transformation was impossible or at the very least would have required a system of education and training that Nietzsche scarcely considered. He undoubtedly imagined that something of the sort would develop and that it would be rooted in new forms of art and poetry, but the if, when, and how of this ennobling of these predators remains uncertain, and his willingness to tolerate levels of brutality shocking.

All of these questions about Nietzsche's final teaching notwithstanding, its ultimate worth and standing is mainly dependent on the status of the doctrine of the eternal recurrence. This notion was the great thought that gave birth to his teaching and that lay at its foundation. However, since Nietzsche did not spell out the meaning of this doctrine before collapsing into madness, coming to terms with it has proven one of the most difficult tasks of Nietzsche scholarship. But without some account of its meaning and importance, the final teaching is left in a limbo of questions without answers.

For some readers of Nietzsche the eternal recurrence is a cosmological doctrine, for others a psychological test, for still others an existential imperative, and for a few a mere literary construct that is meant to paper over the fundamental irrationality of the universe and of Nietzsche's thought as a whole. Rather than examining each of these interpretations in detail, we might be better served to begin by examining the question to which the eternal recurrence is an answer. That question as Nietzsche presents it in *Zarathustra* is very complicated but becomes a bit clearer when we examine it in the context of the dramatic development of the work itself.

The question that leads to the idea of the eternal recurrence arises as a consequence of Zarathustra's attempt to give meaning and purpose to human life in the aftermath of the death of God. After carrying the ashes of his God to the top of his mountain and meditating for ten years, he returns to humanity with what he believes to be a solution. This is the idea of the *Übermensch*, which he assumes will provide a goal for human striving that will enable them to avoid becoming last men. The *Übermensch*, in his view, will become the meaning of the earth. This *Übermensch*, however, can only come into being through a series of metamorphoses that end with the production of a new innocence metaphorically represented by the child spirit. Zarathustra, however, comes to recognize in the course of the work that a renewed, childlike innocence is not enough since the will of the child-*Übermensch* is not free but subject to the dead hand of the past, to the "it was" that fosters the spirit of revenge. As we have seen, the answer to this problem is the eternal recurrence.

To provide a meaningful and convincing answer to this question requires that Nietzsche develop a new notion of time and being, a new ontology that makes it possible to will the past. This in turn requires a new cosmology or account of the natural world, a new anthropology or a new account of human nature and its place in this newly understood world, a new theology that explains the connection between human willing and the motion of the cosmos as a whole, and a new (musical) logic that can serve as the vehicle for articulating this new worldview. This is what I have called Nietzsche's (anti-)metaphysics. Fully understanding and explaining the idea of the eternal recurrence would require the completion of such an (anti-)metaphysics.

The cosmological element here is very important. The modern world rests upon two principles, the notion of causality and the notion of human freedom. The problem is that the two principles contradict one another. The doctrine of the eternal recurrence suggests a possible solution that allows for both a certain kind of freedom of the will and a universal causal necessity.

Understood within the context of the eternal recurrence, I am always determined in every respect by the causal series of all things that produces me. This series is also responsible for producing my will, which is in fact only one moment of the conflicting centers of force struggling against one another that make up the will to power. In this sense I am thoroughly determined in everything I do by the antecedent constellations of forces. But if we look at this from a different perspective, my will is part of the causal force that wills the motion of all matter moving forward into the future, and because the future is also the past, in a sense I will myself, I am my own necessity. Now clearly this is not freedom in the ordinary sense of the term. At best it seems to bear some resemblance to Rousseau's claim that I remain free as part of a general will, here of course understood as a *very* general, indeed a universal or divine, will. Nietzsche recognizes this fact and gives this will the name Dionysus. While my individual will always finds itself constrained by all of the other wills or moments of force past, present, and future, my will can be free if it is identical with this world-will of Dionysus. To be the last disciple of Dionysus is thus to will the whole of what is as it is and becomes, to want nothing to be different in the past or in the future than it has already always been.[15] To will absolutely is to love fate, *amor fati*.

To will in this way, however, is essentially to will all things, to declare as the Old Testament God does of his creation that "It is good." Freedom of the will in the context of the eternal recurrence thus requires the affirmation of everything that has ever been and that will ever be. This alone liberates one from the spirit of revenge and allows one to be active and not merely reactive. As we discussed above, however, this is only possible if one actually wills and declares "good" everything hitherto considered good, evil, great, petty, disgusting, beautiful, ugly, horrible, and so on, everything in short that has been or can be.

There are two questions that stand in the way of belief in this doctrine and thus in the way of the acceptance of Nietzsche's final teaching: the first is whether it is true or even possible, and the second whether accepting and willing it can have the effects Nietzsche believes are necessary. I suggested above that one reason Nietzsche was unable to develop an adequate cosmology to underpin the doctrine was because he lacked sufficient training in the natural sciences. This fact helps to explain why Nietzsche's attempts to explain the eternal recurrence cosmologically are so unconvincing. But the deeper question is whether, even if Nietzsche had obtained such scientific training, he would have been able to develop a convincing cosmological account to support his theory. There is no unequivocal answer to this question. There are in fact still today some well-known scientists who consider something like the eternal recurrence possible, but they are clearly in the minority.[16] While Nietzsche's attempts to explain the doctrine scientifically are thus naive, we cannot simply say that the theory is wrong or impossible.

Nietzsche argues that because time is infinite and matter is finite, there are only a finite number of states of the universe and that as a result the series of states of the universe must inevitably recur. His conclusions for the most part rest upon well-known and often quite ancient arguments that assume that if time is infinite, everything that can happen must have happened, and because the universe has not already come to an end or to an equilibrium (in past infinite time), it will not do so in the future. Nietzsche's argument here finds its foundation in the ancient assumption that the cosmos is eternal, which he sees replacing the Judeo-Christian notion of a finite creation that no longer makes sense after the death of the creator God. Nietzsche's conclusion that in the absence of such a creator the universe must be infinite, however, neglects or at least overlooks other possible explanations of the finitude of the universe and time. Indeed, almost all of the basic notions of time, space, matter, energy, and causality that Nietzsche takes for granted have been rejected or radically transformed by the more recent theories and discoveries of modern science. An actual scientific or cosmological justification of the eternal recurrence would thus have to be much more sophisticated than anything Nietzsche ever imagined.

This notwithstanding, we might still wonder whether, in the absence of such a scientific justification of the eternal recurrence, the doctrine and thus

Nietzsche's final teaching can have meaning for us. In actuality, many of the most serious readers of Nietzsche's thought have assumed that his doctrine does not make any sense cosmologically and believe that Nietzsche himself never intended that it should. I do not accept this latter claim, but what of the former? Does it matter practically for Nietzsche if this element of his final teaching is true? Might it not engender the practical psychological and political consequences Nietzsche believes are necessary if it is treated merely *as if* it were true?

While Nietzsche was concerned with the truth of the doctrine, as he first presents it in his published work, it seems to be more a psychological test. In the penultimate aphorism in book 4 of *The Gay Science*, Nietzsche presents the idea as a hypothetical under the title "The Greatest Weight." He asks what one's response would be to a demon who told one that this life would be repeated over and over in exactly the same way—would the individual see this as an intolerable burden or as a divine blessing (KGW V 2:250)? This suggests an alternative way of reading the doctrine that has many of the same advantages as the doctrine would have if the eternal recurrence were in fact true. It certainly seems to be the case that facing the question of the mere *possibility* of the eternal recurrence and accepting it as true would enable the person in question to overcome the spirit of revenge and live according to *amor fati*, and thus to be active rather than reactive. Whether true or not, it might then act as a kind of existential imperative that produces a new notion of willing and a new sense of responsibility. To affirm the notion of a hypothetical eternal recurrence would be to affirm absolutely without any reservations and thus to say Yes to life with all of its pain and suffering. What is less obvious is whether the doctrine would have the inverse effect on the weak that Nietzsche imagined and hoped for. Would it cause them to throw up their hands in surrender or to commit mass suicide, as he often suggests in his notes? This seems unlikely. Even if the mass of human beings assumed it was a possibility, it would be only one among a number of possibilities and thus perhaps no more effective at convincing the masses than Pascal's wager. Given Nietzsche's analysis of the human, all too human penchant for forgetting (or in Freud's language, repressing) disturbing facts, he could hardly have been unaware of the human capacity for disregarding troubling possibilities. It thus seems unlikely that Nietzsche could have imagined that the idea of the eternal recurrence could have such a debilitating effect on most of humanity unless it was shown to be not merely plausible but at least probable and preferably certain.

It is also important to recognize how extreme Nietzsche's demands are. Why is it necessary to affirm *everything* that has been or will be in order to truly affirm life itself and to escape from the spirit of revenge? Goethe, for example, only imagined that it would be necessary to affirm one perfect moment in order to justify everything else. In this instance we see the underlying theological element in Nietzsche's thought. For Nietzsche everything is connected to everything, the universe is in fact a unity (and not a diversity or a multiverse), ruled as it were by a single principle and with its single goal as the eternal repetition of the same. This is a surprisingly monotheistic vision, in contrast to the more polytheistic world of the Greeks, and points to the hidden but still quite real connection of Nietzsche's thought to Christianity. It also calls into question his early notion of the *gegensätzliche Ureine*, the contradictory primordial one, which he imagines is essential to his tragic view of the world. The contradictory character in a truly tragic vision would seem to suggest the impossibility of conceiving the world as a one or as a unity. With the notion of the eternal recurrence, Nietzsche seems to suggest that the broken heart of things is not ultimately broken at all but a coherent series of thoroughly interrelated events that repeats eternally. His monotheism in this way seems to reinforce the primacy or the *Ureine* or one over the *gegensätzliche* or contradictory.[17]

While Nietzsche thus portrays himself as the antipode to Christianity, and while he certainly imagined himself to be playing such a role, he is in fact only the antipode to a certain form of Christianity. In fact, his thought in many respects is the product of a strain of Christianity that focuses on the priority of divine will and that conceives the human as the *imago dei* to be primarily a willing being. Within this tradition man is conceived on one hand by humanists thinkers such as Pico as a superhuman being capable of emulating God himself, and on the other by thinkers such as Luther as an abject sinner who, however, by God's grace can become the repository and agent of God's will. Nietzsche combines these two elements. Whether he recognized this fact seems doubtful, but the conjunction of the two is strangely evident in his last letters, which he signs randomly either "Dionysus" or "The Crucified." This conjunction is reemphasized in his claim to be "all names in history" (KGB III 5:578).

CONCLUSIONS

In the essays contained in this volume, I have tried to show that beginning in August of 1881 and extending until his breakdown in early 1889, Nietzsche conceived and in large part deployed a final teaching that aimed at the revaluation of all values. This teaching was not just an intellectual exercise but had a practical dimension both in the short term and in the long run. The ultimate goal was the institution of a Dionysian *Reich* and a new tragic age led by a superhuman elite of artist-tyrants that combined the steely hardness of Caesar with the innocence of Christ. The possibility of such a *Reich* and world, however, depended in the short term on the destruction of Christianity in all of its forms and institutions as well as everything that rested on it, including European morality and the European political system. Nietzsche believed that this destruction would be the work of the nihilistic revolutionaries he already saw coming into being around him. Their actions might be various, but the net result would be the instigation of wars of unprecedented violence and magnitude. He believed that it was his fate to initiate this transformation by proclaiming the doctrine of the eternal recurrence.

Nietzsche, however, collapsed into madness before he was able to finish the master work that was to complete his final teaching. While we can piece together his aspirations and plans for the whole from his existing works, his *Nachlass*, and his letters, it is not this teaching that has come to be seen as the core of his thought. In fact, the practical aspects and goals of his teaching have largely been overlooked in the period since World War II.[18] Instead he has been treated as a brilliant critical or experimental thinker whose insights and ways of thinking (and particularly his *Entlarvungspsychologie*) can be employed for purposes quite different than those he intended. This is perhaps not surprising. His late works, including even *Zarathustra*, are for the most part exercises in attack and destruction. It would not be too much of an exaggeration in this sense to characterize him in Goethean terms as "The spirit that always negates."[19] In this sense he has been treated as a resource for the destruction and deconstruction of Christianity and bourgeois society, and thus as someone who has cleared the ground and opened up the possibility for constructing alternative ways of life.

None or at least very few of those who use Nietzsche today share his substantive goals, although they often use him to promote agonistic politics, libertarian individualism, philosophic naturalism, neo-Marxism, or Emersonian self-reliance. That they employ Nietzsche for these projects is not surprising and, as I argued above, hardly illegitimate. The more troubling question, of course, is why they feel compelled to seek his support and whether they can do so without also pointing their readers to the goals Nietzsche endorsed that are quite different than those they intend.[20] Nietzsche is dead, but as he himself pointed out, some men are born posthumously, and this has been true of Nietzsche time and time again. His works allow themselves to be used but also make use of their users. His arguments are not merely passive sources of critique but active, living agents that transform everyone who encounters them, often in ways quite contrary to their users' intentions and expectations.

In the end, I think that many turn to Nietzsche because despite his incisive criticism of almost all existing institutions, he is not a gloomy but an extraordinarily hopeful thinker. He promises a glorious, superhuman future, a future filled with supernal laughter, "that is no human laughter," but he was not able finally to show us the path to this future or to describe it in any detail (KGW VI 1:198). He invites us to ride with him on the back of the proverbial tiger as it joyfully tears contemporary civilization to pieces, assuring us that while many will fall victim to this rampage, a few (which almost all readers take to mean "they") will survive to construct and dwell in a better world. It is a testimony to the power of his language and the depth of his thinking that so many have been willing to ride with him, often in the conviction that they can guide the tiger to their destination or dismount if it carries them in the wrong direction. Whether this is possible, of course, remains a question that deserves our utmost attention.

AC	*The Antichrist*
BGE	*Beyond Good and Evil*
BT	*The Birth of Tragedy*
CW	*The Case of Wagner*
D	*Dawn*
EH	*Ecce Homo*
GL	*History of Greek Literature* (Lecture Course)
GM	*The Genealogy of Morals*
GR	*Greek Rythmics* (Lecture Course)
GS	*The Gay Science*
HAH	*Human, All Too Human*
KGB	*Nietzsche's Briefwechsel: Kritische Gesamtausgabe*, ed. G. Colli and M. Montinari, 18 vols. in three parts and one supplement (Berlin: de Gruyter, 1975–84)
KGW	*Werke: Kritische Gesamtausgabe*, ed. G. Colli and M. Montinari (Berlin: de Gruyter, 1967–)
NL	*Nachlass*
Pl	*Introduction into the Study of the Platonic Dialogues* (Lecture Course)
PP	*Pre-Platonic Philosophers* (Lecture Course)
PTAG	"*Philosophy in the Tragic Age of the Greeks*"
TI	*Twilight of the Idols*
TS	*Introduction to the Tragedies of Sophocles* (Lecture Course)
UM	*Untimely Meditations*
Z	*Thus Spoke Zarathustra*

NOTES

PREFACE

1. All references to Nietzsche's works list title, edition, and relevant division, volume, and page numbers. See the list of abbreviations.

2. The term *Übermensch* is translated in various ways in English, as "overman" or "superman" or "superhuman." All of these translations have their problems, and as a result I use the original German. When a pronoun is necessary, I use "him" because I can find no instance in which Nietzsche does not use the pronoun *er*, "him," in referring to the *Übermensch*. In German the term *Übermensch* takes on a variety of case endings that I have deleted to avoid confusion for the English reader. I use the plural *Übermenschen* on several occasions.

NIETZSCHE'S DEEPEST THOUGHT

1. And particularly after Wagner attacked him publicly in the *Bayreuth Blätter* in 1878.

2. Paul Ricoeur later called this a "hermeneutics of suspicion." David Stewart, "The Hermeneutics of Suspicion," *Journal of Literature and Theology* 3 (1989): 301.

3. This period in Nietzsche's thought has become the centerpiece of interpretation for thinkers such as Robert Pippin who emphasize the "experimental" character of Nietzsche's thought, which they believe puts him in the camp of thinkers such as Montaigne. Robert Pippin, *Nietzsche moraliste français: La conception nietzschéenne d'une psychologie philosophique* (Paris: Odile Jacob, 2006), and his expanded English version *Nietzsche, Psychology, and First Philosophy* (Chicago: University of Chicago Press, 2010). I agree with Pippin and others that the thought of this Nietzsche is more attractive and useful than that of the later Nietzsche I portray in this volume, but I believe it is crucially important to understand the reasons that Nietzsche moved beyond this teaching toward a perhaps less appealing but more metaphysically systematic account. While this turn in Nietzsche's thought may have been a mistake, it is important to recognize that it was a turn away from his earlier approach.

4. As long as this list is, it only begins to capture Nietzsche's impact. On the history of Nietzsche's influence in Germany, France, and America, see Steven E. Aschheim, *The Nietzsche Legacy in Germany, 1890–1990* (Berkeley: University of California Press, 1994); Douglas Smith, *Transvaluations: Nietzsche in France, 1872–1972* (Oxford: Oxford University Press, 1996); Jennifer Ratner-Rosenhagen, *American Nietzsche: A History of an Icon and His Ideas* (Chicago: University of Chicago Press, 2011).

5. On Nietzsche's long and important encounter with pessimism, see Joshua Dienstag, "Nietzsche's Dionysian Pessimism," *American Political Science Review* 95, no. 4 (December 2001): 923–37. Dienstag's essay is one of the best brief but comprehensive accounts of Nietzsche's thought and parallels in many ways the argument developed in what follows.

6. In naming the eternal recurrence, Nietzsche uses a number of slightly different formulations. *Die ewige Wiederkunft des Gleichen*, generally translated as the eternal recurrence of the same but literally the eternal coming again of the identical, is the form he generally prefers, with the term *Wiederkunft* appearing one hundred one times in his published works and notes and *ewige Wiederkunft* forty-one times. He also uses the term *ewige Wiederkehr*, literally the eternal return, seven times while the term *Wiederkehr* itself appears thirty-three times. In his thought before 1881 and occasionally in his later thought, both *Wiederkehr* and *Wiederkunft* are occasionally used in contexts that do not denote his deepest thought. I have not been able to distinguish any significance in this multiple usage and will generally use the phrase "eternal recurrence" to refer to this idea. It is important to note that both *Wiederkehr* and *Wiederkunft* are used in German in describing the return or second coming of Christ. Nietzsche also uses them to describe the eternal recurrence of life, personified as Dionysus. There is a long and complicated scholarly debate over whether this idea was original to Nietzsche and if not, what his sources were. The idea was certainly broadly present in many ancient religions. On this point, see Mircea Eliade, *The Myth of the Eternal Return: Cosmos and History* (Princeton, NJ: Princeton University Press, 1971). Nietzsche was also clearly aware of this fact from his studies of ancient religion in his preparatory work for writing *The Birth of Tragedy*. Different versions of the idea also appear in a number of earlier modern thinkers whom Nietzsche read or may have read. This question, however, is not decisive for the argument here, since wherever the idea came from, it was transformed and employed in decisively new ways by Nietzsche.

7. Lou Andreas-Salomé, *Nietzsche*, trans. Siegfried Mandel (Redding Ridge, CT: Black Swan Books, 1988), 130–31. While the idea of the eternal recurrence, as we will see, is difficult and obscure, scholars have generally rejected the early notion of Bertram that it was a "mocking mystery of a delusion," and of Baeumler that it was an impenetrable religious experience. Ernst Bertram, *Nietzsche: Versuch einer Mythologie* (Berlin: Bondi, 1918), 12; Alfred Baeumler, *Nietzsche der Philosoph und Politiker* (Leipzig: Reclam, 1931).

8. Two of Nietzsche's notes should suffice to make the importance he attributed to

this thought clear. The first was apparently jotted down when he first conceived of the idea: "The new heavy burden (*Schwergewicht*): the eternal recurrence of the same. Infinite importance: for our knowing, erring, for our customs, for the ways of all who are coming. What will we do with the remainder of our lives—we, who have passed most of it in the most essential ignorance? We teach the teaching—it is the strongest means, to incorporate it into ourselves, our sort of bliss (*Seligkeit*), as the teachers of the greatest teaching." He dates the note the beginning of August 1881 in Sils-Maria, and describes it as "6000 feet above the sea and much higher above all human things." *NL*, KGW V 2:392. The second was written between 1882 and 1884 as Nietzsche was planning the decisive third part of *Zarathustra*: "[The idea of the eternal recurrence will] still glow centuries from now. Determining in advance the future. The overpowering of the past: and then the healing forgetfulness, the divine precinct (*Umkreis*). The holy laughter. The song of consolation (according to my music). The teaching of the eternal recurrence is *the turning point of history*." *NL*, KGW VII 1:541. While some have suggested that the idea of the eternal recurrence is derivative from the idea of the *Übermensch* and the will to power, John Nolt argues compellingly that this is not the case. "Why Nietzsche Embraced Eternal Recurrence," *History of European Ideas* (2008): 322–23. That it is compatible with those ideas is not surprising.

9.   And is hardly accidental since it is a modification of the original note describing the idea, quoted above. *NL*, KGW V 2:392.

10. The lives of the Greek gods have meaning as the witnesses (*historoi*) of the struggles of mortals seeking to attain their goals. In this sense they live vicariously. The Judeo-Christian God may have purposes that transcend anything human beings can imagine, but as far as human beings are concerned his principal purpose seems to be establishing a world in which they are tempted and fall, thus demonstrating that they are not like God, but also a world in which once that difference is made clear some of them may be ultimately granted an eternal life with God.

   Nietzsche remarks in one note: "You think that you would have a long rest before rebirth, but don't deceive yourselves. Between the last instant of consciousness and the first appearance of a new life there is 'no time'—as fast as a bolt of lightning it is past . . . timelessness and succession become one when the intellect is not there." *NL*, KGW V 2:462–63. The man-god character of the *Übermensch*-philosopher is thus similar to that of Christ. Dostoevsky recognized this similarity and believed it was crucial to distinguish between the man-god and the man-God. On this point, see my essay "Nietzsche and Dostoevsky on Nihilism and the Superhuman," included in this volume, and C. A. Miller, "The Nihilist as Tempter-Redeemer: Dostoevsky's 'Man-God' in Nietzsche's Notebooks," *Nietzsche-Studien* 4 (1975): 165–226.

11. Karl Löwith, *Nietzsche's Philosophy of the Eternal Recurrence of the Same*, trans. Harvey Lomax (Berkeley: University of California Press, 1997), 10, 169. He believes this necessarily leads Nietzsche to the conclusion that he is god. Krzysztof

Michalski goes so far as to suggest that for Nietzsche time cannot be understood without eternity. *The Flame of Eternity: An Interpretation of Nietzsche's Thought*, trans. Benjamin Paloff (Princeton, NJ: Princeton University Press, 2012), vii.

12. I discuss the new prefaces in "What Was I Thinking?" and *Ecce Homo* in "Life as Music," both included in this volume. He also lays out this development *in nuce* to Georg Brandes in several letters of 1887 and 1888. Brandes asked Nietzsche for biographical information to use as the background for the series of lectures he was planning to deliver on his thought, and Nietzsche happily complied. From a very young age, Nietzsche reflected on his own path and sought to answer the question how he had become what he was. As Rüdiger Safranski points out, between 1858 and 1868 he wrote no fewer than nine autobiographical sketches. *Nietzsche: A Philosophical Biography*, trans. Shelley Frisch (New York: Norton 2002), 25.

13. *Nihilism before Nietzsche* (Chicago: University of Chicago Press, 1995), 174–85, 203–54.

14. Martin Heidegger, "Was Ist Metaphysik?," in *Wegmarken* (Frankfurt am Main: Klostermann, 1967), 1–2.

15. I do not mean to imply that all or even most thinking is intentionally esoteric; some is and some is not. There are many reasons people do not tell the truth about themselves even to those that are closest to them. Some scholars believe that letters to family and friends are especially reliable sources of information, but anyone who has ever written a letter to a family member or to a friend knows how prone we are to exaggeration and concealment exactly in such situations. Nietzsche's letters to his mother and sister in particular are often disingenuous.

16. This is a particularly vexing question in the case of Nietzsche because the persona of the author of his works and the persona that he displays in his letters are often surprisingly at odds with one another.

17. Nietzsche famously claimed that "the Protestant minister is the grandfather of German philosophy." *AC*, KGW VI 3:174.

18. The thoughts of this book were first formulated in 1870 and were delivered as lectures in Basel during the same period. Nietzsche also discussed them at length with Wagner before giving them their final form in the published volume. It seems likely that Wagner also read and perhaps edited the manuscript.

19. At one point he actually considered giving up his academic position to promote the Wagner Society full time.

20. Nietzsche did not recognize that Wagner had little choice since he needed the support of these people to pay the bills. Nietzsche was also shocked by the fact that Wagner seemed to believe that the festival was a great success. Here though Nietzsche was deceived. We know from Cosima Wagner's diaries that Wagner too was devastated, although he clearly knew how to put on a good front.

21. The touchy Wagner was also angry with Nietzsche for what he perceived as neglect when the very sick Nietzsche was unable to visit him. He was also furious with him for his praise of a composition by Brahms and for introducing his

Jewish friend Paul Rée to him (Wagner). Nietzsche almost certainly knew that both of these acts would irritate Wagner.

22. Safranski lays out in some detail the superficiality and phoniness of German culture in the new *Reich*. *Nietzsche*, 117–18.

23. This does not mean that he abandoned drama altogether. Indeed, *Zarathustra* is itself a drama, but a drama that is meant to be read and not performed, a drama experienced in private reading and not as part of a public festival.

24. Nietzsche points toward such a way of thinking in *The Genealogy of Morals*, with his assertion that "we godless anti-metaphysicians still take our fire . . . from the flame lit by a faith that is thousands of years old . . . that God is the truth." KGW VI 2:419. We are prone to interpret Nietzsche as *anti*-metaphysical, but this passage illustrates how important it is to read him as practicing an anti-*metaphysics*.

25. Köselitz, Nietzsche's closest friend, had the greatest immediate impact on the reception and interpretation of Nietzsche's thought, arguing in his foreword to *Zarathustra* in the first edition of Nietzsche's collected works that the center of Nietzsche's thinking was the *Übermensch* with not a single syllable about the eternal recurrence. The philosophically more astute Lou Salome and Franz Overbeck both vehemently disagreed. In conjunction with Nietzsche's sister, Köselitz in his later work on Nietzsche went on to explain that the *Übermensch* for Nietzsche had always been the racially Aryan man. Baeumler picked up on this in this his 1930 edition in an attempt to make Nietzsche the bedrock of National Socialism. Ralf Eichberg, *Freunde, Jünger und Herasubeger: Zur Geschichte der ersten Nietzsche-Editionen* (Frankfurt am Main: Peter Lang, 2009), 81–82, 94–95, 103, 105.

26. Martin Heidegger, *Nietzsche*, 2 vols. (Pfullingen: Neske, 1961); Löwith, *Nietzsche's Philosophy of the Eternal Recurrence of the Same*; Pierre Klossowski, *Nietzsche and the Vicious Circle*, trans. Daniel Smith (Chicago: University of Chicago Press, 1997); Laurence Lampert, *Nietzsche's Teaching: An Interpretation of "Thus Spoke Zarathustra"* (New Haven, CT: Yale University Press, 1986).

27. "Heidegger's Nietzsche," *Political Theory* 15, no. 3 (August 1987): 431–35.

28. *Nietzsche and Philosophy*, trans. Hugh Tomlinson (New York: Columbia University Press, 1983), 48, 69.

29. For an example, see Alexander Nehamas, *Life as Literature* (Cambridge, MA: Harvard University Press, 1985), 142–54.

30. For a summary of the various scholarly interpretations of the eternal recurrence principally although not exclusively in the English speaking world, see Lawrence Hatab, *Nietzsche's Life Sentence: Coming to Terms with Eternal Recurrence* (New York: Routledge, 2005), 115–25. One early work that is now almost forgotten but which presents to my mind a surprisingly accurate interpretation of Nietzsche is George Morgan's *What Nietzsche Means* (Cambridge, MA: Harvard University Press, 1939). Even in the absence of much of the *Nachlass* material now accurately available to us, he presents a straightforward account of Nietzsche's thought that perhaps underemphasizes the importance of the aesthetic/musical

element in Nietzsche and perhaps does not adequately point out the difficulties in reconciling the idea of the eternal recurrence with modern scientific cosmology but is still a light shining in the darkness of its time when it comes to fairly portraying the thought of Nietzsche.

31. Martin Heidegger, *Nietzsche*, 2 vols. (Pfullingen: Neske, 1961), 1:648–58.

32. Safranski, *Nietzsche*, 343.

33. Michalski suggests in his interpretation of Nietzsche's thought that the experience of the eternal recurrence is ultimately unnameable, suggesting that the metaphysical reading of the concept given in *Zarathustra* first by the spirit of gravity and then by Zarathustra's animals is clearly rejected by Zarathustra as insufficient and too metaphysical. *The Flame of Eternity*, 187–95. While the terror of the eternal recurrence may only be fully understood by the participant and not the mere observer, this does not mean that the conceptual reading of it is wrong, only that it is incomplete and insufficient.

34. Lest one assume that this is merely an example of literary hyperbole, Nietzsche repeats this claim in multiple letters to family and friends. For example, he writes to Overbeck on 29 December 1888: "I am no longer a man, I am a fate." KGB III 5:558.

35. To be fair, Nietzsche believed that the development of European nihilism had already turned Europe into a powder keg, and that his announcement would essentially light the fuse of an explosion that was bound to occur in any case.

36. In his letters during the last few months of his life in sanity, he repeatedly says that he will soon "die Welt regieren." See, for example, his letter to Fuchs of 11 December 1888. KGB III 5:522. What this means exactly, however, is unclear. He might mean that he will "rule the world," although the German for this would more likely be "die Welt herrschen." The term "regieren" here is likely more closely related in his mind to "Regisseur," the person who conducts an orchestra or stages a dramatic performance. To "rule" the world in this sense seems to have more to do with staging it as a musical drama, or to use the language of *The Birth of Tragedy* as "an aesthetic phenomenon." This is very much in keeping with his notion that at its heart culture constitutes the foundation of human life. That he believed others would use political power and force to achieve these ends is incontestable as his repeated praise of Caesar, Machiavelli, Borgia, and Napoleon makes clear. While his position here seems to be a model for some form of fascism, it is important to note that fascism in all of its forms was essentially a reactive movement that sought revenge against those who supposedly had corrupted the race or betrayed the people. This is as far as possible from the doctrine that Nietzsche presents.

37. *Reich* can be translated in a variety of ways. The most obvious is "realm," which includes not only the notion of a political realm but also the realm of poetry. More typically in a political context, it refers to a "kingdom" or an "empire" or "imperium," a region subject to rule. The kingdom of God is the *Reich Gottes*, but *Reich* is not simply a kingdom but also, for example, refers to the *Reich* under Hitler. Nietzsche almost certainly does not imagine that this coming *Reich*

will be a kingdom since he is clear in the fourth part of *Zarathustra* that the age of kings has come to an end since their rule was legitimated only by the divine sanction of a God who is now dead. He also does not imagine it to be the instrument of revenge against individuals or a people.

38. On this point, see Paul S. Loeb's insightful "The Dwarf, the Dragon, and the Ring of Eternal Recurrence," *Nietzsche-Studien* 31 (2002): 99, 107–8, 111–12. Loeb, I think, goes a bit too far when he asserts that the proclamation of the eternal recurrence is meant to initiate the suicide of humankind. Nietzsche believes that mass suicide is the likely result of following the current path that in his view ends in the last man. Loeb is closer to the truth in his assertion that the proclamation of the eternal recurrence is meant to end the present existence of humankind by plunging humanity or at least European humanity into a war of unprecedented ferocity that will harden some men in ways that will make some of them capable of living in a world without God and eternal values.

39. He is unequivocal on this point in his late letters. See, for example, his letters to Brandes and to Wilhelm II at the beginning of December 1888 for a description of the apocalypse that he imagines is just over the horizon. KGB III 5:500–504.

40. We also know from Nietzsche's correspondence with his publisher that the works of 1888 were at least in part intended to promote interest in his coming magnum opus. This is evident in remarks throughout these works. In *Twilight*, for example, he remarks, "I have given humankind the most profound book it possesses, my *Zarathustra*; shortly I shall give it the most independent." KGW VI 3:147.

41. Under the burden of the work on the revaluation, Nietzsche at times changed his mind about its structure and even seemed at the very end on the verge of insanity to give up the project altogether, but I believe the weight of the textual evidence shows that it remained a steady goal of his thinking. Whether he *could* have completed it is of course a different question.

42. *Das Leben Friedrich Nietzsches*, 2 vols. (1895–1904); *Das Nietzsches-Archiv, seine Freunde und seine Feinde* (1907); *Der junge Nietzsche* (1912); *Der einsame Nietzsche* (1914); *Wagner und Nietzsche zur Zeit ihrer Freundschaft* (1915); *Friedrich Nietzsche und die Frauen seiner Zeit* (1935).

NIETZSCHE AND THE ANTHROPOLOGY OF NIHILISM

1. An earlier version of this essay appeared in *Nietzsche Studien* 28 (1999): 141–55.

2. On this general point, see Elisabeth Kuhn, *Friedrich Nietzsches Philosophie des europäischen Nihilismus* (Berlin: de Gruyter, 1992). There is some possibility that he used the term to characterize Buddhism in an 1865 lecture, since the term appears in the notebook of one of his students, but there is no way of knowing whether this was his term or the student's. Johann Figl, "Nietzsches frühe Begegnung mit dem Denken Indiens: Auf der Grundlage seines unveröffentlichen Kollegennachschrift aus Philosophiegeschichte (1865)," *Nietzsche-Studien* 18 (1989):466.

3. See Kuhn, *Nietzsches Philosophie*, 21; Curt Paul Janz, *Nietzsche: Biographie*, 3 vols. (Munich: Hanser, 1978–79), 1:677.

4. Bourget, *Essais de psychologie contemporaine*, 2 vols. (Paris: Lemerre, 1885), 2:225, 239; Mérimée, *Oeuvre complètes*, ed. P. Trahard and E. Champion, 12 vols. (Paris: H. Champion, 1927–33), 9:cviii; 11:548. On this point, see Elisabeth Kuhn, "Nietzsches Quelle des Nihilismus-Begriffs," *Nietzsche-Studien* 13 (1984): 266, 269, 271.

5. On this point, see Jean Granier, *La Problème de la vérité dans la philosophie de Nietzsche* (Paris: Seuil, 1966), 284–86.

6. Keith Ansell-Pearson has persuasively argued that Nietzsche details a similar path of overcomings in his 1886 preface to *Human, All Too Human*. "Toward the Übermensch: Reflections on the Year of Nietzsche's Daybreak," *Nietzsche-Studien* 23 (1994):128–30. There is no want of scholarly speculation about the relationship of these figures to other figures and concepts in Nietzsche's work. Richard Perkins sees them as representing the lover, the knower, and the creator. "How an Ape Becomes a Superman: Notes on a Parodic Metamorphosis in Nietzsche," *Nietzsche-Studien* 15 (1986): 180. Marie-Luise Haase in a similar vein sees them as the symbolic repetition of the saint, the philosopher, and the artist. "Der Übermensch in Also Sprach Zarathustra und im Zarathustra Nachlass, 1882–1885," *Nietzsche-Studien* 13 (1984): 236. Eugen Fink argues that they represent the genius, the free spirit, and Zarathustra himself. *Nietzsches Philosophie* (Stuttgart: Kohlhammer, 1960), 72. John Powell Clayton suggests that these three stages mirror Kierkegaard's movement from the religious to the ethical to the aesthetic. "Zarathustra and the Stages on Life's Way: A Nietzschean Riposte to Kierkegaard," *Nietzsche-Studien* 14 (1985): 84.

7. Lampert sees the camel as the heroic spirit while Pieper sees it as the self-humiliating spirit. Both go too far. It is neither heroic in the Greek sense nor self-humiliating in the Christian sense. It obeys the thou shalt and thereby attains a measure of dignity. Laurence Lampert, *Nietzsche's Teaching: An Interpretation of "Thus Spoke Zarathustra"* (New Haven, CT: Yale University Press, 1986), 33; Annemarie Pieper, *"Ein Seil Geknüpft zwischen Tier und Übermensch": Philosophische Erläuterungen zu Nietzsches erstem "Zarathustra"* (Stuttgart: Klett-Cotta, 1990), 112. In his 1959 lecture on *Zarathustra*, Leo Strauss pointed out that Nietzsche's account of the human leaves out the heroic man of the Greek age. I do not think this is correct. Nietzsche characterizes the master of the heroic age as a semi-animal, not as a human being, but certainly containing elements of what Nietzsche in *Zarathustra* calls the lion spirit, although lacking an inner life as he explains in *The Genealogy of Morals*. KGW VI 2:338. This is achieved only by the camel spirit, who one might then characterize as the first fully human being. The reappearance of the lion-spirited man that Nietzsche anticipates is the reappearance of a self-conscious lion-spirited human being, who reappears against the backdrop of a world determined by Christianity and modern rationalism, that is, against the backdrop of institutionalized slave morality. This spirit is thus invariably negative and can only become af-

firmative after this destructive phase as the child, only through a kind of forgetfulness. Even then the spirit can only be fully affirmative as the *Übermensch* who as we will see combines all three forms of the spirit, both master and slave morality.

8. Lampert argues that the camel must destroy what it has hitherto held most dear because this is the most difficult burden to bear. *Nietzsche's Teaching*, 34. That is to say, its metamorphosis is intrinsic to its nature. As we will see in my essay "What Was I Thinking?," included below, Nietzsche made a similar suggestion in the new prefaces he prepared for his earlier works in 1886.

9. Lampert recognizes a similar division of part 1 and sees the lion spirit as the topic of the middle section but does not otherwise recognize the overall meaning of this structure in the context of Nietzsche's philosophical anthropology. *Nietzsche's Teaching*, 35.

10. Lampert also argues that the child must mature into the *Übermensch*. Ibid., 35.

11. *The Brothers Karamazov*, trans. C. Garnett (New York: Random House, 1929), 245–55. On this point, see my essay "Nietzsche and Dostoevsky on Nihilism and the Superhuman" below.

12. How difficult it was for Nietzsche to take this step is indicated by the focus on pity in the fourth part of *Zarathustra* and Nietzsche's repeated consideration in his notes of the dangers of pity for Zarathustra as a result of the consequences of the proclamation of the eternal recurrence. In one of the plans for a continuation of the work, Zarathustra dies of pity, unable to endure the misery his doctrine engenders. *NL*, KGW VII 1:16. How desperate Nietzsche believes this choice to be is made clear by his claim in his notes that if he and the others who stand in opposition to the crisis of the times do not preserve themselves through the teaching of the eternal recurrence, everything will perish. *NL*, KGW VII 1:2. His pity, however, is not for the coming destruction of ordinary human beings but for failures and deaths of the higher men.

13. In one of Nietzsche's unpublished descriptions of Zarathustra's proclamation of the doctrine of the eternal recurrence, one man who hears him goes insane and another kills himself. *NL*, KGW VII 1:16. Nietzsche imagined matters were so desperate that he was willing to risk the destruction of much of humanity in an effort to elevate humanity. *NL*, KGW VII 2:27. It is perhaps indicative of the political meaning of this doctrine that nearly all of Nietzsche's sketches for the second *Zarathustra* project are set wholly or in part in a burning city. See, for example, *NL*, KGW VII 3:29. Those who survive this thought, however, are transfigured. Nietzsche gives us some insight into the character of this new figure in a note for *Zarathustra*: "With the convalescence of Zarathustra, Caesar stands before us, pitiless, gracious—*the cleft between being a creator, goodness, and wisdom is annihilated. Brightness, rest, no excessive longing, happiness in the correctly ordered eternalized moment!*" *NL*, KGW VII 1:16.

14. For a detailed discussion of Zarathustra's account of human psychology, see Alastair Moles' thoughtful *Nietzsche's Philosophy of Nature and Cosmology* (New York: Peter Lang, 1990), esp. 84–100.

15. On this point see, Keith J. Ansell-Pearson, "Nietzsche's Overcoming of Kant and Metaphysics," *Nietzsche-Studien* 16 (1987): 319.

16. This point is developed more fully by Pieper, *Ein Seil*, 48–54.

17. The descent toward the last man for Nietzsche is clearly also a return to what is animal. *NL, KGW* VII 1:15.

18. Ultimately, the descent into animality can only be achieved by the elimination of the wealth of contradictory drives and impulses that make man the lord of the earth. *NL, KGW* VII 2:27. Nietzsche in this sense sees the desire for inner peace as a diminution of life itself.

19. The Great Noon thus divides human history into two halves, from the origin of man (out of the ape) to the death of God and from the death of God to the *Übermensch*. C. A. Miller has pointed out that Dostoevsky's Kirillov similarly divides history into two epochs from gorilla to the annihilation of God and from there to the advent of the new man. "The Nihilist as Tempter-Redeemer: Dostoevsky's 'Man-God' in Nietzsche's Notebooks," *Nietzsche-Studien* 4 (1975): 170. While Nietzsche copied this passage from *The Demons* in his notebooks, it is unlikely that this was the source of his division, since he almost certainly had not read Dostoevsky until 1887, that is, until well after writing *Zarathustra*. On this point, see Nietzsche to Overbeck on 23 February 1887. KGB III 5:27. The Bible is a more likely source. As Pieper points out, the Final Judgment also is imagined to take place at noon. *Ein Seil*, 399. See also Karl Schlechta, *Nietzsches Grosser Mittag* (Frankfurt am Main: Klostermann, 1954), 54. Whatever its origins, the concept of the Great Noon is central to *Zarathustra*. Indeed, the work was originally to be titled "Noon and Eternity." *NL, KGW* V 2:11, KGW VII 1:4.

20. Nietzsche writes in a note that the new notion of good as "I will" stands in contrast to the old notion of good as "I should." He notes further that this is the source of barbarism at the Great Noon. *NL, KGW* VII 1:7.

21. Nietzsche thus argues in a note for a continuation of *Zarathustra* that "the evil man as destroyer is praiseworthy, for destruction is necessary." KGW VII 1:16. As Lampert puts it, *Zarathustra* was meant to loose a storm. *Nietzsche's Teaching*, 241. Or in Stanley Rosen's account, Zarathustra is a philosophical revolutionary who teaches a noble nihilism to eliminate base nihilism. *The Mask of the Enlightenment: Nietzsche's Zarathustra* (Cambridge: Cambridge University Press, 1995), xi.

22. Laughter is the greatest slayer, Zarathustra tells us, but the laughing lion is not simply the spirit of mockery, he is also the spirit that laughs at the destruction of the good. KGW VI 1:388. The lion's laughter, Nietzsche remarks in a note, lifts the stones from Zarathustra's heart, the stones of pity. KGW VII 1:616. The laughter thus makes possible the destruction of morality by freeing the proto-*Übermensch* from pity and guilt.

23. Nietzsche remarks in a note for *Zarathustra*: "Finally, the lion as the third animal of Zarathustra—symbol of his maturity and ripeness." KGW VII 1:543. The lion is the great moment of culmination, the "I will!!!" KGW VII 1:548. Having overcome pity for those who will be destroyed, Zarathustra "can thus struggle

for victory against the great dragon," the creator of all "thou shalts." KGW VII 1:177. Note that Zarathustra speaks here of children, a subtle indication that he expects a race of supermen, not a single one. On this point see Haase, *Der Übermensch*, 243.

24. Or what he called an entr'acte in a letter to Fuchs of 29 July 1888. KGB III 5:374.

25. One of Nietzsche's notes gives us some insight into his decision to abandon *Zarathustra*: "*Zarathustra* is a proof that one can speak with the greatest clarity but be heard by no one." KGW VII 2:26.

26. Active nihilism is thus not a replacement for religion as Leslie Thiele argues. *Friedrich Nietzsche and the Politics of the Soul* (Princeton, NJ: Princeton University Press, 1990), 180.

27. Nietzsche similarly remarks in his notes that "I am happy with the military development of Europe, as well as the anarchic conditions within the states. The time of repose . . . is over. . . . The barbarian in each of us is affirmed, also the wild animal." *NL*, KGW VII 2:26. He is unequivocal about what he sees as the consequences of his teaching: "The consequences of my teaching must rage furiously: but on its account uncountably many shall die." *NL*, KGW VII 2:25. Statements such as these belie the assertions of scholars such as Kaufmann, Nehamas, and Lampert that Nietzsche longs only for spiritual wars. Walter Kaufmann, *Nietzsche: Philosopher, Psychologist, Antichrist*, 3rd. ed. (New York: Random House, 1968), 386–90; Alexander Nehamas, *Nietzsche: Life as Literature* (Cambridge, MA: Harvard University Press, 1985), 224–34; Lampert, *Nietzsche's Teaching*, 283–84. Rosen sees more clearly that Nietzsche's language of war and warriors is the language of global war and not that of professors and café intellectuals. *Mask*, 103. On Nietzsche's politics, see Henning Ottman, *Philosophie und Politik bei Nietzsche* (Berlin: de Gruyter, 1987) and Bruce Detwiler, *Nietzsche and the Politics of Aristocratic Radicalism* (Chicago: University of Chicago Press, 1990). Nietzsche's openness to a coming period of chaos and war, however, should not be taken to demonstrate that he was the father or grandfather of Fascism or Nazism. Nietzsche saw, earlier than most, that the foundations of the old order were rotten and consequently believed that a breakdown of the social and political order was inevitable. That he preferred this to the decadence he saw around him was not surprising. None of this, however, means that he was responsible for Fascism or Nazism. In fact, he went out of his way to criticize the spirit of revenge and the anti-Semitism that characterized both movements.

28. He remarks in a note that they will have no use for parliamentarianism. *NL*, KGW VII 1:16. See also Rosen, *Mask*, 60.

29. See Kuhn, *Nietzsches Philosophie*, 237. The limitation that Nietzsche establishes for this Dionysian *Reich* is an indication of the fundamental subordination of his vision to the doctrine of the eternal recurrence. In the end, like Plato's Kallipolis, Nietzsche's Dionysian *Reich* is subject to the laws of time.

30. F. H. Jacobi, *Werke*, 3 vols. (Leipzig: Fleischer, 1812–25; reprint ed., Darmstadt: Wissenschaftliche Buchgesellschaft, 1968), 3:29.

31. Nietzsche's admiration for such demonic characters is clear and is reflected in his praise of Byron's Manfred and Stendhal's heroes. In my essay, "What Was I Thinking," included below, I show that Nietzsche saw their descent into relativism and lasciviousness as a necessary stage in the development of nihilism.

32. *Literature and Revolution* (New York: Russell & Russell, 1957), 256.

SLOUCHING TOWARD BETHLEHEM TO BE BORN

1. An earlier version of this essay appeared in *Journal for Nietzsche Studies* 30 (2005): 50–70.

2. For a fuller discussion of this matter, see my *Nihilism before Nietzsche* (Chicago: University of Chicago Press, 1995).

3. Eugen Fink has laid out in some detail the series of forms that this development gives rise to in Nietzsche's thought. See his "Nietzsche's New Experience of World," in *Nietzsche's New Seas: Explorations in Philosophy, Aesthetics, and Politics*, ed. Michael Allen Gillespie and Tracy Strong (Chicago: University of Chicago Press, 1988), 203–19.

4. Jürgen Söring, "Nietzsches Empedokles Plan," *Nietzsche-Studien* 19 (1990): 176–211.

5. *Nietzsche's Teaching: An Interpretation of "Thus Spoke Zarathustra"* (New Haven, CT: Yale University Press, 1986).

6. On this point Nietzsche's claims strikingly resembles those Promethean claims made by Giovanni Pico della Mirandola in his famous Renaissance essay, "The Dignity of Man." For a discussion of the Prometheanism of Italian humanism, see my *Theological Origins of Modernity* (Chicago: University of Chicago Press, 2008), 69–100.

7. The mistaken belief that the child is the *Übermensch* is essential to almost all post-structuralist readings of Nietzsche, and leads to the equally mistaken notion that Nietzsche believes only aesthetic and not real violence is necessary. When Nietzsche uses terms like "violence," "war," "destruction," and so on, he is generally referring to actual physical violence, real war, and actual destruction. Even when he refers to wars over ideas, he doesn't imagine that these are merely verbal skirmishes in scholarly periodicals.

8. Or to put the matter in its historical context, from Schopenhauer to Nechayev. On this point see, Kuhn, "Nietzsches Quelle des Nihilismus-Begriffs," *Nietzsche-Studien* 13 (1984): 262–63.

9. Nietzsche makes this clear in "The Ass-Festival" in *Zarathustra*, where the ass in parodying Zarathustra repeatedly says I-A, which is the equivalent of *Ja* or Yes. KGW VI 3:384.

10. To put this in the context of his own life, he first had to overcome disgust at the eternal recurrence of the smallest and most petty individuals (whom he identifies as his mother and sister), but then his pity for those who were higher, but not high enough, and here he clearly has in mind Wagner and Schopenhauer whom he would have to leap over and thus send (figuratively) to their death. His

critique of both but especially of Wagner (in *The Case of Wagner* and *Nietzsche contra Wagner*) was a first step in that direction.

11. See notes 22 and 23 to the preceding essay above. This lion is also strongly reminiscent of the pitiless Jester who leaps over the tightrope walker. Laughter (and apparently particularly the laughter of the *Übermensch* that Nietzsche so longs for) thus makes possible the destruction of morality by freeing human beings from pity and guilt. The German word for courage is *Mut*. The courage of the *Übermensch* is *Übermut*, which is a "wanton exuberance that looks down on and makes fun of things."

12. In contrast to Christ, Zarathustra thus has not merely a second but a third coming, a third *Wiederkehr*.

13. In the *Nachlass*, when Zarathustra proclaims the eternal recurrence, one man who hears him goes insane and another kills himself. KGW VII 1:543.

14. Lampert, *Nietzsche's Teaching*, 233.

15. He remarks in "The Greek State," a short piece originally intended to be included in *The Birth of Tragedy*, that the sole purpose that can justify humanity individually or collectively is the production and service of genius. *NL*, KGW III 2:258–60.

16. For an example of this view, see Leslie Thiele, *Friedrich Nietzsche and the Politics of the Soul: A Study of Heroic Individualism* (Princeton, NJ: Princeton University Press, 1990).

WHAT WAS I THINKING?

1. *Interpretation*

    Interpreting myself, I always read myself in:
    I cannot be my own interpreter.
    But he who climbs on his own path,
    Also carries my image up to brighter light.
    (*GS*, KGW V 2:29)

2. And the corollary, "Everything in measure!" meant act according to the human measure and not as if you were a god. Or taking the two maxims together, "Avoid hubris!"

3. Heracleitus, fragment 101.

4. Freud apparently thought so, asserting, according to his close friend Ernest Jones, that, "Nietzsche developed a more penetrating knowledge of himself than any other man who ever lived." A. H. Chapman and M. Chapman-Santana, "The Influence of Nietzsche on Freud's Ideas," *British Journal of Psychiatry* 166, no. 2 (February 1995): 251–53.

5. Andreas Urs Sommer, *Kommentar zu Nietzsches Der Antichrist, Ecce Home, Dionysos-dithyramben, Nietzsche contra Wagner* (Berlin: de Gruyter, 2013), 325.

6. There is some debate about whether *Ecce Homo* is autobiographical. See Fried-

rich Nietzsche, *Ecce Homo*, trans. R. J. Hollingdale (New York: Penguin, 1979), "Translator's Introduction," 7.

7. Here Nietzsche seems to anticipate the hermeneutic approach most prominently presented in the twentieth century by Hans-Georg Gadamer that rests on the notion of a fusion of horizons. He also certainly provides some support for those who want to use his thought for their own purposes.

8. Alexander Nehamas is representative of this view in the Anglo-American world. *Life as Literature* (Cambridge, MA: Harvard University Press, 1985). Nehamas, however, fails to appreciate the transformation in Nietzsche's thought that occurred with the realization of the idea of the eternal recurrence, and interprets all of his late works from an Emersonian perspective that is more appropriate to the works of his middle period. Nehamas in my view goes astray because he discounts Nietzsche's notion of the eternal recurrence. Ibid., 6–7, 141–69. In part this is the result of his decision not to examine any of Nietzsche's letters or any of the *Nachlass* other than the problematic material collected together by his sister as *The Will to Power*. Ibid., 9–10. Like many of the French post-structuralists whom he relies upon, he is less interested in what Nietzsche actually thought and said and more interested in what can be made out of him. His Nietzsche thus may be more attractive to modern readers that the actual, historical Nietzsche, but it is important to note the difference and not to mistake one for the other.

9. As we see in his discussion with the dwarf in "On the Vision and the Riddle" in *Zarathustra*. KGW VI 1:195–96.

10. This notion has a long history. Shakespeare's Macbeth and Goethe's Mephistopheles are only two of many examples of literary characters that echo this sentiment. Shakespeare, *Macbeth*, 5.5.18–28; Goethe, *Faust*, 2.5.11599–606.

11. The difference between Nietzsche's middle and late work is particularly evident if we compare this notion with the end of *Dawn* where he imagines he and his fellow free spirits as birds flying out to sea who eventually become tired and settle down on the water but take joy in the fact that other birds fly farther. D, KGW VI 1:335. At that point Nietzsche still imagined that in some sense we always set sail for the infinite. In the context of his final teaching rooted in the idea of the eternal recurrence, the infinite has disappeared and is replaced by a notion of the whole, and the tired birds resting on the surface of an infinite sea are replaced by a golden boat with a wondrous golden passenger arriving on a new shore.

12. On Nietzsche's acceptance of Schopenhauer's pessimistic critique of all notions of progress but a rejection of Schopenhauer's resulting despair, see Christopher Janaway, "Schopenhauer as Nietzsche's Educator," in *Willing and Nothingness: Schopenhauer as Nietzsche's Educator*, ed. Christopher Janaway (Oxford: Clarendon, 1998), 25.

13. Or to put it in simple terms, while all are necessary and must be affirmed this does not mean one cannot distinguish better and worse. The argument that he

develops with respect to life is surprisingly similar to the scholastic argument about orders of being and imagines a spectrum from weak to strong rather than a binary notion of good and evil.

14. *NL*, KGW VII 1:541.

15. I do not mean to assert here that Nietzsche is correct in this conclusion. Without a number of subsidiary assumptions, for example, it is not obvious that absolute affirmation is more able to distinguish perspectives from one another. How would we determine from Nietzsche's perspective, for example, if Shakespeare is more life-affirming and life-enhancing than Henry Ford? It seems that if one recognizes the highest thing, it should be easy to recognize the relative height of everything else, but this is not as obvious as it seems. The Stoics, for example, faced a similar problem with their assertion that the life of the sage was the perfect good, but then were unable to avoid the conclusion that all other forms of life were equally bad.

16. While Nietzsche saw Judaism as the preeminent example of a priestly as opposed to a warrior culture and as the source of Christianity, this did not produce a personal animus toward Jews or lead him to conclude that Jews could not be good Europeans. On the contrary, perhaps his best friends Heinrich Köselitz, Paul Rée, and Helen Zimmern were Jewish, he admired Heinrich Heine as one of the two greatest German stylists (along with himself), and maintained a friendly correspondence with the Danish Jewish scholar Georg Brandes who was the first to popularize his work.

17. On the publication history of Nietzsche's works, see William H. Schaberg, *The Nietzsche Canon: A Publication History and Bibliography* (Chicago: University of Chicago Press, 1995).

18. Nietzsche seeks somewhat disingenuously to mitigate the already tepid nationalism of *The Birth of Tragedy*. He took a leave of absence from his professorial position in Basel and volunteered to serve as an orderly in the war, even though he had previously been discharged from military service due to injury and had given up his Prussian citizenship. This suggests a greater dedication to the nationalist cause than the text of the new preface suggests.

19. In *Ecce Homo* he hints at such a connection, remarking that *The Birth of Tragedy* "smells offensively Hegelian."

20. On Nietzsche's understanding of the relation of tragedy and pessimism, see Joshua Dienstag, "Tragedy, Pessimism, Nietzsche," *New Literary History* 35, no. 1 (Winter 2004): 83–101.

21. For more on this point, see my *Nihilism before Nietzsche*, 241–46.

22. Because Nietzsche had a reductionist view of Christianity that did not take account of the many and deep theological differences among different sects, he apparently did not understand the way in which his own thought was deeply indebted to the divine voluntarism of the nominalist thinkers from Ockham to Luther. Ibid., 203–57.

23. While there was no new preface for the *Untimely Meditations*, and especially

to the two meditations dealing with Wagner and Schopenhauer, respectively, Nietzsche does discuss his treatment of them in this section of the new preface to *Human, All Too Human*.

24. Cf. "On the Tree on the Mountainside," in *Zarathustra*. KGW VI 1:47. This is an important trope in many Romantic works such as Tieck's *William Lovell* and Byron's *Manfred*.

25. *HAH*, KGW IV 2:44.

26. Nietzsche's emphasis here on psychology needs to be understood within the context of his final teaching as bound up with what I have called his new (anti-) metaphysics and particularly his new anthropology. Since the time of Plato, but particularly within the context of Christianity, philosophical anthropology has understood human beings to be a combination of body and soul. Already in the prologue, but more extensively in the first part of *Zarathustra*, Nietzsche had argued that there was no body-soul duality because there was no soul. Psychology for Nietzsche thus does not mean the study of the soul but the study of what he calls the self, which he identifies with the body, although the body itself is no longer understood as mere matter but as the organization of the passions or force vectors.

27. Nietzsche's comments here about this unpublished essay are a clear warning to anyone who wants to draw on the arguments in this work—as many post-structuralists do—that its conclusions are not reflective of Nietzsche's mature teaching, but in fact an indication of a mistaken path that the mature Nietzsche was convinced he had overcome. The later Nietzsche may of course be wrong to have rejected the truth the younger Nietzsche grasped, but it does suggest that anyone who bases an interpretation of Nietzsche on his earlier position is on shaky ground if he or she uses the later work to support it.

28. The draft of the new preface to *Dawn* was finished on 13 November 1886, but Nietzsche did not receive the final revised copy of the manuscript until 24 June 1887, after much back and forth over the manuscript with his publisher. Schaberg, *The Nietzsche Canon*, 135–39. Nietzsche first mentions reading Dostoevsky to Overbeck on 23 February 1887. Nietzsche was thus deeply engaged with Dostoevsky when he was writing his new preface and particularly with his story of the *The Underground Man*.

29. In characterizing morality in this way, Nietzsche suggests that he is playing the role of Odysseus. The analogy to Odysseus is a prominent trope in his late work and especially in *Beyond Good and Evil*.

30. In this respect his self-description mirrors Bazarov's description of himself as a nihilist in Turgenev's *Fathers and Sons*. Miller, "The Nihilist," 212.

31. Here he analogizes his role to that of Christopher Columbus, a comparison he often used in *Dawn*. This is not surprising since the works are clearly intimately connected. Nietzsche originally conceived of *The Gay Science* as the continuation of *Dawn*. On this point, see Nietzsche to Köselitz, 18 December 1881, KGB III 1:149–50. The motif of Odysseus is also not far away.

32. Nietzsche explicitly defends this view in his own case in *Ecce Homo*, as we will

see below. This concern with physiology is part of his new anthropology or what he calls psychology in his late work.

33. See "The Problem of Socrates," in *Twilight of the Idols*. KGW VI 3:61–66.

34. The demon of "The Greatest Weight," of course, appears again in *Zarathustra* as the Spirit of Gravity.

35. In the new preface, Nietzsche suggests that *incipit tragoedia* could also be read as *incipit parodia*. Robert Gooding-Williams has argued that what this suggests is that *Zarathustra* is not merely a tragedy but also a parody of Neoplatonism and a Pauline reading of the Bible. "Nietzsche's Descent: *Incipit Tragoedia, Incipit Parodia*," *Journal of Nietzsche Studies* 9/10 (Spring/Autumn 1995): 50–69.

36. On this point, see Sarah Kofman, "Baubô: Theological Perversion and Fetishism," in *Nietzsche's New Seas: Essays in Philosophy, Aesthetics and Politics*, ed. Michael Allen Gillespie and Tracy Strong (Chicago: University of Chicago Press, 1988), 175–202.

NIETZSCHE'S MUSICAL POLITICS

1. An earlier version of this essay appeared in *Nietzsche's New Seas: Essays in Philosophy, Aesthetics and Politics*, ed. Michael Allen Gillespie and Tracy B. Strong (Chicago: University of Chicago Press, 1988), 117–49.

2. The distance between his thought and that of analytic philosophy, which sought to purge philosophical language of metaphor and construct an analytically rigorous logic based on mathematics to serve as a handmaiden to science, could not be clearer.

3. Curt Paul Janz, *Friedrich Nietzsche: Biographie*, 3 vols. (Munich: Hanser, 1978–79), 2:265.

4. See, for example, the initial review in the *Allgemeiner Schweizer Zeitung* (Basel), 9 February 1889.

5. Julius Kaften, "Aus der Werkstatt des Übermenschen," *Deutsche Rundshau* 32 (1905): 90–110, 237–60; Janz, *Nietzsche*, 2:620.

6. Martin Heidegger's seminal Nietzsche lectures of the 1930s were, for example, not published until 1961. *Nietzsche*, 2 vols. (Pfullingen: Neske, 1961), 1:486.

7. Karl Jaspers, *Nietzsche: Einführung in das Verständnis seines Philosophierens*, 4th ed. (Berlin: de Gruyter, 1974), 17–21.

8. Jacques Derrida, for example, doubted there was any totality in Nietzsche's text. *Spurs: Nietzsche's Styles/Éperon: Les Styles de Nietzsche* (Chicago: University of Chicago Press, 1979), 134.

9. In a letter of 14 September 1888, Nietzsche recommends to Deussen that he "read this piece once from the standpoint of taste and style: no one writes like this in Germany today"; and to Meysenbug, he remarks in a letter of 4 October 1888 that "in the end I myself am now the single refined German stylist." KGB III 5:426, 447. Statements of this kind have led scholars such as Alexander Nehamas to correctly conclude that Nietzsche was deeply concerned with style. *Life as Literature* (Cambridge, MA: Harvard University Press, 1985). Nehamas,

however, also takes a narrow view of Nietzsche's "logic," characterizing it as literary, and thus doesn't recognize the importance of music in Nietzsche's way of thinking. Ibid., 3.

10. Nietzsche may have begun by building upon Wagner's attempts to unite music and words into a *Gesamtkunstwerk*, but he goes beyond this in looking back to the Greek notion of *musikē*, seeking to reincorporate the arts of all of the muses—epic poetry, history, astronomy, comedy, tragedy, choral hymns, erotic poetry, lyric poetry, and dance—into a comprehensive whole, in this way also reconstituting a primordial Mnemosyne, the mother of the muses, whose name derives from the Indo-European root *men-, "think" or "remember." This is then combined with Socratic philosophy. In this way he seeks to play the role he laid out in *The Birth of Tragedy* for a future musical Socrates. KGW III 1:98. He points out in his lectures on pre-Platonic philosophy that the term *sophos* in the Greek of the tragic age did not mean merely "wise" in our modern sense but also "having an extended sense of taste." PP, KGW II 4:217. While Klaus Kropfinger is correct that music is the foundation of everything for Nietzsche, it is not music in the narrow modern sense that plays this role but music understood in the more expansive ancient sense. "Wagners Musikbegriff and Nietzsches 'Geist der Musik,'" *Nietzsche-Studien* 14 (1985): 11. On music understood in the narrower modern sense, Janz has given us a considered account of Nietzsche's substantive concern with music in his Nietzsche biography cited above; his edition of Nietzsche's *Der Musikalishe Nachlass* (Basel: Barenreiter, 1976); his "Die Kompositionen Friedrich Nietzsches," *Nietzsche-Studien* 1 (1972): 172–84; and his "The Form-Content Problem in Nietzsche's Conception of Music," in *Nietzsche's New Seas: Explorations in Philosophy, Aesthetics, and Politics*, ed. Michael Allen Gillespie and Tracy B. Strong (Chicago: University of Chicago Press, 1988), 97–116. For a brief but very useful summary of earlier scholars' concerns with this question, see Babette Babich, "On Nietzsche's Concinnity: An Analysis of Style," *Nietzsche-Studien* 19 (1990): 65; and for an excellent bibliography of Nietzsche and music, see her "Nietzsche and Music: A Selective Bibliography," *New Nietzsche Studies* 1, nos. 1/2 (1996): 64–75.

11. Janz, "Kompositionen," 185.

12. Janz, *Musikalische Nachlass*, 341–43.

13. Janz, *Nietzsche*, 2:215.

14. The symphonic structure of *Zarathustra* has long been suspected by musicians and others. On this point, see Paul Miklowitz, "Also Sang Zarathustra: Reflections on Friedrich Nietzsche and Music," *Piano Quarterly* 158 (Summer 1992): 43–48.

15. Janz, *Nietzsche*, 2:211–21; Janz, "Kompositionen," 175. Roger Hollinrake has shown the multiple ways in which *Zarathustra* was modeled upon Wagner's *Ring of the Nibelung*. *Nietzsche, Wagner and the Philosophy of Pessimism* (London: Allen and Unwin, 1982). See also Paul S. Loeb, "The Dwarf, the Dragon, and the Ring of Eternal Recurrence: A Wagnerian Key to the Riddle of Nietzsche's *Zarathustra*," *Nietzsche-Studien* 31 (2002): 91–113.

16. Werner Dannhauser notes the almost musical cohesion of the work in *Nietzsche's View of Socrates* (Ithaca, NY: Cornell University Press, 1974), 203. Janz suggests that in *Twilight*, "the 'music' becomes dissonant" (*Nietzsche*, 2:220).

17. Frederick Love points out that even in his admiration for the romantic elements in Bizet, Nietzsche recognized and applauded the fact that it was structured according to classical taste. "Nietzsche, Music, and Madness," *Music & Letters* 60, no. 2 (April 1979): 197. In reflecting on his own compositional efforts, he wrote in 1858 that he had formed an inextinguishable hatred of modern music and everything that was not classical, mentioning Mozart and Hayden, Schubert and Mendelssohn, Beethoven and Bach, as the columns on which German music was built. "Aus meinem Leben," in Friedrich Nietzsche, *Werke in Drei Bänden*, 3 vols., ed. K. Schlechta (Munich: Hanser, 1954–56), 3:27.

18. My analysis of *Twilight* focuses on the way in which it is composed. On the way in which this musical logic might be heard or received, see Tracy Strong's "Introduction," in Friedrich Nietzsche, *Twilight of the Idols; or, How to Philosophize with the Hammer*, trans. Richard Polt (Indianapolis: Hackett, 1997), vii–xxviii.

19. The structures of the other four works of 1888 also seem to be based upon musical forms. *Ecce Homo* is also written in sonata form. For a detailed discussion of this, see my essay "Life as Music" below. Both *The Case of Wagner* and *The Antichrist* are apparently in ternary form (ABA). They might be schematized as follows: *The Case of Wagner*: A (1–4), B (5–7), A (8–11), Coda (12); *The Antichrist*: A (1–23), B (23–43), A (44–61), Coda (62). A demonstration of these structures would of course require a more thorough explanation than cannot be given here. The fourth work, *Nietzsche contra Wagner*, which consisted of a number of Nietzsche's earlier aphorisms directed against Wagner, is structured as a theme and variations. Each variation begins with a "w" word *Wo, Wagner, Wir, Wohin, Wagner,* and *Wie*, with an intermezzo between the second and third variations entitled *Eine Musik der Zukunft*, and a coda pointing to Nietzsche himself, entitled *Der Psycholog*.

20. On the development of *Twilight* as a manuscript, see Mazzino Montinari, "Nietzsche Lesen: Die Götzen-Dammerung," *Nietzsche-Studien* 13 (1984): 69–79. On its publication history, see Schaberg, *The Nietzsche Canon*, 166–69.

21. On Nietzsche's thought process as he reformulated the title, see David Thatcher, "A Diagnosis of Idols," *Nietzsche-Studien* 14 (1985): 250–68.

22. Richard Wagner, *Götterdämmerung*, act 3, scene 2, lines 189–92.

23. Nietzsche did not invent the image of thinking with a hammer—this was already used by Thomas Müntzer on the title page of his sermon attacking false belief in 1524. Andreas Urs Sommer, *Kommentar zu Nietzsches Der Fall Wagner, Götzen-Dämmerung* (Berlin: de Gruyter, 2012), 212.

24. In the printed text, there are actually 181 words below the Latin line, but the word "Das" in line 3 of KGW VI 3:52 is not present in the draft of the text in Nietzsche's notebooks. KGW IX 10 WII 8:79. There are other changes from the original draft, but all of them are substantive and not grammatical, and this change is contrary to Nietzsche's practice in the rest of the preface. The change

was probably made by Köselitz (who transcribed Nietzsche's text for publication) or the publisher. On this point, see Ralf Eichberg, *Freunde, Jünger und Herausubeger: Zur Geschichte der ersten Nietzsche-Editionen* (Frankfurt am Main: Peter Lang, 2009), 72, 75. With respect to some of his changes, Köselitz claimed that he was simply following Nietzsche's penciled corrections, but these have never been found, and Overbeck and others at the time doubted they existed. Ibid., 136. While such subtlety on Nietzsche's part may seem unlikely to many readers, one should note that Nietzsche was deeply concerned with such numerology in his classical scholarship. See Christopher Middleton, "Nietzsche on Music and Meter," *Arion* 6 (1967): 58–65. Moreover, at precisely the time he was writing *Twilight*, he received a very long letter from Carl Fuchs of 31 August 1888 focusing on the mathematical character of musical architecture and rhythm, which demonstrates their common dedication to such issues and detail. KGB III 6:275–94. Nietzsche responds on 9 September 1888 telling Fuchs he has finished *Twilight* and continuing the discussion of musical forms. KGB III 5:413–16.

25. TS, KGW II 3:14–17; GL, 5:147–51. While in Basel, Nietzsche often taught courses on both Greek meter and Greek rhythm.

26. For the draft of an earlier preface to *Idleness*, see KGW VIII 3:345–47. The sense of Nietzsche's isolation in this version is palpable. Nietzsche portrays himself as a hermit living in mountains penning words that can tear the heart of a god to pieces but almost completely neglected and misunderstood by human beings. It is dated at the beginning of September 1888 and is in remarkable contrast to the very engaged and personalistic preface that he eventually included (at Köselitz's urging) in the revised book and dated 30 September 1888.

27. Thatcher has suggested several other interpretations of Nietzsche's use of the term "hammer." "Diagnosis of Idols," 250–68. He concludes that Nietzsche's use of the hammer is less to destroy than to diagnose as a doctor might use a hammer to examine a patient. This seems to me an important and quite plausible point that deepens the meaning of the term in Nietzsche's work. It points toward Nietzsche's diagnosis of the sickness of the age that is certainly central to the substantive argument of *Twilight*, but it underestimates the deeper sense in which Nietzsche identifies the hammer throughout this period with the eternal recurrence, which he repeatedly says will break the history of humanity in half. Thomas Brobjer emphasizes this point as well: "To Philosophize with a Hammer: An Interpretation," *Nietzsche-Studien* 28 (1999): 38–41.

28. Nietzsche, of course, is comparing himself here to God who rests on the seventh day after the creation of the world. On this point, see Babette Babich, "Nietzsche's Imperative as a Friend's Encomium: On Becoming the One You Are, Ethics, and Blessing," *Nietzsche-Studien* 32 (2003): 45. Cf. also Nietzsche's proposed conclusion to *The Antichrist*: "Law against Christianity. Given on the day of convalescence, on the first day of the year one (—on 30th of September 1888 of the false chronology)" (KGW VI 3:252). The idea of convalescence here is reminiscent of Zarathustra's convalescence after calling forth and surviving the thought of the eternal recurrence.

29. On this point, see "On the Thousand and One Goals," in *Zarathustra*. KGW VI 1:70–72. Such a connection is not new. Hegel, following Montesquieu and others, argued that the spirit of each people is manifest in the god, gods, or idols it worships, and this notion was picked up by many nineteenth-century thinkers. Nietzsche actually applies this insight not merely retrospectively but to contemporary states as well.

30. Nietzsche's identification of his philosophy as psychology here points to the centrality of his new anthropology for his (anti-)metaphysics, to the rootedness of his understanding of the human in terms of the passions and thus of the will to power that is made whole and intelligible only within the context of the eternal recurrence.

31. Dannhauser, *Nietzsche's View of Socrates*, 207.

32. Although it is not stated here, what underlies this fatalism is of course the central element of Nietzsche's final teaching, the eternal recurrence of the same.

33. Kathleen Higgins remarks that "Nietzsche understands the interplay of tones in melody and harmony as a symbolic expression of the oneness of the universe." "Nietzsche on Music," *Journal of the History of Ideas* 47, no. 4 (October–December 1986): 668. See also David Allison, "Some Remarks on Nietzsche's Draft of 1871, 'On Music and Words,'" *New Nietzsche Studies* 1, nos. 1/2 (1996): 18.

34. And to be clear, the Nazis. Nietzsche's anti-German sentiment is manifest throughout his late work and without his sister's distortions may very well have prevented his misuse by Hitler, Baeumler, Rosenberg, and others.

35. Nietzsche here touches on the topic that he dwelt on at greater length in his early unpublished lectures "*On the Future of Our Educational Institutions*" (1872).

36. As Babette Babich points out for Nietzsche, "art seeks to harmonize *dissonance*." "Musik und Wort in der antiken Tragödie und *La gaya scienza*," *Nietzsche-Studien* 36 (2007): 250.

37. For Nietzsche this is the affirmation of the eternal recurrence, although he does not bring that out at this point in his argument. The eternal recurrence appears only at the end of the work in preparation for his magnum opus where he intended to explicitly proclaim the idea.

38. Nietzsche recognizes Spinoza as his precursor in a letter to Overbeck of 30 July 1881. KGB III 1:111. He refers to Schopenhauer in a similar vein at *NL*, KGW VII 3:254.

39. This becomes even more apparent in *Ecce Homo*, as we will see below.

40. He describes this distinction explicitly in *Beyond Good and Evil* and *The Genealogy of Morals*.

41. He is thinking here of figures such as Byron's Manfred whose greatness transcends the moral and legal strictures of his time and leads him into vice and criminality. As we saw above, for Nietzsche such moral decadence is the inevitable consequence of perspectivism.

42. Goethe, *Faust*, line 11,989 (KGW VIII 3:324). He is one who has become free, a free spirit in Nietzsche's sense.

43. He is a preeminent example of what Nietzsche characteristically refers to as the good European.

44. Nietzsche suggested in a letter to Köselitz of 12 September 1888 that "the book can serve to introduce and whet the appetite for my *Revaluations of All Values.*" KGB III 5:417.

45. Nietzsche's sonata form in this respect seems to end up midway between the classical sonata of Hayden and Mozart, which was preeminently about movement, and the Romantic sonata, which was less driven by the necessity of forward movement and relied on image and meaning. Nietzsche believed in the superiority of music to image; indeed, he was convinced one could move from music to image but not vice versa, and in this respect he was more classic than romantic. Allison, "Some Remarks," 25, 28. Nietzsche's use of sonata form in *Twilight* in this respect is not so different from that of Schumann. On this point, see the illuminating essay by Mosco Carner, "Some Observations on Schumann's Sonata Form," *Musical Times* (October 1935): 884–86. This is perhaps not so surprising since many of Nietzsche's own musical compositions are Schumannesque. See also Gary Lemco, "Nietzsche and Schumann," *New Nietzsche Studies* 1, nos. 1/2 (1996): 43–56.

46. Nietzsche tells Köselitz in a letter of 30 October 1888 that he hopes that now people will be finally able to appreciate this passage, which was neglected like the rest of *Zarathustra* but which according to Nietzsche still gives him shudders every time he reads it. KGB III 5:462.

47. Nietzsche's goal was to convince a small and select group to follow the path he lays out, not the masses. Concerning the distribution of *Twilight of Idols*, for example, he remarks to his publisher Naumann on 27 December 1888 that he "should give away as few copies as possible and keep in mind that the book is meant only for those who are closest to me and who understand my intentions and my mission." KGB III 5:525–26. There is no mistaking his belief in the necessity of a new aristocracy, although in his mind it will be a European and not a German aristocracy. On this point, see Bruce Detwiler, *Nietzsche and the Politics of Aristocratic Radicalism* (Chicago: University of Chicago Press, 1990).

48. In a note in the *Nachlass*, Nietzsche tries to express his own experience of this world harmony: "Five, six seconds and no more: there you suddenly feel the presence of the eternal harmony. . . . In these five seconds I live an entire human existence, for them I would give my entire life and I would not have paid too much" (*NL*, KGW VIII 2:388).

49. On the way in which dissonance produces a longing for consonance, see Strong, "Introduction," xvi.

LIFE AS MUSIC

1. Michael Platt, "Behold Nietzsche," *Nietzsche-Studien* 22 (1993): 66.

2. Friedrich Nietzsche, *Ecce Homo*, trans. R. J. Hollingdale (New York: Penguin,

1979), "Translator's Introduction," 7. It is more a prospective work that looks forward to the great task Nietzsche sees in the immediate future than a retrospective work that seeks to explain who he is in terms of his past development. Sommer, *Kommentar*, 327.

3. Here the relationship to Montaigne, one of Nietzsche's favorite authors, suggests itself. Montaigne famously describes the *Essays* in the preface to the work as "The book of the self." The title *Ecce Homo* may also be an allusion to Goethe. In *Twilight*, for example, Nietzsche refers to Napoleon's remark upon meeting Goethe, "Voilà un homme!" which can effectively be translated as *ecce homo*. Sommer, *Kommentar*, 352. In its manifest rejection of Christianity, it also seems to serve as a mirror image of Augustine's *Confessions*. Ibid., 340. And at times it does resemble a catechism. Ibid., 343.

4. For a discussion of this point, see Julian Young, *Friedrich Nietzsche: A Philosophical Biography* (Cambridge: Cambridge University Press, 2010), 518–27. Daniel Conway believes Nietzsche is completely delusional at this point. *Nietzsche's Dangerous Game* (Cambridge: Cambridge University Press, 1997).

5. Although, since he proclaims himself, the title at least subliminally also suggests an analogy to Pilate, the representative of Caesar. Together these point toward the *Übermensch* who, as we have seen, Nietzsche describes as "Caesar with the soul of Christ." *NL*, KGW VII 2:289.

6. Consciously or unconsciously it is also an eerie prediction of imminent death and by analogy rebirth, posthumously, to play on Nietzsche's famous remark. *EH*, KGW VI 3:296.

7. He sees this coming world as a Dionysian *Reich*, thus an anti-Christendom. *NL*, KGW VIII, 2:41, 313, 431.

8. And perhaps also as Caesar, who in his own way is an antipode to Christ.

9. Insofar as it also points toward Caesar, it similarly abandons the notion of peace that is so essential to Christianity.

10. His focus on the what as opposed to the who is clear in the difference between this passage and the passage in *Zarathustra*, where the phrasing is "You should become who you are." KGW V 2:197.

11. While Strauss, Higgins, and Berkowitz, to take just three examples, want draw a clear distinction between Nietzsche and Zarathustra, I do not find this argument convincing. Leo Strauss, "Note on the Plan of Nietzsche's *Beyond Good and Evil*," in *Studies in Platonic Political Philosophy* (Chicago: University of Chicago Press, 1983), 174–91; Kathleen Higgins, "*Zarathustra* Is a Comic Book," *Philosophy and Literature* 16 (1992): 1–14; and Peter Berkowitz, *The Ethics of an Immoralist* (Cambridge, MA: Harvard University Press, 1995). While Nietzsche and Zarathustra are not identical, the poem at the end of *Beyond Good and Evil* suggests a deep connection, and the biographical details on this point convincingly argue that at least as far as the teaching of the idea of the eternal recurrence, the Great Noon, and everything that follows from this are concerned, there is very little difference between Zarathustra's role in the book and the role Nietzsche imagines for himself in the later 1880s. On this point, see Hugh Silverman,

"The Autobiographical Textuality of Nietzsche's *Ecce Homo*," *Boundary 2* 9/10 (Spring–Autumn, 1981): 145.

12. The connection that is often made to Walt Whitman is thus not as far-fetched as one might imagine.

13. Curt Paul Janz, "The Form-Content Problem in Friedrich Nietzsche's Conception of Music," trans. Thomas Heilke, in *Nietzsche's New Seas: Explorations in Philosophy, Aesthetics, and Politics*, ed. Michael Allen Gillespie and Tracy B. Strong (Chicago: University of Chicago Press, 1988), 101. On Nietzsche's musical training and sensibilities, see Benjamin Moritz, "The Musical Thought of Friedrich Nietzsche," diss., Northwestern University, available online at http://music.mansfield.edu/faculty/benjamin-moritz/nietzsche -research/dissertation/.

14. These aspects of his music were unrecognized by his contemporaries and have only recently become apparent to scholars. Moritz is one of the few who has provided the technical analysis of Nietzsche's music compositions to demonstrate in detail the deep connection between his musical, philological, and philosophical works. Ibid.

15. The connection of the work structurally to Wagner's *Ring of the Nibelung* has also been spelled out by Roger Hollinrake in his *Nietzsche, Wagner and the Philosophy of Pessimism* (London: Allen and Unwin, 1982).

16. Nietzsche to Fuchs, August 1888, KGB III 5:399–403.

17. Nietzsche clearly did not understand the larger symphonic structures of Wagner's music, but that notwithstanding, his critique of the effects of Wagnerian music on even the musically literate listener still rings true in many respects. Georges Liébert has argued that Nietzsche was mistaken about Wagner on many levels. *Nietzsche and Music*, trans. David Pellauer and Graham Parkes (Chicago: University of Chicago Press, 2004). Liébert's musical points are often persuasive, but his reasoning is often obtuse. Instead of focusing on what Nietzsche actually argues, he is prone to explain Nietzsche's later attacks on Wagner as a by-product of his migraines, which made it hard for him to listen to music for the length of time necessary to appreciate Wagner. Ibid., 69. For a similar reason, he believes Nietzsche himself was only capable of thinking in aphorisms and was unable to think in larger, more systematic terms. Ibid., 98. The essays in this volume present a different reading of Nietzsche's thought.

18. I have discussed the nature of sonata form in the preceding essay. For a fuller account, see James Webster, "Sonata Form," in *Grove Music Online*, ed. L. Macy (accessed 27 March 2008), http://www.grovemusic.com. See also Charles Rosen, *Sonata Forms*, 2nd ed. (New York: Norton, 1988).

19. A musical argument creates tension through the relation of expressive content and musical form. Wim Mertens, *American Minimal Music: La Monte Young, Terry Riley, Steve Reich, Philip Glass* (London: Kahn & Averill, 1999), 88. The musical argument may be characterized as the primary flow and current idea being presented in a piece. The very definition of musical argument is some-

thing that keeps going, and you uncover new details and new combinations. A musical argument is not the same as a verbal argument that has two sides. A musical argument makes the two sides one thing, as in counterpoint.

20. In music texture is the way the melodic, rhythmic, and harmonic materials are combined in a composition. Texture is often described in regard to the density, or thickness, and range or width between lowest and highest pitches, in relative terms as well as more specifically distinguished according to the number of voices, or parts, and the relationship between these voices. Marilyn Saker and Bruce Benward, *Music: In Theory and Practice*, 8th ed., 2 vols. (New York: McGraw-Hill, 2009), 1:145.

21. This analysis is complicated by the fact that Köselitz along with Overbeck and Nietzsche's mother and sister deleted some passages in the work as Nietzsche left it, claiming that they did so because they considered these passages works of madness. Even the manuscripts for these sections were for the most part destroyed by the mother and sister. However, we know that one of these passages referred to both the mother and sister in particularly unflattering terms and that another was a declaration of war against Kaiser Wilhelm II. Sommer, *Kommentar*, 331–33. Where these passages would have fit into the work is unclear, but presumably the passage on Wilhelm II would fit in connection with other sections dealing with great politics. We also know from a letter to his editor that he intended the work to end with the poem "Ruhm und Ewigkeit," in which he discounts the importance of the fame that is the reward paid to virtue in favor of a love of necessity and eternity, that is, what he calls *amor fati* and identifies with the affirmation of the eternal recurrence. Nietzsche to Naumann, 29 December 1888, KGB III 5:557–58; see also Sommer, *Kommentar*, 333. Within the musical structure laid out here, the poem would have served as a coda to the work, in much the same sense that "The Hammer Speaks" serves as a coda to *Twilight* as I argued above in "Nietzsche's Musical Politics." He thought very highly of the poem and remarks in the draft of a letter to Köselitz of 30 December 1888 that one would could die if one read it without being prepared. KGB III 5:566.

22. After the introduction/preface, Nietzsche inserted one page, which I will discuss below.

23. The first and last works listed are principally concerned with music.

24. I agree with Tracy Strong that Nietzsche had a communitarian conception of music and tragedy in his early work, but I believe that he abandoned this position for a more aristocratic conception in his later work. Tracy Strong, "Nietzsche and the Song of the Self," *New Nietzsche Studies* 1, nos. 1/2 (Fall/Winter 1996): 1–14.

25. It is difficult in the context of the idea of the eternal recurrence to keep the individual self separate from the god for whom one speaks, not to become the world-song one sings.

26. I thus disagree with scholars such as David Parker who claim that, "for Nietz-

sche, then, expressing his identity involves articulating his key beliefs and values; saying who he is involves saying what qualities of being he holds most important—in other word, say *what it is good to be*." "Nietzsche's Ethics and Literary Studies: A Reading of *Ecce Homo*," *Cambridge Quarterly* 33, no. 4 (2004): 307. Nietzsche does not express his ideas, beliefs, and values, but tells us about his body. He most certainly does not tell us what he thinks is good—in fact he tells us he is not good. And finally he does not set himself up as a model but explains to us why he is unique and thus not why we should emulate him but why we should follow him.

27. In a letter to Meysenbug of 18 October 1888, he calls himself the highest instance of decadence on earth. KGB III 5:452.

28. In this way he connects Wagner's decadence with that of his father. Both were born in the same year.

29. Notice here that he says "as if fated," which suggests that his claims are more circumspect than his apparently megalomaniacal language at other times suggests.

30. This remark suggests scholars should use great caution in using Nietzsche's discussion of his earlier works here for interpreting them.

31. It thus covers some of the same ground that he traversed in the series of new prefaces to his older, pre-*Zarathustra* works written in 1886 discussed above.

32. It is important to note that Nietzsche does not say here "Dionysus versus Christ." In *The Antichrist* Nietzsche decisively distinguishes Christ from the Crucified. In his view Christ was a being free from the spirit of revenge, an innocent, who taught not faith but a new way of life. He even refers to him as an idiot, drawing either on the Greek meaning of the term or Dostoevsky's novel. *AC*, KGW VI 3:198. Christ, however, is not part of Christianity as it has come to be understood. Nietzsche in fact declares that the last Christian died on the cross and that the Church was constructed in opposition to the evangel. *AC*, KGW VI 3:206. Christianity in his view is in fact the production of Paul, who was driven by resentment and who used the small Christian sect as a vehicle for his revenge against the master class. He, not Christ, put the crucifixion at the center of Christianity. *AC*, KGW VI 3:214–15. While Nietzsche thus sees the Crucified as antithetical to the Dionysian, he can describe the Dionysian *Übermensch* as Caesar with the soul of Christ (*NL*, KGW VII 2:289).

33. See Nietzsche's letter to Deussen of 14 September 1888, KGB III 5:428.

34. He like the grape has become ripe and ready for the harvest by the god of the grape and of wine, Dionysus, the vintager with his diamond knife.

35. "In *Ecce Homo* Nietzsche shapes himself to what he is; his autobiography is the history of the incarnation of himself—and at the end of this incarnation stands the fatality of Nietzsche becoming god. . . . Nietzsche recounts in *Ecce Homo* how the god Dionysus came to be out of him." Martin Kornberger, "Zur Genealogie des 'Ecce Homo,'" *Nietzsche-Studien* 27 (1998): 326, 328. Werner Stegmaier similarly remarks, that "just as Nietzsche as Zarathustra is a Prophet, so as Dionysus he is a god." "Nietzsches Kritik der Vernunft seines Lebens," *Nietzsche-Studien* 21 (1992): 179.

NIETZSCHE AND DOSTOEVSKY ON
NIHILISM AND THE SUPERHUMAN

1. An earlier version of this essay entitled "Dostoevsky and Nietzsche: Murder, Madness, and Suicide; Nihilism and the Doctrine of the Eternal Recurrence" appeared in *Nietzsche and Dostoevsky*, ed. Jeffrey Metzger (Evanston, IL: Northwestern University Press, 2016).

2. Nietzsche wrote to Overbeck on 23 February and 7 March 1887 describing his discovery of Dostoevsky and comparing it to his discovery of Schopenhauer. C. A. Miller, "Nietzsche's Discovery of Dostoevsky," *Nietzsche-Studien* 2 (1973): 202. For Nietzsche's references to Dostoevsky in his letters see KGB III 5:21, 24, 27, 41–42, 50, 75, 106, 451, 457, 483.

3. Nietzsche knew Dostoevsky only through French translations. On the texts Nietzsche read, see Janko Lavrin, "A Note on Nietzsche and Dostoevsky," *Russian Review* 28, no. 2 (April 1969): 160. The *Landlady* and *Notes from the Underground* were presented in the French translation as two chapters of a single story. For suggestive evidence that he read *The Idiot*, see NL, KGW VIII 3:59.

4. The idea of the eternal recurrence solves in its own way the question of free will that had troubled European thought at least since the advent of the Reformation. On this point, see Ken Gemes and Christopher Janaway, "Nietzsche on Free Will, Autonomy and the Sovereign Individual," in *Proceedings of the Aristotelian Society, Supplementary Volumes*, 80 (2006): 321–57.

5. Miller, "The Nihilist as Tempter-Redeemer: Dostoevsky's 'Man-God' in Nietzsche's Notebooks," *Nietzsche-Studien* 4 (1975): 166.

6. On this point, see Erik von der Luft and Douglas Stenberg, "Dostoevskii's Specific Influence on Nietzsche's Preface to *Daybreak*," *Journal of the History of Ideas* 52, no. 3 (July–September 1991): 442. Miller suggests that the mole imagery is not necessarily an allusion to Dostoevsky and may have come from *Beyond Good and Evil*. Miller, "Nietzsche's Discovery," 210–12. See also Richard Avramenko, "Bedeviled by Boredom: A Voegelinian Reading of Dostoevsky's Possessed," *Humanitas* 17, nos. 1–2 (2004): 108–38.

7. Miller, "Nietzsches 'Soteriopsychologie' im Spiegel von Dostoevskys Auseinandersetzung mit dem Europaischen Nihilismus," *Nietzsche-Studien* 7 (1978): 130–31.

8. Ibid., 132–33.

9. Luft and Stenberg, "Dostoevskii's Influence," 446–47. See also Lavrin, "A Note," 165, and Ekaterina Poljakova, "Die 'Bosheit' Der Russen: Nietzsches Deutung Russlands in der Perspektive Russischer Moralphilosophie," *Nietzsche-Studien* 35 (2006): 213.

10. Miller, "Nietzsches 'Soteriopsychologie,'" 142–44.

11. On this matter he was deeply influenced by the nineteenth-century revival of Russian monasticism led by monks at the Optina Monastery, and by the philosophical-theological work of his young friend Vladimir Soloviev. On Soloviev, see L. M. Lopatin, "The Philosophy of Vladimir Soloviev," *Mind* 25, no. 100 (October 1916): 425–60.

12. What is not clear is whether Nietzsche understood the differences between Western Christianity and Eastern Orthodoxy and particularly the role that *theosis* played among the Orthodox. It is hard to believe, however, that even if he did grasp these differences, it would have changed his approach to Christianity since he was a radical reductionist in his critique of Christianity, simplifying and condensing all differences into a simple psychopathology.

13. On this matter Nietzsche, intentionally or due to misrepresentations by the French translators, transforms Dostoevsky's praise of the decency of these men into a praise of their criminal and militaristic backgrounds. See Hartwig Frank, "Die Metaphor Russland im Denken Nietzsches," *Nietzsche-Studien* 36 (2007): 351–53. In other words he assimilates them to Stendhal's antiheroes rather than portraying them as Dostoevsky actually described them. This misunderstanding or misconstruction makes it difficult to draw any more-certain conclusions about the impact of this work on Nietzsche.

14. For a fuller account of the depiction of nihilists in Russian literature, see my *Nihilism before Nietzsche*, 135–73.

15. He was misled on this point by Mérimée and Bourget. Kuhn, "Nietzsches Quelle," 262–63. Feuerbach was more important for their thinking than Schopenhauer.

16. Miller, "The Nihilist," 212.

17. Ibid., 193.

18. On Kirillov's man-god, see ibid., 168, 188; and Lavrin, "A Note," 166.

19. Miller, "The Nihilist," 209.

20. *The Brothers Karamazov*, trans. Constance Garnett (New York: Modern Library, 1996), 242.

21. Kirillov is ultimately dominated by logic rather than life, and is defeated by his idea. He is a decadent who overintellectualizes everything. Miller, "The Nihilist," 205–8.

22. A great deal in this story reflects Dostoevsky's hatred of Catholicism and the Jesuits in particular, who, he believed, sought dominion of the sort that the Grand Inquisitor exercises. But Ivan discounts this element, suggesting that this Inquisitor is motivated not by self-interest or a longing for power but by a love of humanity. For a thoughtful discussion of the chapter, see Ellis Sandoz, "Philosophical Anthropology and Dostoevsky's 'Legend of the Grand Inquisitor,'" *Review of Politics* 26, no. 3 (July 1964): 353–77.

23. Michael Stoeber argues that the devil is Ivan's hallucination. "Dostoevsky's Devil: The Will to Power," *Journal of Religion* 74, no. 1 (January 1994): 38.

24. Goethe, *Faust*, line 1338.

25. As Lavrin points out, if God is dead, then universe is a vaudeville of the devil. "A Note," 162.

26. The argument for the man-god that the devil develops here and that Kirillov articulates in *The Demons* has its origins in the thought of the Left Hegelian Ludwig Feuerbach who claims that the necessary turning point of history will be the moment when man becomes aware and admits that his consciousness of God is nothing but the consciousness of man as a species. Ludwig Feuerbach,

The Essence of Christianity, trans. Marian Evans (London: Chapman, 1854), 267. This notion played a powerful role among Russian nihilists.

27. Stoeber, "Dostoevsky's Devil," 36.

28. On the similarity of the Grand Inquisitor and Zarathustra, see Lavrin, "A Note," 167.

29. Dostoevsky's devil mentions this possibility in his discussion with Ivan but considers it only in passing, and draws no conclusions about its significance.

30. In this respect he perhaps most closely resembles Shigalov who was also willing to sacrifice 90 percent of the population so that the other 10 percent could be truly free and creative.

31. Miller, "The Nihilist," 185.

32. On this point, see Geoff Uyleman, "Nietzsche and Dostoevsky's Creative and Resolving Existential Despair," *Aporia* 15, no. 1 (2005): 32; Lavrin, "A Note," 170; and Stoeber, "Dostoevsky's Devil," 42.

33. Miller, "Nietzsche's Discovery," 254. Miller suggests that Dostoevsky's treatment of Kirillov can be read as a critique of Nietzsche. Miller, "The Nihilist," 224. Lavrin sees Ivan's conversation with the devil as a proleptic critique of Nietzsche. Lavrin, "A Note," 167.

34. On this point, see Mark Lilla, *The Stillborn God* (New York: Vintage, 2007), 18–39.

35. Stoeber believes that both thinkers draw on Jacob Boehm's mysticism of the will. Stoeber, "Dostoevsky's Devil," 27, 38. While there is much to be said for this argument in Dostoevsky's case, there are many more immediate and plausible sources for Nietzsche's notion of the will.

36. For a defense of Dostoevsky's position, see David Walsh, "Dostoevsky's Discovery of the Christian Foundation of Politics," *Religion and Literature* 9, no. 2 (Summer 1987): 49–73.

NIETZSCHE AND PLATO ON THE FORMATION OF A WARRIOR ARISTOCRACY

1. An earlier version of this essay appeared under the title "Toward a New Aristocracy: Nietzsche contra Plato on the Role a Warrior Elite," in *Nietzsche, Nihilism and the Philosophy of the Future,* ed. Jeffrey Metzger (London/New York: Continuum, 2009).

2. He would also have been rendered apoplectic by his sister's misrepresentation of him and distortions of his work that made their appropriation by the Nazis possible.

3. I do not intend in this way to deny the legitimacy of efforts to make use of Nietzsche's thought for ends at odds with his own, but I do want to suggest that it is not as easy as one might imagine to make use of Nietzsche without being made use of in return, and that as a result it is crucial that we not overlook the darker and less hospitable aspects of his thought in our efforts to make use of what is bright and inspiring.

4. *Two Treatises of Government*, ed. Peter Laslett (Cambridge: Cambridge University Press, 1967), 268.

5. Some have mistakenly concluded that the political is merely institutionalized violence. In this respect, Carl Schmitt and his postmodernist followers such as Agamben and Žižek go astray in imagining that the political realm is defined by the one who can determine the state of exception, that is, the person who can decide when the rule of law can be set aside in favor of the rule of force. Carl Schmitt, *The Concept of the Political*, ed. Tracy Strong, trans. George Schwab (Chicago: University of Chicago Press, 1996); Giorgio Agamben, *State of Exception*, trans. Kevin Attell (Chicago: University of Chicago Press, 2005); Slavoj Žižek, *The Universal Exception* (New York: Continuum International, 2006). In fact, the political comes to an end whenever mere violence rules. As Montesquieu recognized, political authority is then replaced by despotic or tyrannical force. The effort of postmodernism to show that all order is a form of organized violence thus distorts the meaning of both violence and the political and erases the differences between citizens and subjects.

6. *Iliad* 1.177.

7. Ibid. 1.3–5. We might prefer that all of our defenders be more like Hector, more reluctant warriors, but then we might also want to see that all of those with a willingness to use violence to get their way are operating under military discipline and civilian control.

8. Ibid. 18.104.

9. Such philosophic precepts are articulated in the *Laws* and made the basis of the education of the warrior class. In the *Crito*, Socrates suggests that those who are incapable of philosophizing on their own and have no philosopher or philosophic precepts to follow should obey the existing laws of the city. In that case they will at least not make anything worse.

10. In Nietzsche's view, Plato here stands in contrast to Socrates who overcame his fear of death (*PP*, KGW II 4:360).

11. Nietzsche enlisted in the artillery from 1867 to 1868 and was released after a riding injury. Even though he had given up his Prussian citizenship when he assumed his position at the University of Basel, he asked for a leave to serve as an orderly in the Franco-Prussian War in 1871.

12. Nietzsche gives us some idea of how difficult such a transformation will be in his discussion in the "Second Essay" of *The Genealogy of Morals* of the enormous amounts of violence needed to breed an animal that can keep promises. KGW VI 2:305.

13. Even his early *On the Future of Our Educational Institutions* is only concerned with promoting liberal education and culture versus the predominant form of education at the time that he believed aimed at producing technically proficient, effective moneymakers. It is of course not inconceivable that Nietzsche would have articulated such a system of education had he been able to continue his work.

14. In the last year of his life, Nietzsche wrote the prologue for a work that explained

how virtues could come to rule in his great politics. He explicitly states that such a politics is not for everyone and lays out his own brand of "pure Machiavellianism" that he asserts is fit only for superhuman beings not for men. He compares it to Plato's efforts but distinguishes the rule of virtues from the rule of morality. It remains, however, merely a prologue without any further specifications. It is possible that he intended to include something like this in one or another version of the *Revaluation of All Values*. KGW VIII 2:267–70.

WHAT REMAINS

1. Leonard Sax, "What Was the Cause of Nietzsche's Dementia?," *Journal of Medical Biography* 11 (2003): 47–54.
2. Surprisingly, even his apparently most outrageous claim, that his thought would mark the separation between two world ages, has been at least partially confirmed by the fact that later thinkers have treated his thought as the end of modernity (or even Western metaphysics) or the beginning of the postmodern age. In this respect he does apparently mark the boundary between two world ages.
3. Pierre Klossowski, *Nietzsche and the Vicious Circle* (Chicago: University of Chicago Press, 1997), xv–xvii.
4. As we have seen, the pity Nietzsche is concerned with here is not for the fate of ordinary human beings, but for the higher men, many of whom also will perish in the coming cataclysm.
5. One might object here that the absence of pity that characterized this period was only characteristic of sociopaths and that the number of such people as a percentage of the human population is quite small. The question from Nietzsche's point of view, however, is not whether the number is large or small but whether it is large enough. Machiavelli, for example, observed that the vast majority of human beings simply want to be left alone and that only a few want to dominate others, and yet it is those few who rule and exploit the rest. *The Prince*, 2nd ed., trans. Harvey Mansfield (Chicago: University of Chicago Press, 1998), 39. Nietzsche clearly imagines that, as a result of his war on Christianity and his revaluation of all values, the passions and will to power of these "sociopathic" men will be affirmed, and that out of this group a new aristocracy will arise.
6. *Nietzsche's Philosophy of the Eternal Recurrence*, 94.
7. His plans for scientific study were also derailed by his break with Paul Rée and Lou Salomé with whom he had planned to travel and study. Safranski, *Nietzsche*, 251.
8. *Nihilism before Nietzsche* (Chicago: University of Chicago Press, 1995).
9. See especially 203–57.
10. Of course, had he actually obtained such an education, he might well have recognized that his notion of the will to power was untenable.
11. Heidegger, *Nietzsche*, 2:335–98.
12. Thomas Altizer, *The Gospel of Christian Atheism* (Philadelphia: Westminster

Press, 1966); Jean-Luc Marion, *God without Being* (Chicago: University of Chicago Press, 1991).

13. Here Nietzsche's thinking may have been impeded by a lack of knowledge of primate behavior. His model for the predator is the lion and for the herd the cow, but humans are omnivorous primates who have inherent social structures of their own that include monogamous, polyandrous, and polygamous family groups in which there are struggles for dominance among both males and females but in which cooperation and the survival of the group are primary and not simply the result of the dominance of a single alpha male or a ruling group.

14. Nietzsche in this respect sees the predatory side of our human nature best represented in what Hegel called the life and death struggle that characterized early self-consciousness and was the source of the master-slave dialectic. Hegel was convinced that modern humans had internalized the self-control demanded earlier of the slaves by their masters and in that sense were capable of self-government. Nietzsche rejects this possibility. For him there are natural masters (predators) and slaves (herd animals) whose natures can be further cultivated to perfect their natural characteristics.

15. Here Nietzsche remains within the tradition that beginning with Luther understands freedom to be possible only by being one with God, thus only when God possesses the individual and takes him away from Satan. I thus can will freely only when I am entirely one with God.

16. Roger Penrose, Paul Steinhardt, and Neil Turok are perhaps the best known defenders of such a cyclic view, but their views are not widely accepted, and their theories rest on quite different assumptions and come to different conclusions than Nietzsche's.

17. This point is reinforced by Nietzsche's suggestion even in his early work that all of the rest of the gods were born from the smile of Dionysus and all men from his tears. *BT*, KGW III 1:68.

18. These goals were still relatively clear to scholars in the interwar period. See, for example, George Morgan, *What Nietzsche Means* (Cambridge, MA: Harvard University Press, 1941).

19. *Faust*, l.1338.

20. George Kateb seems to me to offer a more sensible approach in his *Emerson and Self-Reliance* (Lanham, MD: Rowman and Littlefield, 1995). He points out the connections between Emerson and Nietzsche but argues that a democratic politics has to rely on a democratic thinker.

INDEX

Achilles, 163–64

active nihilism, 34, 35, 36, 38, 148

Adler, Alfred, 4

Adorno, Theodor, 4

aei on (ever-being), 6, 125

Aeschylus, 44, 87, 96, 112, 176

Agamben, Giorgio, 232n5

Albrechtsberger, Johann Georg, 89–90

Alexandrian culture, 73

Altizer, Thomas, 189

amor fati, 20, 54, 101, 134, 135, 136, 147, 155, 173, 186, 194

Andreas-Salomé, Lou, 10, 204n7, 207n25, 233n7

Ansell-Pearson, Keith, 210n6

anthropology of nihilism: appearance of the lion and, 34, 212–13nn22–23; characterization of the will to power, 33; Christianity and, 35; consequences of the death of God for European humanity, 33–34, 212nn17–18; diagram of the span of human possibilities of being, 30, 33, 35; discussion of the three possibilities of being human, 31, 211nn9–10; the Great Noon's position on the diagram of human possibilities, 33; implications if passion is the essence of the human being, 32; meaning of the last man, 29; Nietzsche's belief in active nihilism, 34, 38; Nietzsche's decision to abandon Zarathustra, 34, 213n25; stages of nihilism, 35, 36; tightrope analogy, 29; unexpected strengths of the liberal

democratic worldview and, 38–39; vision of the *Übermensch* and, 29, 30, 31, 37–38, 46–47, 211n13; will to power's connection to the psychology of the passions, 32–33

Antichrist, The, 10, 27, 34, 35, 98, 109, 114, 122–23, 184, 187, 225nn7–9

(anti-)metaphysics: basis of, 188; concept of the Dionysian and, 13, 72–73; concepts defining, 13, 207n24; distinguishing feature of, 19; doctrine of the eternal recurrence in the framework of classical metaphysics, 13–14, 17–18; notion of time and being in, 194; ontology of, 16, 18; psychology and, 77, 218n26; theological crisis created by scientific knowledge, 18

antinomy doctrine, 13, 73, 79, 93

anti-Semitism, 70, 114, 161, 188, 213n27

Apollo/Apollinian, 58, 73, 98, 104, 110, 116, 125, 129

architect, 104

architectonic, 110, 113, 115, 116, 118, 119

Arendt, Hannah, 4, 50

Ariadne, 56

aristocracy. *See* warrior aristocracy

Aristotle, 6, 18, 37, 97, 98, 111, 190

artist: Dionysian, 100, 117, 129–30, 198; metaphysics and, 44, 72; Nietzsche's perception of himself as, 109; Nietzsche's understanding of the use of art, 129–30; Plato's view of, 170; tragic artist's redemption of humanity, 101, 104, 105, 106, 223n37